PRINCIPLES

OF

SPORT

BIOMECHANICS

Seventh Edition

Joe D. Bell
Tony Grice
Linus J. Dowell

american press
BOSTON, MASSACHUSETTS
www.americanpresspublishers.com

Cover photograph by Oxana Rishnyak. Used with permission from 123RF.com

Preface

Kinesiology, as it is known in physical education, is the science of human motion. In the early days of physical education, the content of a course in human motion was confined chiefly to functional anatomy and subjective evaluation of movement. Gradually, as sports emerged as a more integral part of the physical education curriculum, the concept of human motion was broadened to include the study of mechanical principles which applied to sport techniques. The principles were applied not only to the movement of the body itself, but also to the movements of the projectiles related to the various sports.

The state of our knowledge in Biomechanics is rapidly growing primarily due to better and better computer technology. Any growth must, however, have as its base a foundation of laws, theories and principles which are grounded in the study of the mechanical nature of human movement.

This textbook is designed with the undergraduate kinesiology major in mind. It is not intended to be the end-all text for graduate studies. We deliberately kept the concepts simple enough to be easily understood by students who tend to have less background in mathematics and physics. The text takes the student through foundational concepts and solutions that could be reached using basic algebra and trigonometry tools.

A great deal of time, experience, and research has gone into the preparation of this book. The authors are grateful to the many students of kinesiology over the years who contributed to this work through their athletic prowess, scholarly insight, and research. A special word of thanks goes to the late Dr. Linus Dowell for his initial development of this book and for his active role in much of the research that went into it. Dr. Dowell will be missed, but fondly remembered, by those who were fortunate enough to sit in his classes and to serve as his colleagues.

And, of course we cannot forget the Master of All Movement.

Joe D. Bell
Tony Grice

Contents

1

WHY STUDY THE PRINCIPLES OF SPORT BIOMECHANICS?

The study of human motion is generally considered essential for the physical education teacher, coach, athletic trainer and/or biomechanist. Kinesiology is the study of human motion. It includes both the structural and the mechanical aspects of human movement. Webster's New Collegiate Dictionary defines Kinesiology as "the study of the principles of mechanics and anatomy in relation to human movement". Understanding one's ability to move anatomically is generally referred to as structural kinesiology. The study and analysis of mechanical kinesiology or human performance through the principles of mechanics has more recently become known as biomechanics.

The Principles of Sport Biomechanics is designed to study the effects of physical forces that relate to the human body while engaged in sport. Factors that affect motion include gravity, friction, air resistance and water resistance. The relationship between the performer, the sports implements being manipulated and/or the objects which the performer strikes, throws, kicks or in some other manner applies force requires investigation. Biomechanical principles must be studied in terms of the performance objectives. In teaching, a three-step sequence is generally followed which includes telling them, showing them and correcting them. Stated less simply, the physical education teacher typically describes the skill, demonstrates the manner in which it is to be performed and then analyzes the student's performance on each individual effort. The information provided by the teacher must be based on scientific data and an accurate interpretation of the performance of that particular sport skill.

The analysis of a sport skill includes the effects of the forces applied sequentially throughout the performance. The human body acts as a single lever or link system executing the proper sequence of joint motions in order to accomplish the desired skill. For the desired improvement of the performer to occur, the teacher or coach must adequately describe, demonstrate and analyze sports skills based on scientific procedures known as biomechanical analysis.

Principles and techniques for performance analysis are presented ranging from simple observation to more complex assessment methods utilizing sophisticated high-speed motion video and film equipment interfaced with computers. Quantitative analyses of this kind are used quite often to evaluate the performance of elite athletes, but, the cost and availability of this equipment and the expertise and/or training needed may not be practical. However, newer, more sophisticated technology that is less expensive to acquire may soon be accessible.

Tom Crawford, Head of Coaching Development for the United States Olympic Committee, suggests: "include the training of all coaches, from P.E. teachers to volunteer parent-coaches, in the teaching of fundamental movement skills. Rather than fielding a ground ball, for instance, coaches would learn how to break the activity down into its basic motion." The more technical equipment will not typically be available in the physical education or athletic departments of the average secondary school, but the physical educator or coach in the field should be knowledgeable of research in biomechanics and human performance. Practical experience and hands-on computer software have been incorporated with laboratory problems involving the very latest in scientific technology. The physical educator in teaching-coaching situations must be able to select and incorporate the appropriate level of biomechanical analysis for any given situation.

In conclusion, a knowledge of the principles of sports biomechanics will provide physical educators, athletic trainers, coaches and scientists with the information needed to analyze sports skills, assess and correct problems that affect one's performance. Thus, valid qualitative and quantitative analyses can be used to identify and possibly eliminate recurring weaknesses in sport biomechanics.

2
BASIC TOOLS

Principles of Sport Biomechanics are often discussed in mathematical terms. Therefore, it is essential to have an understanding of basic arithmetical concepts. When a mathematical computation requires more than one step or operation, certain rules regarding the order of operations in mathematics are a necessity. Often the acronym, PEMDAS, is used to memorize the correct order of operations. A common word association phrase used to help students to remember this acronym is as follows: "Please Excuse My Dear Aunt Sally."

P = **Parentheses**
E = **Exponents**
M = **Multiplication followed by**
D = **Division from left to right**
A = **Addition followed by**
S = **Subtraction from left to right**

When **parentheses** are used, the mathematical operations within are completed first, before any other computations are performed.

Exponents refer to integers or numbers that have increased in size exponentially. This is another way of saying that they have been squared or cubed, or increased by a factor of 2, 3, 4, et cetera. Exponents are usually shown as superscript numbers that follow immediately to the right and slightly above a whole number or integer. The exponent indicates the number of times that the whole number is to be multiplied times itself.

Multiplication and **Division** within a mathematical expression have precedence over addition and subtraction. If numerous computations are involved within an algebraic expression or equation, multiplication and division are calculated first from left to right as they occur.

Next, any **Addition** and/or **Subtraction** are calculated as they occur in the equation from left to right. An example of these operations follows:

$$X = 3 \times 5 + (9 - 6) + 2^3 \qquad \textbf{Parentheses cleared first}$$
$$X = 3 \times 5 + 3 + 2^3 \qquad \textbf{Exponent calculated}$$
$$X = 3 \times 5 + 3 + 8 \qquad \textbf{Multiplication is next}$$
$$X = 15 + 3 + 8 \qquad \textbf{Addition follows}$$
$$X = 26 \qquad \textbf{Final value for X}$$

Algebra sometimes refers to X as the unknown quantity. Many problems in algebra involve the calculation for one or more unknown quantities. These unknowns may be represented by X or any other letter or variable. Unknown variables are often expressed in an **equation**, which implies that the values shown on the left side of the equal sign are equal to the values shown on the right. The solution to calculating the value of a variable on one side of the equation is to clear out that side leaving only the variable. The ultimate value of the variable can be determined by clearing out all of the other numbers and/or operations to the other side of the equation. This is accomplished by performing the same calculation on **both sides** of the equation using the order of operations. Several examples are shown below:

$$b - 5 = 13$$
$$b - 5 + 5 = 13 + 5 \qquad \textbf{Add 5 to both sides}$$
$$b = 18$$

$$2(y - 4) + 6 = 32$$
$$2(y - 4) + 6 - 6 = 32 - 6 \qquad \textbf{Subtract 6 from both sides}$$
$$2(y - 4) = 26$$
$$2y - 8 = 26$$
$$2y - 8 + 8 = 26 + 8 \qquad \textbf{Add 8 to both sides}$$
$$2y = 34$$
$$\frac{2y}{2} = \frac{34}{2} \qquad \textbf{Divide 2 into both sides}$$
$$y = 17$$

Square Roots

The **square root** of a positive number is calculated by performing the inverse operation of squaring a number. The calculation of the square root gives a number which when squared or multiplied times itself results in the original number from which the square root was determined. Square roots may be determined from whole numbers or decimal fractions, but **not** negative numbers. For example, the square root of 36 is 6. Square roots may be either positive or negative because any number multiplied times itself will always result in a positive number. Thus the square root of 36 could also be –6. However, if you multiplied –6 times +6, the result would be – 36. Therefore, the square root of – 36 cannot be determined.

Several examples of square roots are as follows:

1.00 = ±1.00	7.25 = ± 2.6925824
4.00 = ±2.00	11.86 = ± 3.4438351
9.00 = ±3.00	33.00 = ± 5.7445626
16.00 = ±4.00	196.00 = ± 14.00
25.00 = ±5.00	999.00 = ± 31.606961

Percentages

A percentage is based on the principle that the whole of any quantity or object necessarily represents one hundred percent of that quantity or object. Therefore, a percentage is any one of the one hundred parts. This is very similar to one cent being one-one hundredth of a total dollar. Twenty-five cents is 25% or one-fourth of one dollar. Percentages are often shown as decimal fractions. Twenty-five percent is written as 0.25 or 25%. Thirty-three percent of 85 is the same as stating 0.33 multiplied times 85 is equal to 28.05. One might also say that the number 28.05 is 33.33% of 85.

Angles

Angles in biomechanics are utilized in several ways. The numerous joints in the human body create various angles. Angular motion or velocity is often needed to describe the movement of body segments. **Goniometers** are used to measure the angle at any specific joint in the body. **Protractors** are often used to measure angles.

A **radian** is equal to 57.3 degrees and is often used to measure the kinematics of human motion. It is the angle subtended at the center of a circle by an arc equal in length to the radius. One radian equals 360 degrees divided by 2 times pi. **Pi** is always a constant value of 3.1416. The circumference of any circle is determined by multiplying 2 times pi times the radius. Radians may be converted to degrees or revolutions or vice versa. If one wishes to convert:

    (1) radians to degrees, multiply by 57.3;

    (2) radians to revolutions, divide by 6.28;

    (3) degrees to revolutions, divide by 360;

    (4) degrees to radians, divide by 57.3;

(5) revolutions to radians, multiply by 6.28; or

(6) revolutions to degrees, multiply by 360.

Trigonometry

Trigonometry is based on mathematical calculations relating to the **angles** and **sides** of triangles. Two of the most common trigonometric relationships are applicable to **all** triangles.

The **Law of Sines** states that the ratio between the length of any side of a triangle and the angle(sin) opposite that side is equal to the ratio between the length of any other side of the triangle and the angle(sin) opposite that side:

$$\frac{A}{\sin a} = \frac{B}{\sin b} = \frac{C}{\sin c}$$

The **Law of Cosines** states that the length of any side of a triangle is equal to the sum of the squares of the lengths of the other two sides of the triangle minus two times the product of the lengths of the other two sides and the cosine of the angle opposite the original side:

$$A^2 = B^2 + C^2 - 2BC \cos a$$
$$B^2 = A^2 + C^2 - 2AC \cos b$$
$$C^2 = A^2 + B^2 - 2AB \cos c$$

The **right triangle** is probably the most commonly used triangle. All right triangles contain a ninety degree angle or right angle. The **hypotenuse** is the side opposite the right triangle. It is also the longest side. The **Pythagorean Theorem** describes the relationship between the hypotenuse and the other two sides of the right triangle. It states that the square of the length of the hypotenuse is equal to the sum of the squares of the lengths of the two sides of a right triangle:

$$C^2 = A^2 + B^2$$

The **sine**(sin) of an angle is the ratio of the length of the side opposite the angle to the length of the hypotenuse:

$$\sin a = \frac{opposite}{hypotenuse} = \frac{A}{C} \quad \text{or} \quad \sin b = \frac{opposite}{hypotenuse} = \frac{B}{C}$$

The **cosine** (cos) is the ratio of the length of the side adjacent to the angle relative to the length of the hypotenuse:

$$\cos a = \frac{\textbf{adjacent}}{\textbf{hypotenuse}} = \frac{B}{C} \quad \text{or} \quad \cos b = \frac{\text{adjacent}}{\text{hypotenuse}} = \frac{A}{C}$$

The **tangent** (tan) of an angle is the ratio of the length of the side opposite the angle of the side adjacent to the angle:

$$\tan a = \frac{\textbf{opposite}}{\textbf{adjacent}} = \frac{A}{B} \quad \text{or} \quad \tan b = \frac{\text{opposite}}{\text{adjacent}} = \frac{B}{A}$$

Often, marathon runners and other long distance runners use this concept when running on a road course. They refer to this as "running the tangents". In other words, instead of running the curves of the road, they shorten the distance by running a straight line or tangent across the curves. This utilizes an old geometry axiom which states that the shortest distance between two points is a straight line.

Values of trigonometric functions up to ninety degrees are provided in Table 1 on page 9. They may also be determined with calculators which have trigonometric function capabilities.

$$\sin 30° = .5000$$
$$\cos 75° = .9659$$
$$\tan 42° = .9004$$
$$\cot 58° = .6249$$

Angles greater than 90° but less than 180° are calculated by simply subtracting the given angle from 180°. Trigonometric functions in this range are all negative except for the sine.

$$\sin 135° = \sin 45°$$
$$\cos 160° = -\cos 20°$$
$$\tan 150° = -\tan 30°$$
$$\cot 174° = -\cot 1°$$

Angles greater than 180° but less than 270° are calculated by subtracting the angle in question from 270°. Functions in this range are negative for the tangent and cotangent but positive for the sine and cosine.

$$\sin 235° = \sin 35°$$
$$\cos 260° = \cos 10°$$
$$\tan 190° = -\tan 80°$$
$$\cot 214° = -\cot 56°$$

Angles greater than 270° but less than 360° are calculated by subtracting the given angle from 360. Trigonometric functions in this range are all negative except for the cosine.

$$\sin 275° = -\sin 85°$$
$$\cos 330° = \cos 30°$$
$$\tan 295° = -\tan 65°$$
$$\cot 344° = -\cot 16°$$

Hand Held Calculators

The hand held calculator is a very helpful tool in computing problems in biomechanics. Several functions are essential. Most calculators now have **square root** functions and **memory**. Some also have the automatic calculation of trigonometric functions, such as, sines, cosines, and tangents programmed onto the microchip. Calculators also have their own rules of operations. For example, in order to display a negative number, you must punch the **equal key** after entering the negative number or the negative sign will not appear.

Table 2.1
Trigonometric Functions

Degrees	Sines	Cosines	Tangents	Cotangents	
0	.0000	1.0000	.0000		90
1	.0175	.9998	.0175	57.290	89
2	.0349	.9994	.0349	28.636	88
3	.0523	.9986	.0524	19.081	87
4	.0698	.9976	.0699	14.301	86
5	.0872	.9962	.0875	11.430	85
6	.1045	.9945	.1051	9.5144	84
7	.1219	.9925	.1228	8.1443	83
8	.1392	.9903	.1405	7.1154	82
9	.1564	.9877	.1584	6.3138	81
10	.1736	.9848	.1763	5.6713	80
11	.1908	.9816	.1944	5.1446	79
12	.2079	.9781	.2126	4.7046	78
13	.2250	.9744	.2309	4.3315	77
14	.2419	.9703	.2493	4.0108	76
15	.2588	.9659	.2679	3.7321	75
16	.2756	.9613	.2867	3.4874	74
17	.2924	.9563	.3057	3.2709	73
18	.3090	.9511	.3249	3.0777	72
19	.3256	.9455	.3443	2.9042	71
20	.3420	.9397	.3640	2.7475	70
21	.3584	.9336	.3839	2.6051	69
22	.3746	.9272	.4040	2.4751	68
23	.3907	.9205	.4245	2.3559	67
24	.4067	.9135	.4452	2.2460	66
25	.4226	.9063	.4663	2.1445	65
26	.4384	.8988	.4877	2.0503	64
27	.4540	.8910	.5095	1.9626	63
28	.4695	.8829	.5317	1.8807	62
29	.4848	.8746	.5543	1.8040	61
30	.5000	.8660	.5774	1.7321	60
31	.5150	.8572	.6009	1.6643	59
32	.5299	.8480	.6249	1.6003	58
33	.5446	.8387	.6494	1.5399	57
34	.5592	.8290	.6745	1.4826	56
35	.5736	.8192	.7002	1.4281	55
36	.5878	.8090	.7265	1.3764	54
37	.6018	.7986	.7536	1.3270	53
38	.6157	.7880	.7813	1.2799	52
39	.6293	.7771	.8098	1.2349	51
40	.6428	.7660	.8391	1.1918	50
41	.6561	.7547	.8693	1.1504	49
42	.6691	.7431	.9004	1.1106	48
43	.6820	.7314	.9325	1.0724	47
44	.6947	.7193	.9657	1.0355	46
45	.7071	.7071	1.0000	1.0000	45
	Cosines	Sines	Cotangents	Tangents	Degrees

Practice Problems

1. $\begin{array}{r} +10 \\ +\ 7 \\ -\ 3 \\ +14 \\ \hline \end{array}$

2. $(8 - 3) - (9 + 2) + (25 + 4) - (7 - 5) = \underline{\hspace{2cm}}$

3. $\begin{array}{r} 17.065 \\ -4.0915 \\ \hline \end{array}$

4. $\begin{array}{r} -17 \\ -\ 6 \\ \hline \end{array}$

5. $(+75)(-17) = \underline{\hspace{1.5cm}}$

6. $(-66)(-21) = \underline{\hspace{1.5cm}}$

7. $(319)(0) = \underline{\hspace{2cm}}$

8. $\dfrac{17.334689}{.5014} = \underline{\hspace{1.5cm}}$

9. $\dfrac{0}{87} = \underline{\hspace{1.5cm}}$

10. $\dfrac{14}{2/3} = \underline{\hspace{2cm}}$

11. $\dfrac{7}{5}$

12. $17 + 2/3 \times 12 =$ _____

13. $6 \times 25 \quad =$ _____

14. $4^2 + 4^2 =$ _____

15. $(5 \times 10)^2 =$ _____

16. $(4/5)^2 =$ _____

17. $(4 + 9)^2 =$ _____

18. If a = 9 and b = 4, what does ab equal _____?

    What does a + b = _____ ?

    or $\dfrac{a}{b}$ = _____?

19. If c = 42 and d = 18, what does cd equal _____?

    What does c + d = _____?

    or $\dfrac{c}{d}$ = _____?

20. $c + \dfrac{a-b}{5} \times d$ = _____?

II.   **Using a protractor, construct the following angles:**

1. 45°   2.   60°   3.   130°

III.   **Using a goniometer, determine the number of degrees in the following:**

1.   a partner's elbow at full flexion? at full extension?

2.   a partner's knee at full flexion? at full extension?

3.   a partner's ankle during plantar flexion? during dorsiflexion?

3

BASIC HUMAN MOVEMENT

The human body is a wonderfully complex machine. The body's biomechanical and physiological processes that provide the energy for muscular contractions and movement are indeed complex and beyond the scope of this textbook. However, we will observe the results of these muscular contractions as they exert forces upon the various anatomical and mechanical structures of the body. The combinations of muscles and joints in the body make for very favorable analogies to several simple machines.

Examples of some of the simple machines which result from the various anatomical structures of the body are shown in Figure 3-1. These mechanisms are powered by the muscles to produce movements of the body. **(P.1.0)**

"Machines" refer to any device that is used to accomplish work by applying force in some way to gain a mechanical advantage. In essence, the function of a machine is to change the magnitude or direction of a force in order to gain a mechanical advantage or to assist movement.

Probably the five simplist machines are the pulley, the wheel and axle, the lever, the inclined plane and the screw. Of the five, the first three are readily found in the human body. The pulley is an example of how the direction of pull is changed to gain a mechanical advantage. The action of ligaments and tendons at the knee and ankle are good examples. The head rotating on the neck or shoulders represents the movement of a wheel and axle. Most levers in the body sacrifice force to gain speed. Because approximately 75 percent are Third Class levers, it is said that the human body is built for speed and range of motion.

As shown in Figure 3-1, the structures of the body vary in design and in function. The pelvic bones of the body support weight like an arch into which the lower spine fits like a keystone. The muscles of the leg pull across the patella much in the same fashion that the cable of a crane pulls across its pulley wheel. A classic example of the ball and socket is seen in the shoulder joint and the hinge is evident in the joints of the fingers, elbows and knees.

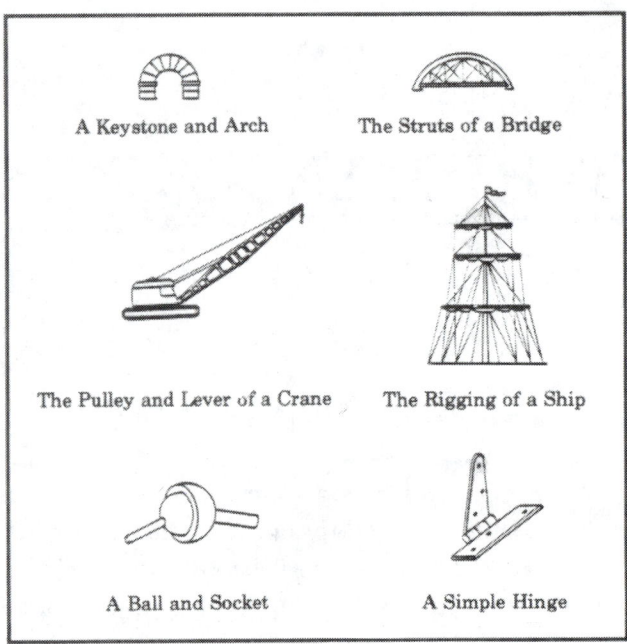

Figure 3-1 Mechanical Mechanisms of the Body

Anatomical Structures

The reference position used in this text for fundamental movements of the body is a slight variation of the standard reference position used in most anatomical studies. The position used for this text is an erect standing position with the feet slightly apart and parallel, the arms hanging freely at the sides, and the palms facing the body. **(P.2.0.)**

Fundamental body positions are described with reference to three anatomical planes of the body: 1) the *sagittal plane*; 2) the *frontal plane;* and 3) the *transverse plane.* See Figure 3-2. All of the rotary movements of the body occur around axes that are at right angles to these planes **(P.3.0.)**.

The movements of the body may be described in reference to these various planes or as movement about the axises that are created at the junction of these axises. Some movements occur essentially in only one plane and are referred to as uniaxial. Flexion, extension and hyperextension are examples of uniaxial movements at a hinge joint, such as the elbow. If movements occur in two planes, they are called biaxial and if in three or more, triaxial. The knee is a biaxial joint allowing flexion and extension, and some rotation. Examples of triaxial joints are the shoulder and the hip, that are ball and socket joints. They allow flexion, extension, abduction, adduction, circumduction and rotation to take place. Another example of a triaxial

14

joint is the thumb which is a saddle joint. Other movements that result in a gliding or sliding action occur in plane joints and are **nonaxial**. Nonaxial joints, such as, the intercarpal and intertarsal joints allow gliding or twisting articulations.

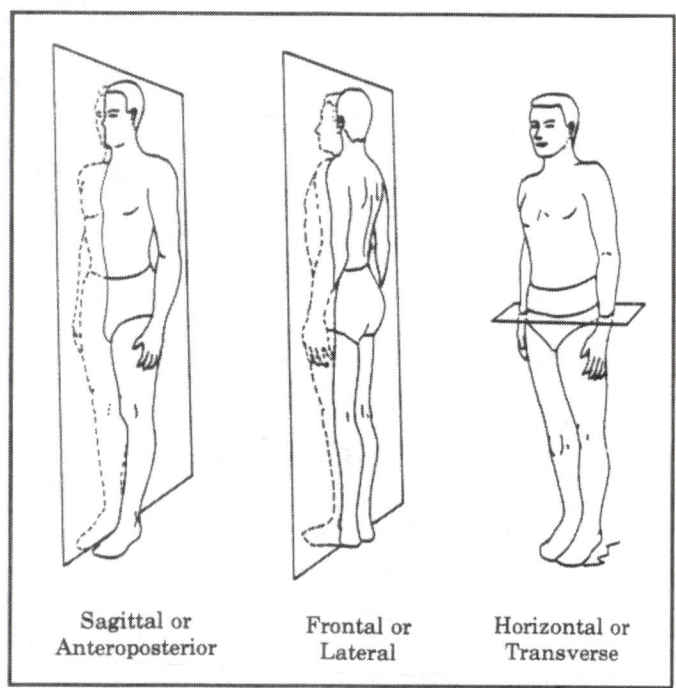

Sagittal or
Anteroposterior

Frontal or
Lateral

Horizontal or
Transverse

Figure 3-2   Planes of the Body

The human skeleton is usually divided into two categories: the axial skeleton and the appendicular skeleton. The appendicular skeleton includes the arms and legs or appendages. The axial skeleton encompasses the skull and the torso. Approximately 180 of the 206-210 bones that make up the human skeleton are capable of voluntary movement. These bones serve as a link system of individual levers that articulate with one another to allow range of motion around various joints. Bones are generally classified by shape into one of four types: flat, irregular, long, or short.

Joints or articulations are classified into two broad kinds: those with a joint cavity and those without a joint cavity. Those with a joint cavity are further classified as freely movable or **diarthrodial**. Those without a joint cavity have two classes; slightly movable or **amphiarthrodial** and immovable or **synarthrodial**. See Table 3-1.

Most joints in the body that allow voluntary movement are diarthrodial. Several characteristics of diarthrodial joints are as follows: (1) joint cavity present; (2) freely (movable; (3) synovial fluid or membrane present; (4) articular surface covered with

Table 3-1
Classification of Joints by Structure and Action

Kind	Classification	Generic	Type — Technical	Explanations and Examples
Without a joint cavity	I. Synarthrodial (immovable)	A. Fibrous	Suture – from the Latin word meaning "seam"	The edges of two bones grow together, united by a thin layer of fibrous, periosteum tissue between. Sutures of the skull are examples.
	II. Amphiarthrodial (slightly movable)	A. Ligamentous	Syndesmosis – from Greek word meaning "with ligament"	Slight movement permitted by elasticity of a ligament joining two bones. examples are coracoacromial joint, mid radio-ulnar joint, and mid tibio-fibular joint.
		B. Cartilaginous	Synchrondrosis – from Greek work meaning "with cartilage"	Joints that are united by hyaline or fibro-cartilage. Hyaline cartilage allows slight deformation by compression only. Epiphyseal unions are examples. Fibro-cartilage permit motion of a bending and twisting nature, such as, intervetebral discs.
With a joint cavity	III. Diarthrodial (freely movable)	A. Synovial	Arthrosis – from Greek word meaning "separation or cavity"	
		1. Gliding	Plane	**Non-axial** — Permits gliding or twisting. Examples: Intercarpal and intertarsal joint
		2. Hinge	Ginglymus	**Uni-axial** — Concave surface glides around the convex surface, such as, the elbow joint. Allows flexion and extension.
		3. Pivot	Trochoid	**Uni-axial** — Allows rotation around a vertical or long axis. Examples are the atlanto-axial joint and the proximal radio-ulnar joint.
		4. Condyloid	Ovoid-Ellipsoid	**Bi-axial** — Oval or oblong convex surface fits into similarly shaped concave surface. Allows flexion, extension, abduction, adduction and circumduction, but not rotation. The wrist and 2nd to 5th metacarpophalangeal (finger) joints are examples, but not the thumb.
		5. Ball and Socket	Spheroid/Enarthrosis	**Tri-axial** — Spherical head of one bobe fits into the concave or cup-line cavity of the other bone. This swivel motion allows flexion, extension, abduction, adduction, circumduction, and rotation on the long axis.
		6. Saddle	Reciprocal reception	**Tri-axial** — Both bones articulate like a reciprocally concave-convex surface. Allows flexion, extension, abduction, adduction and circumduction. The thumb is only example.

16

hyaline cartilage; (5) encapsuled with ligaments; and possibly; (6) intra-articular fibrocartilage discs. Figure 3-3 illustrates several types of diathrodial joints.

The starting position for defining the movements of the joints of the body is the **anatomical position.** This is a standing position with the hands held facing palms forward normally. For the purpose of this text, the neutral position described earlier will be used.

Movements or activities made primarily in the **sagittal** plane around the horizontal-frontal axis might also be described as bending or stretching. Sit-ups or bicep curls occur primarily in the sagittal plane. Movements in the **frontal** plane around the sagittal-horizontal axis are side-ways in nature. Examples are lateral flexion or bending of the spinal column from left to right, as well as, abduction, adduction, elevation, depression, inversion, and eversion. In addition, ulnar and radial deviation are often referred to as ulnar and radial flexion often seen in jumping jacks, and possibly the round off in gymnastics occur. Movements in the **horizontal** plane around the sagittal-frontal axis encompass all forms of rotation. Often they are called twisting type movements around a vertical axis. These include right or left

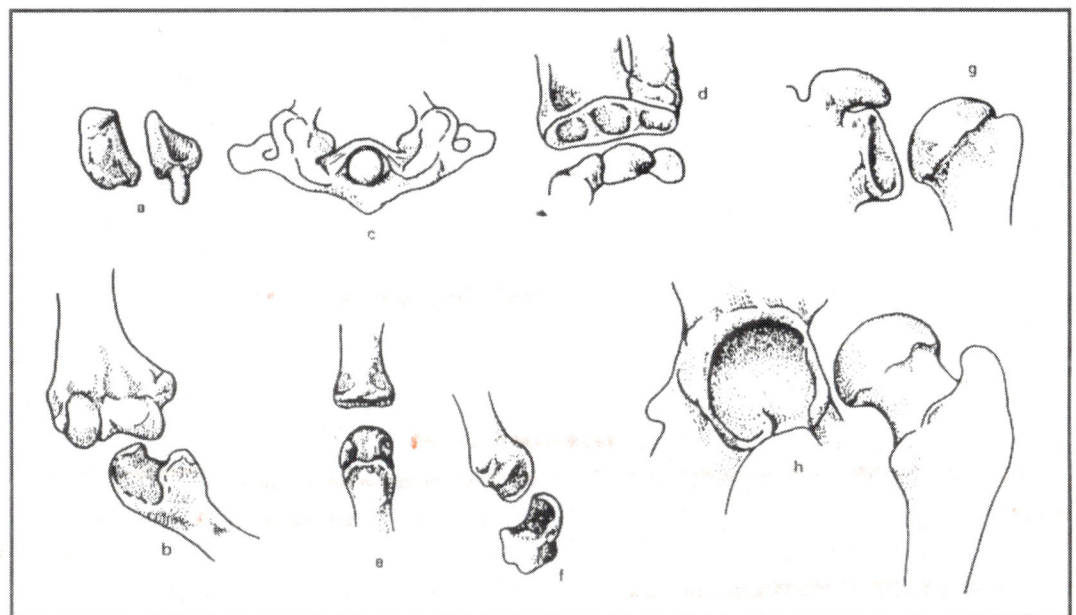

Figure 3-3   Major types of diarthrodial joints. (a) Plane (intercarpal).
(b) Hinge (elbow or humeroulnar). (c) P)ivot (atlantoaxial). (d) Condyloid (radiocarpal). (e) Condyloid (metacarpophalangeal). (f) Saddle (thumb or carpometacarpal). (g) Ball-and-socket (shoulder). (h) Ball-and-socket (hip).
[adapted from Hollinshead, W.H., and Jenkins, D.B.: *Functional anatomy of the limbs and back.* 5th ed. Philadelphia: W.B. Saunders, 1981]

rotation, lateral or outward rotation, medial or inward rotation, pronation and supination. The pirouette in ballet or the spin in figure skating best identify this movement in sports.

A fourth plane of movement is the **diagonal or oblique** plane that occurs around an oblique axis. Circumduction is a complex combination of oblique movements in which a body segment describes the shape of a cone. Movement in an oblique plane is probably the largest of all sports movements that involve ballistic motion, that is, a vigorous muscular contraction followed by a coasting phase. This coasting or deceleration phase is usually referred to as one's follow-through.

In throwing and kicking sports, it is the diagonal motion created by arching the back, rotating the torso, shifting one's weight and propelling one's body from a preliminary backswing or wound-up position through contact or propulsion. This initial stretch or "wind-up" motion has often been referred to as **Deraption**. Following deraption, the body acts as a single unit pulling the arm or leg forward through a diagonal plane. This oblique, concentric contraction is called **Seraption**. This term originates from the Mexican serape or shawl which hangs from the shoulders in a diagonal fashion. The resulting diagonal movements executed in throwing, spiking, serving, punting or kicking have collectively become known as the **Serape Effect**.

Simple Levers

The simplest and most common machines in the body are represented in the various types of levers that are present at most of the joints where movements take place. Due to variations in the location of the fulcrum (pivot point) about which the lever rotates, the location at which the force is applied, and the location of the weight resistance, differing degrees of *mechanical advantage* can be gained by the body segments **(P.4.0)**.

There are three types or classes of levers to be found in the human body which are defined by the relationships between the force, the weight, and the fulcrum of the body segment in question. The *first class lever* is defined as a lever that has the fulcrum located between the point of force application and the weight being moved **(P.5.0)**. First class levers are designed for either speed or force or a combination of the two. An example of a first class lever in the human body is the forward and backward movement of the head, as in nodding in the affirmative. The best example used to demonstrate the first class lever is the see-saw. It can be shown that by manipulation of the distance from the fulcrum of either of the occupants of a see-saw people or unequal weights can achieve balance.

The *second class lever* is defined as a lever having the weight to be moved located between the fulcrum and the point of force application (P.6.0). Second class levers generally produce movements of greater force at the expense of speed. There is some speculation regarding the existence of a true second class lever in the body.

18

The most commonly used example in which the foot in a weight supporting position is plantar flexed (as seen when rising upon on the toes). The most commonly associated machine to the second class lever is the wheelbarrow. The mechanical advantage gained from this configuration results in the ability to carry very heavy loads.

The most commonly occurring lever in the body is the ***third class lever.*** This lever is the one most responsible for human movement. In the third class lever, the point of force application is located between the fulcrum and the weight to be moved (P.7.0). There are many examples on the body of this type of lever. The hamstring muscles in the leg creating flexion and the biceps muscle of the upper arm flexing the forearm are typical examples. The third class lever is better designed to produce speed of movement. Examples of the common levers of the body are shown in Figure 3-4. It is unlikely that the third class lever would be widely demonstrated as a machine because of the great strength disadvantage seen in these levers.

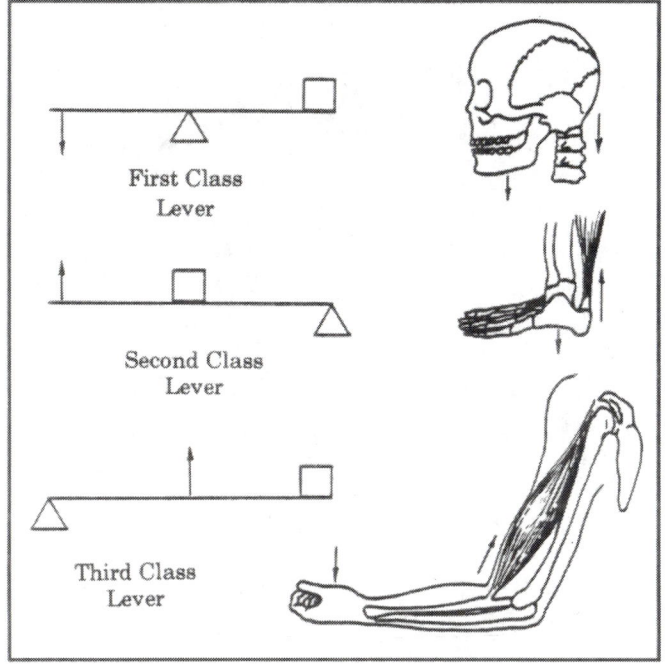

Figure 3-4   Levers of the Body

The key elements of the lever system in general are distinguished by their locations relative to the fulcrum of the lever. The ***weight arm*** of the lever is defined as the distance of the center of mass of the resistance (weight to be moved) from the fulcrum of the lever. Further, the ***force arm*** of the lever is the distance from the point of force application to the fulcrum of the lever and the ***fulcrum*** is the point about which the lever rotates. **(P.8.0)** As previously mentioned, using a lever allows for the development of a mechanical advantage when doing work. The ***mechanical advantage*** of a lever is the ratio of the length of the force arm to the length of the weight arm of a particular lever. Mathematically, it is defined thusly:

$$MA = FA / WA \quad (P. 9.0)$$

It can be logically deduced from this equation that the length of the force arm plays a major role in the production of a mechanical advantage in a lever. So, the longer the force arm a lever has, the greater the mechanical advantage it can produce. **(P.10.0)** Notice in Figure 3-5 the relative locations and proportions of the force arms and weight arms in the three types of levers.

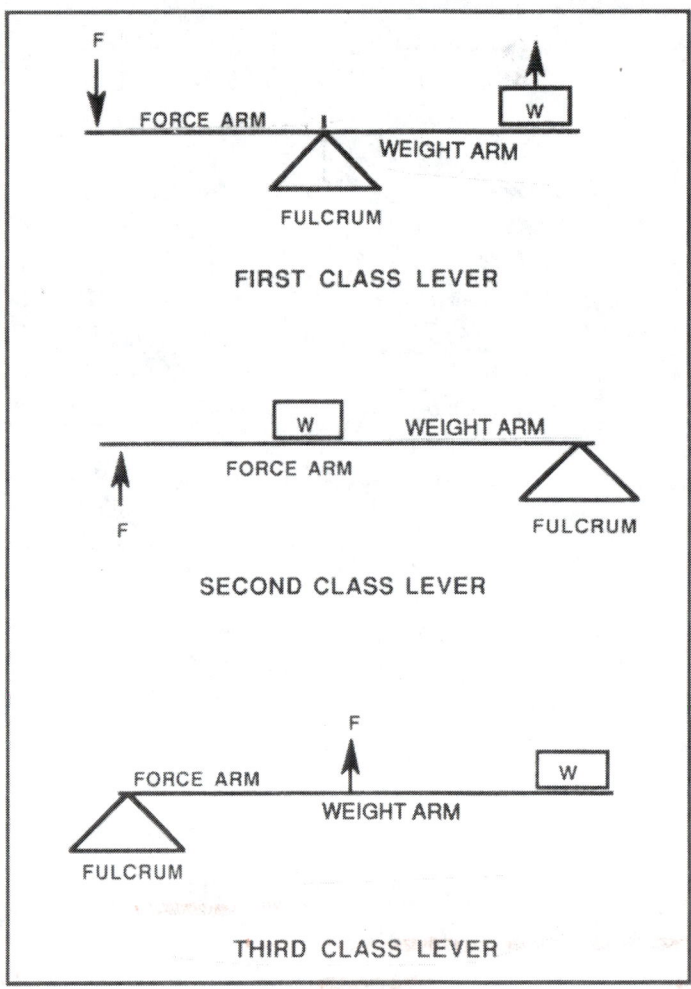

Figure 3-5   Classes of Levers and their Components

In order for any force to have its greatest effectiveness, it must be applied at right angles to the lever. (P.11.0) The force created by any simple lever system can be quantified by the simple equation:

$$F \times FA = W \times WA \quad \text{(P.12.0)}$$

This equation only applies for forces that are exerted at right angles to the lever in question.

Example

What is the force that the biceps muscle must exert to hold a 10-lb weight with the forearm in a parallel position, if the muscle connects to the forearm at a right angle two inches from the elbow joint. The distance from the center of gravity of the weight to the elbow is 16 inches?

To solve, first define the parameters:

$$W = 10 \text{ pounds}$$
$$WA = 16 \text{ inches}$$
$$FA = 2 \text{ inches}$$
$$F = ?$$

Then, plug parameters into the equation:

$$F \times FA = W \times WA \quad \text{or} \quad F \times 2 = 10 \times 16$$

Solve:

$$F \times 2 = 10 \times 16$$
$$F = 160 \,/\, 2$$
$$F = 80 \text{ lbs}$$

A schematic representation of the above problem is seen in Figure 3-6. The relative positions of the force arm, the weight arm and the center of mass of the resistance are also shown in this diagram. The basic formula, as previously mentioned, applies only to forces that are applied at right angles to a lever. However, in more complex problems requiring non-right angle force applications, the formula is still used as a first step in the solutions.

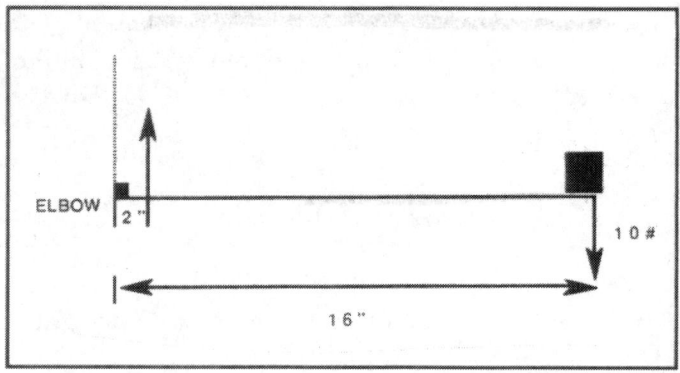

Figure 3-6

In order to progress beyond this initial step, it becomes necessary to understand some basic trigonometric and geometric functions as discussed in Chapter 2. The concept of Sine, Cosine, and Tangent relationships revolves around the ratios of the sides of a right triangle. With the knowledge of any angle (other than the right angle), or of any side of the triangle, one can solve for all the other parts of that triangle. The ratios of the lengths of the sides have been worked out and tabulated in the form of the Sine, Cosine, and Tangent tables shown in Table 2-1. Figure 3-7 clearly shows these relationships by example in triangle ABC.

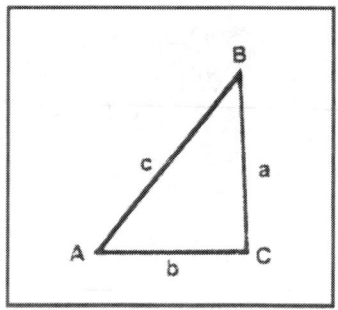

Figure 3-7

The **Sine** (abbreviated as *sin*) of an angle is the ratio of the side opposite that angle and the hypotenuse of the triangle. The **Cosine** (abbreviated as *cos*) of an angle is the ratio of the side adjacent to that angle and the hypotenuse of the triangle. And, the **Tangent** (abbreviated *tan*) is the ratio of the opposite to the adjacent side. All three of these relationships are important to the solutions to leverage and motion problems.

22

Then, if the biceps muscle happens to be exerting force at some angle other than 90 degrees, which is often the case, the construction of a simple right triangle of force vectors located at the point of force application is necessary. This construction is somewhat abstract, but a simplified and understandable one is shown in Figure 3-8.

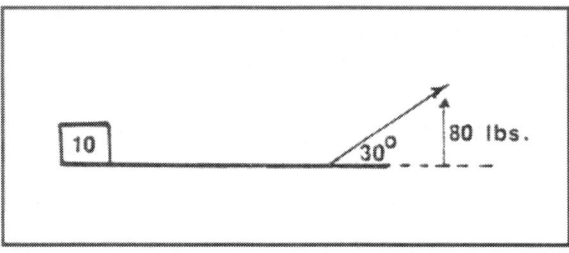

Figure 3-8

Notice that the theoretical force vector, marked as 80 lbs, represents the previously solved for force that was applied at 90 degrees to the lever. However, if the biceps were exerting force at 30 degrees, additional work must be done to solve the problem. In our construction the hypotenuse represents the actual force vector and the vertical vector represents the theoretical 90-degree force vector. Since we have already solved for the vertical vector and we know the angle of the hypotenuse, we are able to solve using the Sine of the 30 degree angle:

$$Sin\ 30 = 80\ /\ F$$
$$F = 80\ /\ Sin\ 30$$

Looking in the Sine tables for the value of Sin 30, we find that it is .5. Thus, we can solve the problem:

$$F = 80\ /\ .5 = 160\ lbs$$

So, it can be seen from the above examples, that, in order for the biceps muscle to support a weight even as small as 10 lbs., it must exert 160 lbs. of force when placed at a 30-degree angle. This solution applies to situations in which the lever is perpendicular to the force of gravity (i.e., parallel to the ground). The problem becomes more complex when the lever angle is below the horizontal.

Suppose, though, that we have a situation in which the lever is not parallel to the ground. This scenario presents a different set of problems due to the fact that the downward weight forces are not at right angles to the lever, and their true effective weights must be calculated. This is simple to do; although, it appears quite complicated at first. The first step (shown in Figure 3–9) is to calculate the true effective weights for the resistant forces in question. By simply constructing a perpendicular to the lever and using some simple geometric principles we can solve for the effective weights.

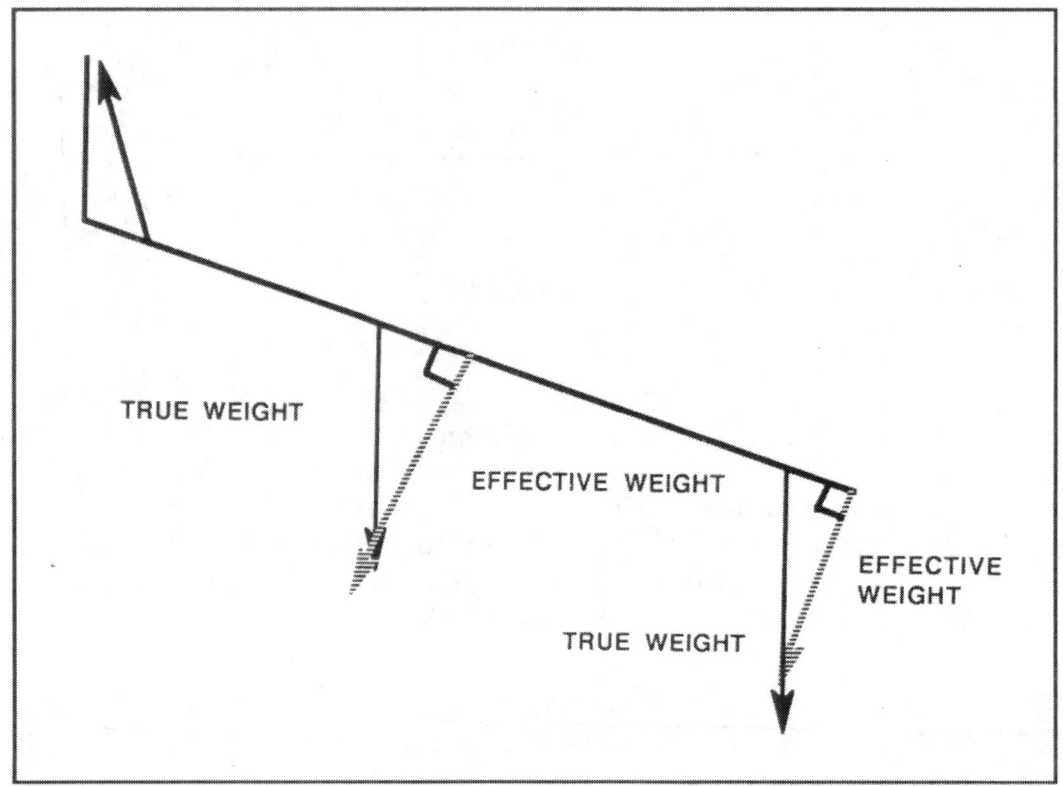

Figure 3-9

After the effective weights have been calculated, the solution follows the previously demonstrated problems: 1) Applying the equation for force at perpendicular to the lever; then 2) solving for non-right angle force applications.

Problems

1. From Table I, or on a calculator, determine:

    a. Sin 30, Sin 75, Sin 120

    b. Cos 25, Cos 50, Cos 80

    c. Tan 20, Tan 40, Tan 45

2. Determine the force necessary to lift a 100 lb. weight given a force arm of 1 in. and a weight arm of 5 in. What is the mechanical advantage of this lever system?

3. A mother weighs 150 lbs. and wants to see-saw with her daughter who weighs 75 lbs. Where should the fulcrum be placed on a 12-foot see-saw in order for the mother to balance the daughter

4. Joe has his forearm parallel to the floor with his biceps perpendicular to his forearm. Joe's bicep muscle connects to the forearm at a distance of 3 inches from the elbow joint. A 40-lb. weight is placed in Joe's hand with its center of gravity a distance of 9 inches from where the biceps inserts on the forearm. How much force must be exerted by the biceps just to hold the 40-lb. weight?

    Joe moves his arm such that his biceps is at an angle of 160 degrees with the forearm. What force must the biceps now exert to hold the weight?

5. A weight lifter is lying on her back, with her thigh fixed in a vertical position. The knee is bent at 90 degrees, resulting in a horizontal position of the lower leg. The quadriceps muscle inserts 4 inches below the knee joint and pulls at a 5-degree angle. The lower leg weighs 15 lbs. and its center of mass is located 10 inches from the knee joint.

    How much force do the quads have to exert just to hold the lower leg in this position?

    How much force is exerted when a 30 lb. weight is added at a distance of 18 inches from the knee?

6. John has his forearm parallel to the floor with his biceps perpendicular to it. John's biceps muscle inserts on the forearm at a distance of 2 inches. from the elbow joint. The forearm weighs 20 lbs. and its center of gravity is located 6 inches from the elbow. How much force must the biceps exert to hold the forearm parallel to the floor?

An 80 lb. weight is placed in John's hand with its center of gravity a distance of 12 inches from where the biceps inserts on the forearm. How much total force is needed to hold the weight in this position?

John moves his arm such that his biceps makes an angle of 150 degrees with the forearm. What force is now necessary to hold the weight in this position?

7. Jill is in a standing position with her thigh held parallel to the floor. Her thigh weighs 20 lbs. and its center of mass is located 10 inches from the hip joint. The hip flexor muscle inserts on the femur at a distance of 4 inches from the joint at an angle of 45 degrees. Her knee is bent at a 90-degree angle and the distance from her hip to knee is 18 inches. Her lower leg weighs 12 lbs.

   How much force must the hip flexor exert to hold this position?

   If Jill were to extend her lower leg, resulting in a shift of the center of mass of the entire leg to a location 1 inch above the knee, how much force would then be needed?

8. Mike holds a weight of 50 lbs. in his hand with his forearm at an angle of 60 degrees below the horizontal. The center of gravity of the weight is located 12 inches from the elbow joint. Mike's forearm weighs 25 lbs. and its center of mass is located 4 inches from the point of insertion of the biceps muscle. The biceps muscle inserts at a distance of 2 inches from the elbow joint at an angle of 120 degrees to the forearm.

   a) What is the effective weight of the weight and of the forearm?

   b) How much force must the biceps exert to hold the weight in this position?

9. A shot putter holds an 8 lb. shot at her neck in a position ready to put it. It is 12 inches from the center of the shot to the elbow joint and the triceps muscle attaches on the forearm at a distance of 2 inches from the elbow joint at a 2° angle. The forearm weighs 5 lbs. and its center of mass is located 4 inches from the elbow. The forearm is positioned at a 30-degree angle to the horizontal. How much force must her triceps muscle exert to start the shot in motion?

Exercises

1. List the mechanical mechanisms that operate in the body—hinges, ball and socket, pulley, wheel and axle

2. Explain why a muscle needs to be strongest under stretch.

3. Locate three levers in your body and give the fulcrum, force point, and weight point in each. Identify the class of lever represented and tell the kind of movement desirable with each type.

4. Identify the following mechanisms as they exist in the human body:

   a. hinges

   b. ball and socket

   c. pulley

   d. wheel and axle

5. Give a sports example for each of Newton's laws of motion:
   a.

   b.

   c.

EXPERIMENT 3.1

Purpose

The purposes of this experiment are to:

1. Demonstrate the mechanical disadvantage of third class levers.
2. Compare the weight lifted and the force produced by prime movers.
3. Relate the mechanical principles employed in the human body with levers.

Procedures

With the help of a partner execute the following conditions. Record the required information in the results section of this report.

Condition 1. With the help of your partner, determine the maximum weight you can hold for 4 seconds in the curl position with your elbow at a 90 degree angle.

Condition 2. With the help of your partner, determine the maximum weight you can lift by rising up on your toes.

Condition 3. Perform as many pull-ups as possible. Count 4 points for each complete pull-up with the chin over the bar. Give 1 point for elbow bend to 135 degrees; 2 points for bend to 90 degrees; 3 points for bend to 45 degrees.

Results

Condition 1   Record maximum weight held for 5 seconds   _____

Condition 2   Record maximum force on toes   _____

Condition 3   Record pull-up points   _____

1. What prime mover did you energize to hold the weight? How much force were you able to exert?

2. What prime mover did you contract to lift the weight? How much force was exerted to lift this weight?

3. At what position did you fail on your last pull-up? Why do you feel you stopped at this point rather than the extended position?

4. What principle is involved here?

EXPERIMENT 3.2

Purpose

The purposes of this experiment are to:

1. Experience the effect of air resistance on falling balls.
2. Compare the effect of air resistance on falling balls of different weights.
3. Compare the effect of air resistance on falling balls of equal weight but different cross sectional areas.

Procedures

With the help of a partner execute the following conditions. Record the required information for each condition in the results section of this report.

Condition 1. Drop a golf ball, table tennis ball, and a cotton ball a distance of 16 feet or more. The balls are to be dropped at the same time from the same height. A partner is to record the order in which they hit the ground.

Condition 2. Drop a table tennis ball that is weighted so that it is the same weight as a plastic baseball. Drop both balls from a height of 16 feet or more. Drop both balls at the same time. With the help of a partner, record the order in which they hit the ground. Note: The Table tennis ball can be weighted by injecting water into it or by filling it with sand. Be sure to cover the hole in the ball with tape.

Results

Condition 1. Record the order of contact with the ground:

_____3_____ cotton ball

_____1_____ golf ball

_____2_____ table tennis ball

Note: The table tennis ball can be weighted by injecting water into it or by filling it with sand. Be sure to cover the hole in the ball with tape.

1. Where was the velocity of the balls the greatest? The least?

2. Where was the acceleration of the balls the greatest? The least?

3. If dropped from a high level, the acceleration of each would approach _____ ? Which ball would reach this acceleration first? Last?

4. Upon which ball did air resistance have the greatest effect? Why?

5. Upon which ball did air resistance have the least effect? Why?

Conclusions

State conclusions that will explain your results:

1.

2.

3.

4.

5.

6.

7.

8.

Key Terms from Chapter 3

Efficiency —Quality or degree of effective operation in comparison with cost in energy. Work output / work input.

Fulcrum—The point about which a lever rotates.

Force Arm—The distance from the fulcrum to the point of force application on a lever.

Lever—A rigid bar that revolves about a fixed point, the fulcrum.

Mechanical Advantage—The ratio of the force that performs useful work of a machine to the force which is applied to the machine.

Pulley—A simple machine used to change the direction of a pulling force by means of a band, belt, etc.

Frontal Plane (Coronal)—A vertical plane passing through the body laterally dividing it into a front (anterior) and back (posterior) half.

Sagittal Plane—A vertical plane passing through the body dividing it into left and right sides. If it occurs at the mid-line, it is referred to as the mid-sagittal plane and divides the body into equal halves.

Transverse Plane (Horizontal)—A plane at right angles to the sagittal and frontal planes, dividing the body into upper and lower sections.

Weight Arm—Distance from the fulcrum to the point of resistance on a lever.

4
LINEAR MOVEMENT
AND PROJECTILES

The primary objective of most physical education activities is linear movement of some type. Whether propelling the body through space, or hurling a projectile across a great distance, the outcome is linear movement. All linear movements are the result of a series of rotary movements involving the many leverage systems of the body. Movement is basic to most sports. Sports either entail actual movements of the whole body (**translations**) as in sprinting and swimming, or movements of an object (**projectile**) as in throwing or striking. Movements may also involve activities that resist the movement of others as in wrestling or football. Often, activities involve movements of body segments, such as in modern dance.

Kinematics is the branch of mechanical analysis that involves the description of movements or of the results of movements. The movements may be either vertical or horizontal, but most often are neither completely vertical nor horizontal, but a combination of the two. When a shot putter delivers the shot, the key component of interest is the horizontal displacement of that shot. But, it is obvious to even the inexperienced observer that the path (**trajectory**) taken by the shot consists of more than simple horizontal components (see Fig. 4-1).

Time is a very important element in studies of various types of motion. If a person is running a race, the most important consideration is how long it took that person to reach the finish line. Generally, **in kinematics, motion is characterized in terms of velocity and acceleration (P.1.0).** These are both vector quantities and are two-dimensional. The velocity of a body is defined as the rate of change of position of that body. Velocity and speed are often mistakenly used interchangeably. Velocity refers to displacement of a given body in a given direction and is thus a vector quantity. Speed is properly referred to as the rate of movement in a non-specified direction and is scalar or one-dimensional.

The distance a body travels is equal to its average velocity times the length of time it traveled (P.2.0).

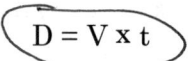

$$D = V \times t$$

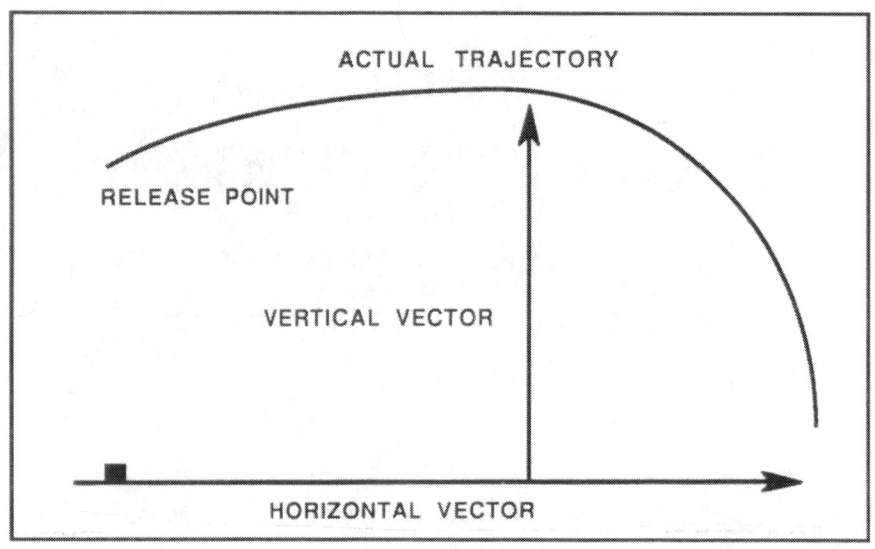

Figure 4-1 Horizontal and Vertical Components of Trajectory for a Shot

A runner averages 10 meters/sec for 100 meters. What time for the 100 meter dash can be expected?

$$D = V \times t \qquad 100 = 10 \times t \qquad t = 10 \text{ sec.}$$

In the human body, velocity is created by the action of third class levers which creates rotary motion that is converted into linear motion (P.3.0). With the exception of falling bodies, all human movements and projectile motions are the result of this phenomenon.

Extremely important to the consideration of movement are two elements over which we have little control: gravity and air resistance. Many of the physical laws which govern how far, how fast, or how high an athlete may travel function differently in the real world, than could be expected in a vacuum.

Many kinesiology activities are affected by the pull of gravity (P.4.0). Anytime an object is thrown, hit, or kicked or a person jumps, tumbles or vaults, gravity plays a vital role in the quality of that performance. The attractive force of the earth causes an acceleration of any projected body toward the earth at a rate of approximately 32.2 ft/sec/sec (9.i m/sec/sec). In many cases, this acceleration due to gravity is not constant. The more dense (small area, high weight) an object is the more predictable the acceleration is. **Most objects, however, accelerate at 32.2 ft/sec/sec until air resistance retards the rate of acceleration (P.5.0).** If an object is dropped or projected, the most important force acting on it is gravity. In fact, if two objects of the same weight and density are used, it can be shown quite dramatically that gravity will affect both in the same way. If one of these objects is projected horizontally and the other dropped from the same height, they will contact the ground at exactly the same instant; even if these objects are cannon balls and one is fired from a cannon!

The effects of gravity upon a body or an object are focused around a point referred to as its center of mass or center of gravity. The location of the center of mass in humans has been well documented and the effect of movements upon that center of mass can be shown experimentally with relative ease. **When a person jumps into the air, the height to which the center of mass can be raised above the supporting surface cannot be changed by body position; but, the position of the center of mass within the body can be changed (P.6.0).**

Examples

In diving, the path the center of gravity of the diver will take after leaving the board cannot be changed, but the position of the body about the center of gravity may be changed by limb movements.

When jumping center in basketball, the legs drive the center of gravity only to a certain height above the floor. However, the position of the center of gravity in the body may be lowered by limb movements (i.e, lowering one arm, pointing toes, straightening legs) at the height of the jump and thus allowing the jumper to tip the ball at a greater height (See Fig. 4-2).

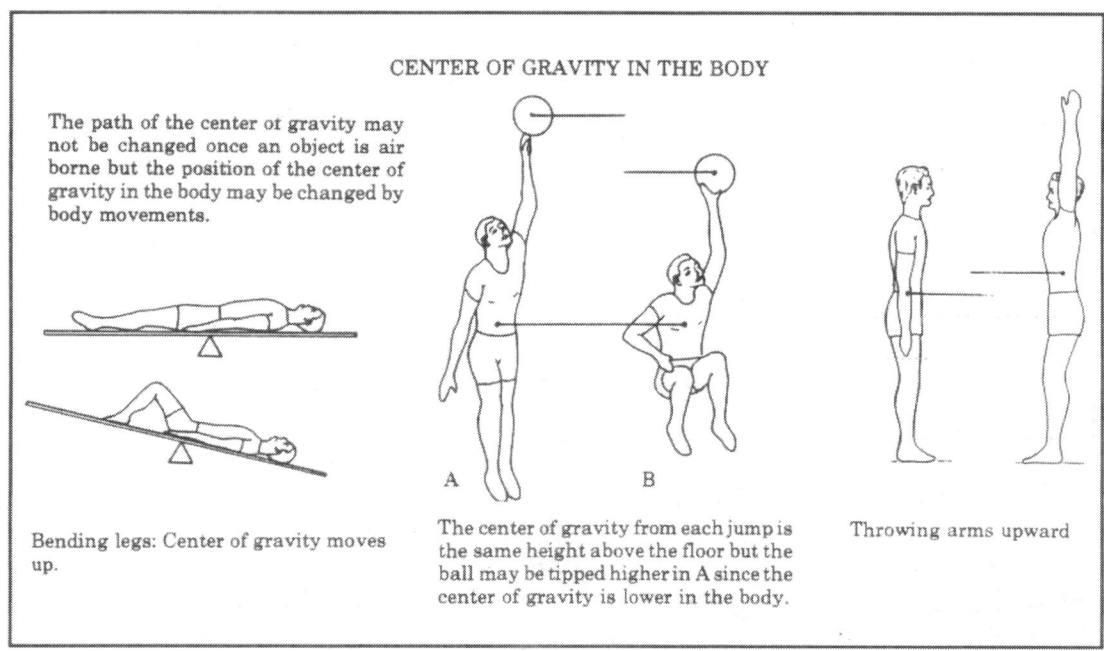

CENTER OF GRAVITY IN THE BODY

The path of the center of gravity may not be changed once an object is air borne but the position of the center of gravity in the body may be changed by body movements.

Bending legs: Center of gravity moves up.

A   B

The center of gravity from each jump is the same height above the floor but the ball may be tipped higher in A since the center of gravity is lower in the body.

Throwing arms upward

Figure 4-2

The movement of the center of mass upward or downward within a body create an interesting effect called <u>Transfer of Momentum</u>. This phenomenon occurs when the <u>kinetic energy created by one of the limbs of the body is actually transferred to the center of gravity of the body.</u> A dramatic example of this important effect was seen in the ancient Olympics, when jumpers in the running long jump were able to span distances in excess of modern world records. Their secret was the use of hand weights that were swung forward at takeoff and released backward at the peak of the jump. Experts agree that in modern day high jumping, the use of the swing leg and arms contributes approximately 70% of the total vertical component of lift in that event.

The principal of transferring momentum from the part to the whole suggests that momentum from any part of the body can be transferred to the body as a whole (P. 7.0). When executing a vertical jump, a person will swing both arms vigorously upward in order to achieve a vertical acceleration (movement) of the center of gravity at takeoff. This can be dramatically shown by standing and vigorously thrusting the arms upward without attempting to jump with the legs. The body is literally pulled into the air a small amount. Another dramatic example is seen when a gymnast executes a kip-up. The momentum of the legs is transferred to the entire body literally pulling it off the floor (see Fig 4-3.

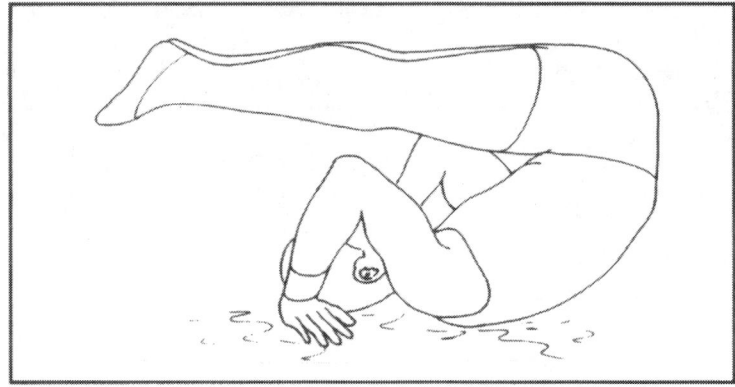

Figure 4-3 Kip-Up:
Application of transferring momentum from the part to the whole

Another example of the manipulation of the location of the center of gravity in the body can be seen in the **Principle of the Ends and the Middle. When a body is in the air free of support, and the head and feet move downward, the hips will move upward (P.8.0.).** When a pole vaulter assumes a jack-knifed position over the bar by lowering his or her legs the hips rise over the bar. The same is true when a high jumper arches over the bar. The advantage of when a high jumper arches over the bar. The advantage of these positions lies in the fact that the center of mass of the body moves to a position outside the body and actually passes under the bar in both cases (see Fig. 4-4).

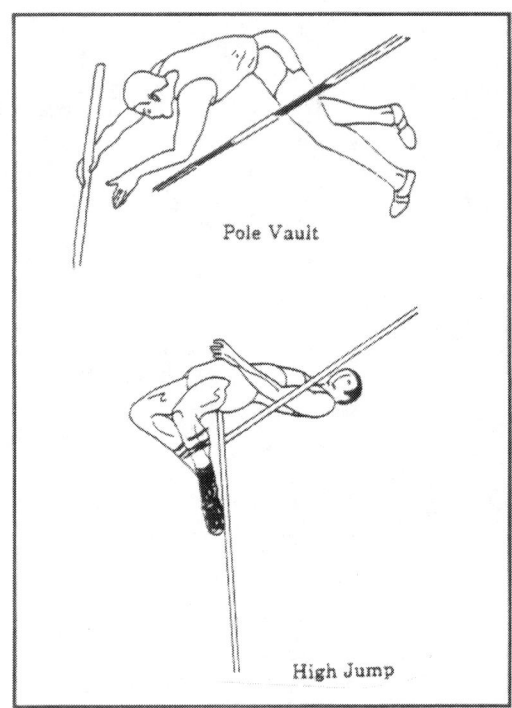

Pole Vault

High Jump

**Figure 4-4 Application of the Principle
of the Ends and the Middle**

The two principle components acting upon an object that has become a projectile are gravity and air resistance. Once an object has been thrown, kicked, or shot, these two forces act to retard acceleration. With the exception of a dropped object, all projectiles lose speed once they are released. **Gravity pulls all bodies toward the earth at a rate of approximately 32 feet/sec/sec (or 9.8 meters/sec/sec) until air resistance retards acceleration (P.9.0).**

Examples

A shot dropped from a height will be traveling at the rate of 32 ft/sec at the end of the first second, 64 ft/sec at the end of the second two, and so on until it is affected by air resistance. The shot will drop 16 feet in the first second; 48 feet in the next second; 80 feet in the next, and so on. If the shot was put at an angle of 40 degrees with the horizontal at a velocity of 36 ft/sec, what would be its horizontal velocity at release?

$$\text{Cos } 40 = V_h / 36 \text{ fps}$$
$$V_h = 36 \text{ (Cos 40)}$$
$$V_h = (36) \text{ (.7660)}$$
$$V_h = 27.58 \text{ ft/sec}$$

What would be the vertical velocity of the shot at release under the same parameters?

$$\text{Sin } 40 = V_v / 36 \text{ fps}$$
$$V_v = (36) \text{ (.6428)}$$
$$V_v = 23.14 \text{ ft/sec}$$

How high did the shot rise from the point of release?

$$V_i^2 = 2ad$$
$$(23.14)^2 = (2) \text{ (32) (d)}$$
$$d = 535.46 / 64$$
$$d = 8.37 \text{ ft.}$$

(or)

$$H = V_i^2 \text{ (Sin } \theta)^2 / 2g$$
$$H = (36)^2 \text{ (.6428)}^2 / 64$$
$$H = (1296) \text{ (.4132) } / 64$$
$$H = 8.37 \text{ ft.}$$

It is important to note that vector representations of velocity and distance have both vertical and horizontal components and can be solved with knowledge of the angle of projection and one of the other components of the triangle relationship. Care must be taken, however, to make sure that velocities are used when they should be and that displacements are used when they should be.

Observation of different objects that are projected in sports activities, reveals that the paths which they take are different. The path taken by a projectile is called the **trajectory** of that object. Depending upon the relative density (weight vs. volume) of the object, the trajectory will be somewhat parabolic in nature. For most projectiles, the trajectory is a **skewed parabola**. There are some generalities that can be made concerning trajectories. **The trajectory that an object will travel is a skewed parabola. Its upward limb will be longer than the downward limb placing the apex closer to the spot at which the object falls. The time** it takes for the object to reach the apex is less than the time it takes it to come down from the apex. The angle of projection is also smaller than the angle down (P. 10.0).

Example

A baseball thrown from center field to home plate follows a skewed curve and has a vertical deceleration until it reaches its highest point and its vertical velocity is zero. It then begins to fall down towards the ground and is accelerating due to gravity.

The key factor in the shape of the path the projectile takes is air resistance. A typical skewed parabolic path is shown in Figure 4-5. An obvious example of this phenomenon can be seen when a badminton shuttle is cleared. The effects of spin will be discussed in a later chapter plays an important role in the trajectory of a projectile. Also, the more dense an object the less skewed its trajectory will be. A 16-lb. shot normally has a trajectory that is nearly parabolic because of its relativity high density and slow velocity.

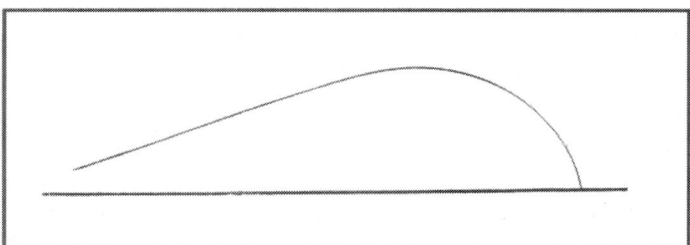

Figure 4-5 Trajectory of a ball in flight in a sea of air

The displacement of various projectiles can be estimated using two formulae. **For a heavy object with low initial velocity and a parabolic trajectory, the range of the object from release to return to the same height as projected can be estimated using the range formula for a parabola (P.11.0).**

$$R = V_i^2 \ \mathrm{Sin}\ 2\theta\ /\ g$$

Where:

      R = range in feet

      V_i = initial velocity in feet per second

      g = 32 feet per second per second

      θ = angle of projection with the horizontal

Example

A hammer leaves the hand and lands at the same height as it was released. It leaves at a 45 degree angle with the horizontal at a velocity of 50 ft/sec. How far did the hammer travel?

$$R = (50)^2 \text{ Sin } (2)(45) / 32$$
$$R = \quad 2500 \text{ (Sin 90) } / 32$$
$$R = \quad 2500(1) / 32$$
$$R = 78. \text{ 13 feet}$$

The range formula that is used above does not take into account air resistance and density of the projectile. Therefore, it can only be used as an estimate. It is fairly reasonable to use this equation for high-density projectiles that are released at low velocities. Table 4–1 shows some parameters for the range of various balls used in sports and games.

Table 4–1
Research Report
(Kinematic Laboratory Results)
Summary of Factors Influencing the Angle of Projection
and Range of Selected Balls Thrown for Distance

Ball	Diameter (inches)	Cross-sectional area	Weight (oz.)	Mean Initial Velocity (ft./sec.)	Mean Initial Angle (degrees)	Mean Range (ft.)	Parabolic Mean (ft.)	Mean K
Tennis Ball	2.50	4.91	2.08	90.66	32	125.33	230.30	.57
Baseball	2.89	6.49	5	105.99	27.50	220.05	288.91	.77
Softball	3.82	11.46	6.75	90.88	38.80	198.25	248.25	.82
5" Playground Ball	5.57	24.37	6	74.24	27.10	113.70	138.71	.83
Water Polo Ball	8.59	58.00	15	76.80	37.60	93.92	174.38	.59
10" Playground Ball	9.40	69.40	15.51	62.76	35.20	86.43	116.61	.77
Basketball	9.55	71.65	21	57.81	34	92.82	96.43	.96
12" Playground Ball	10.25	86.55	15.03	69.52	42.06	89.97	150.28	.60
MEAN	6.57	41.10	10.80	78.58	34.30	127.56	180.48	.74

In attempting to find an equation to account for air resistance, researchers have developed a range formula that applies only in the following, very specific conditions. **The formula for determining the range that a thrown *softball* or *baseball* will travel, when thrown at the optimal angle of *30 degrees* with an initial velocity of *90 – 120 ft/sec* is: $R = 2\,WV\,/\,\pi\,(r)$ (P.12.0).**

Example

A baseball weighing 5 oz. with a radius of 1.4 inches is thrown for distance at a 30-degree angle with the horizontal and an initial velocity of 120 ft/sec. How far did the baseball travel down range before it hit the ground?

$$R = 2WV\,/\,\pi\,r$$

Where: W = 5 oz.

r = 1.4 inches

π = 22 / 7   3.14

V = 120 ft/sec.

R = (2) (5) (120) / (22/7) (1.4)

R = (2) (5) (120) / (3.142) (1.4)

R = 1200 / 4.3988

R = 277 ft.

Compare this scenario using the earlier mentioned range formula and it is easy to see that there is a major difference. What is this difference? Of course, it is the effect of air resistance that is accounted for in the latter formula.

So, it can be seen here that there are four major components that affect the flight of a projectile. **As an object becomes airborne, the path of its center of gravity is determined by initial velocity, direction, air resistance and weight (P. 13.0).**

In all types of activities where greatest distance is the goal, maximum initial velocity is desired along with an initial angle of projection of the center of gravity of the object of approximately 30-degrees to the horizontal. **Because air resistance is a major factor in the flight of most balls used in sports it has been found that the optimum angle of projection to get the greatest distance is around 30 degrees (P.14.0).**

Principle 14.0 should be viewed in light of the other factors that affect trajectory, as well. One consideration is the aerodynamic properties of the projectile being observed. A javelin, a discus, and a baseball have very different aerodynamic properties and, therefore, have different optimal angles of projection.

The time of flight of a projectile is determined by the angle of projection and the initial velocity of the object. The formula for estimation of the time of flight is:

$$T_f = 2V_i \, \text{Sin} \, \theta \, / \, g$$

Where:

T_f = time of flight

V_i = initial velocity

θ = angle of projection

g = 32 ft/sec/sec

Of course, consideration must be given for the relative density of the object. Objects with a large weight to cross sectional area ratio that are released at relatively low velocities yield better application of the formula.

Example

If a shot is put at an angle of 45 degrees with the horizontal and with an initial velocity of 36 ft/sec. in the direction of the put, what will be its time of flight from the point of release to the same level at which it was released?

$$T_f = (2) \, (36) \, (\text{Sin} \, 45) \, / \, 32$$

$$T_f = (2) \, (36) \, (.7071) \, / \, 32$$

$$T_f = \ 50.91 \, / \, 32$$

$$T_f = 1.59 \ \text{sec.}$$

If the shot were released at a 30 degree angle the time of flight back to the same level as release would be:

$$T_f = (2) \, (36) \, (\text{Sin} \, 30) \, / \, 32$$

$$T_f = (2) \, (36) \, (.5) \, / \, 32$$

$$T_f = \ 36 \, / \, 32$$

$$T_f = \ 1.125 \ \text{sec.}$$

If time of flight is an important factor in performance, then it is most convenient to reduce the angle of projection to as flat an angle as possible. For example, when executing a drop shot in badminton, the shuttle must have a downward angle in order to reduce the time of flight, thus, allowing the shot to be effective. A baseball outfielder must throw the ball from the outfield at a flat angle for his or her throw to be effective.

The converse is true for this situation as well. In order to optimize height gained and to allow time for execution of skills, the takeoff angle or projection angle should be increased. Although a punter could most likely punt the ball much farther with a low angle of projection, he must allow time for his defenders to get down field. Consequently, the optimal angle for a punted football it approximately 50 degrees. A gymnast who is executing a tumbling pass and wishes to perform a back flip takes off at a near vertical angle in order to achieve greater height.

For objects having nearly parabolic trajectories (those with relatively high density and low initial velocities), the optimal angle is generally around 45 degrees. **If a heavy object is projected the same number of degrees above and below 45 degrees, it will attain the same distance in each case when measured to the horizontal level of the point of release (P. 15.0).** In other words, with release velocity constant, a steel ball thrown at 30 degrees will travel the same distance as one thrown at 60 degrees (see Fig. 4-6).

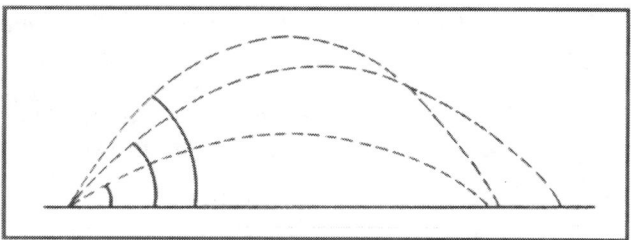

**Figure 4-6 Path of an object
when air resistance is not a factor**

Although it seems obvious to most of us, it should be noted here that one very important principle has been left out. Logically, consideration of human motion and of projectile motion is not complete without quantification of the linear displacement of the person or object. In other words, **the shortest distance between two points is a straight line (P. 16. 0).** At a glance this seems like a trivial principle, but track coaches spend a great deal of time teaching their sprinters to run in a straight line. A baseball or softball player who is attempting to score from second base will be more successful if third base is *not* rounded too widely.

Problems

1. (A) A cross country runner travels a cross country course of 3 miles in 15 minutes. What is average speed in miles per hour? What is the average speed in yards per second?

(B) If while you are driving down the highway at 80 miles per hour you allow your mind to wander from the road for 0.5 seconds, how far do you travel during this time that you are not paying attention to the road?

(C) What is the instantaneous velocity of a falling shot at the end of 3 seconds of its fall? How many feet did the shot fall during the third second of its fall? How far did the ball fall during the first 4 seconds of its fall?

2. Nolan Ryan has been clocked on his fast ball at 100.9 miles per hour. What is the velocity of the ball in feet per second? How much time elapses before the ball gets to the plate? (assume that the ball is released at 55 feet from the plate)

3. If a long jumper achieves a 2-foot elevation of his center of gravity and takes off at an angle of 20 degrees, what is his horizontal velocity at the takeoff?

4. If 8 kg. shot is put at an angle of 42 degrees with the horizontal with a velocity of 25 ft/sec. in the direction of the put, what will be its upward velocity at the moment of release? How high will the shot go if released from a height of 6 feet?

5. At the moment of takeoff, a long jumper has a forward velocity of 20 ft/sec. Vertical velocity is 20 ft/sec. What is the angle of takeoff?

How high does his center of gravity rise if at takeoff it is at a height of 3ft.?

6. A high jumper leaves the ground with a velocity of 12 ft/sec. at an angle of 85 degrees. The center of gravity is 2.5 feet above the ground at takeoff. What was the total height of the center of gravity above the ground at the peak of the jump?

7. If a 16 lb. shot is put at an angle of 40 degrees with the horizontal and with a velocity of 38 ft/sec. in the direction of the put, what will be its time of flight and distance traveled from the point of release to the return to the same level at which it was released? What would be the time of flight and distance if the angle were 30 degrees?

8. Two girls at their elementary school field day are participating in the softball throw. Erin throws at an angle of 30 degrees and with an initial velocity of 100 ft/sec. Lyn on her final toss lets her ball go at an angle of 30 degrees but with an initial velocity of 90 ft/sec. Which girl won the contest? What was the winning distance? (the weight of the softball is 6.67 ounces and the diameter is 3.8 inches)

9. An outfielder in baseball throws a baseball at an angle of 30 degrees to the horizontal at a velocity of 98 ft/sec. What is the range of the ball?

How much did air resistance affect the range of the baseball?

Exercises

1. Describe sports activities that are affected by the law of falling bodies.

2. Describe conditions that exist which make the optimum angle for putting the shot less than 45 degrees.

3. If one wants to obtain good coverage by the defending team punting the football, at what angle should the ball be punted? Is this angle the optimal angle for distance? Explain.

4. Practice jumping for height as in trying to touch the rim of a basketball goal. What helps you get height? Describe the technique you used.

5. Perform several actions that demonstrate the principle of transfer of momentum from the part to the whole. Describe what happened.

6. What is meant by linear movement? How is it described?

7. If a rifle bullet is shot horizontally three feet above the ground and another bullet is dropped at the same instant from the same height, which bullet will hit the ground first?

8. What angle will get the greatest distance for a projectile? How is this affected by wind conditions?

9. What angle will get the same distance but in less time than a 60 degree angle? (Give specific conditions for your answer.)

EXPERIMENT 4.1

Purpose

The purposes of this experiment are to:

1. Experience height reached in jumping by the use of various techniques.

2. Compare the height obtained under conditions using various techniques.

3. Relate the mechanical principles employed to the techniques used to obtain height in jumping.

Procedures

Secure two partners and administer the two-foot jumping test under the various conditions listed below to each other.

Using a chair or table on which to stand, hold a yardstick at the height your partner jumps for each condition and measure that height above the floor. Record the maximum height jumped for each condition in the results section of this report. Summarize and discuss the results in the form of a lab report.

Task

Execute a one step vertical jump under each of the following conditions and record the maximum head height of three trials for each condition.

Condition 1: Execute the jump with the arms held firmly at the sides of the body.

Condition 2: Execute the jump by forcefully throwing the arms upward above the head.

Condition 3 Execute the jump by forcefully throwing the arms upward at take-off and then forcefully bringing them down to your sides at the peak of the jump.

Condition 4: Place the yard stick against the wall at the highest height achieved for any condition. Using any technique including running or stepping into the jump, attempt to touch the yardstick with your head. Make notes of the technique you used.

Results

In tabular form record the results for each condition. Display your results in graphic format.

Key discussion questions

What condition was best for you to jump off of both feet and attain greatest height?

Describe the mechanical principles you used in your best jump.

Why do you think you were able to achieve greatest height using this technique?

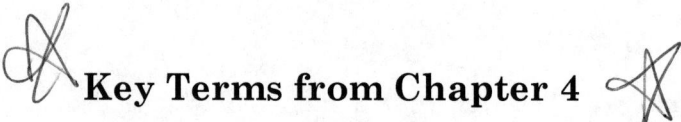# Key Terms from Chapter 4

Acceleration—rate of change of velocity

Displacement—movement of an object in a specific linear direction

Inertia—property of an object that requires an effort in order to change its position

Linear Motion—change of position in a straight line from one point to another

Motion—continuing change of place or position

Momentum—product of the mass of an object and its velocity

Movement —change of position, destroying or upsetting the equilibrium of a body

Projectile—a thrown or kicked or shot object

Speed—rate of motion

Trajectory—path of a projectile

Velocity—rate of change of position

5
STABILITY

The performance of most sports requires the athlete to maintain balance of the body, to the extent demanded by the particular sport. However, in many cases the athlete who is successful must operate on a very fine line between being off balance and stable. To be successful as an professional running back requires excellent control of the center of gravity; but stability becomes very relative. In this chapter, the control of this property known as stability, and the importance of the location of the center of gravity relative to the base of support is discussed. When a body is at rest it is said to be in a state of equilibrium. The primary difference between equilibrium and stability is a matter of semantics. But, simply stated, stability is a degree of equilibrium. It is important here to note that bodies come in all shapes and sizes. The study of **Morphology** is a process by which bodies are classified according to general shapes. Typically, there are three fundamental shapes used to describe a person.

Mesomorph, is the shape defined by a triangular appearance. That is, the person has wide shoulders and a relatively narrow waist. The **Endomorph** is characterized by roundness. Frequently, endomorphs may be described as "pear-shaped." The **Ectomorph** is the body type sometimes called, "string bean." This person is tall and thin in appearance.

People can be on the extremes of these body types or they can possess some characteristics seen in more than one type. Most often, though, a person will fall into one of these categories.

Certainly, morphology plays an important role in the location of the center of gravity within the body. Likewise, there are significant differences due to gender. Typically, the male center of gravity is a few centimeters higher than the female. This is not always the case, because a mesomorphic female may actually have a higher center of gravity than an endomorphic male.

Because the typical toddler is somewhat top heavy, the center of gravity is very high. The relative weight of the head of a toddler is much greater than that of an adult. Also, the toddler will typically add to the problem by holding the arms high during early walking development.

There are four important factors that determine the amount of stability a body possesses:

1) **Stability is directly proportional to the area of the base of support upon which the body rests (P. 1. 0).**

Therefore, the larger the area of the base of support upon which a body rests, the greater its stability.

Examples

When a wrestler assumes the down or referee's position, he creates as wide a base of support as possible in order to resist his opponent.

A skier who wishes to be more stable in bad snow conditions assumes a wider position or "wide track."

There are many instances in sport where manipulation of the area of the base plays a vital role in the successful performance of that sport. It should likewise be noted that the converse is true regarding the relationship between base area and stability. That is, the smaller the area of the base, the less stable the body. A swimmer enhances his or her starting position by assuming as small a base of support as possible.

2) **Stability in a given direction is directly proportional to the horizontal distance of the center of gravity from the edge of the base toward the given direction of movement (P. 2. 0.).**

In almost any sporting event, athletes will shift their centers of gravity in the direction of intended movement. Those who do not will often be unsuccessful in their trials. In order to fully understand the concepts of stability, one must understand the concept of **center of gravity** of the body. Center of gravity or center of mass is defined as **the point in the body about which the mass or weight of the body is equally distributed.** The location of the center of gravity in individuals varies depending upon gender and morphology (shape). A summary of selected gender differences can be seen in Table 5-1.

The location of the center of gravity in a body can change depending upon the alignment of the body segments. The movement of a body segment in a given direction causes a shifting of the center of gravity toward the direction of movement. There are often situations in sport in which the center of gravity is located outside of the body, as was discussed in Chapter 4. Manipulation of the location of the center of mass plays a vital role in the performance of sport skills.

Certainly the location of the center of gravity within the body of each of the morphologies is affected. There is obviously a significant difference between genders in location of center of gravity. Typically, the male center of gravity is a few centimeters higher than that of the female. This is not always the case, because a mesomorphic female may actually have a higher center of gravity than an endomorphic male.

50

Table 5-1
Research Report
(Kinematic Laboratory Results)
The Effect of the Movement of Body Parts on height of Center of Gravity

	Mean Men (N = 30)	Mean Women (N = 30)	Average (N = 60)
Center of Gravity, Both hands at side	99.72 cm 56.28%*	91.68 cm 55.78%	95.70 cm 56.03%
Center of Gravity, One hand up	103.08 cm 58.16%	94.28 cm 57.36%	98.68 cm 57.75%
Center of Gravity, Two hands up	106.31 cm 60.01%	96.73 cm 58.46%	101.52 cm 59.23%
Center of Gravity, Knees up	107.82 cm 60.87%	99.47 cm 60.52%	103.64 cm 60.70%

*Percent of total body height.

Examples

If a person wishes to resist force from another in a given direction, one should widen his/her base in the direction opposite the force and shift the center of mass toward that base.

Any athlete attempting to stop movement in one direction should shift the center of mass in the direction opposite of that movement.

A sprinter in track leans forward in the starting block in order to decrease stability in the forward direction.

Obviously, stability is compromised when the center of gravity is shifted to a position outside the base of support. One needs only to observe a toddler beginning to walk to see this phenomenon. Humans are innately equipped to regain stability quickly. As we grow to adulthood we become more adept at this skill. Rarely do we see adults stumbling and running before they topple over as infants do. Toddlers are actually not running as at first it appears. They are merely trying to control the location of their centers of mass. Because the typical toddler is somewhat top heavy, the center of gravity is very high. The relative weight of the head of a toddler is much greater than that of an adult. Also, the toddler adds to the problem by holding the arms high during early walking development. In other words, they simply are not coordinated walkers.

The importance of the horizontal distance of the center of gravity from the forward edge of the base is rarely more evident than it is in running. In order to run fast, the runner's center of gravity must pass over the forward foot beginning with contact and continuing through support. Taking too long a step results in movement of the forward edge of the base to a greater horizontal distance from the center of mass. This is not conducive to running successfully. Stability is increased and there is literally a series of stops and starts resulting from too long a stride.

3) Stability is indirectly proportional to the distance of the center of gravity of the body above the base of support (P. 3. 0).

The height of the center of gravity above the base is another key factor in stability. Athletes attempting to gain stability accomplish this by simply lowering their centers of gravity.

Examples

A wrestler increases his stability by lowering his center of gravity.

Human pyramids that are built with low centers of gravity are most stable.

A basketball or football player in stopping quickly usually must lower the center of gravity to become more stable.

The converse is also true concerning the height of the center of gravity. Many sports require less stability in order to enhance movements. The higher the center of gravity of a body the less stable that body becomes.

Examples

A swimmer in starting quickly has the center of gravity as high as possible in order to upset equilibrium more easily.

At the start, a track sprinter becomes less stable by raising the center of gravity as high as reasonably possible to move more quickly into position for the proper sprinting technique .

Some typical examples of the manipulation of the height of the center of gravity are seen in Figure 5-1.

Figure 5–1

The key for each of the above conditions regarding the stability of a body lies in the location of the center of mass of that body relative to its base of support. **For equilibrium to exist, the center of gravity of a body must fall within its base (P.4.0).** Though this seems obvious to most observers of human movement, the importance of this principle plays a vital role in the performance of sport skills.

4) **The stability of a body is directly proportional to the weight of that body (P.5.0).**

This principle is directly related to the mass of the body being considered. The greater mass a body possesses, the more difficult it is to move that body off of its base of support. This is particularly true if all other factors relating to the position of the center of gravity are similar.

Examples

A 300-pound defensive tackle in football is more difficult to block or move than a 250 pound defensive tackle.

A 450-pound sumo wrestler will possess greater stability than a 350-pound sumo. Other variables, such as, comparable strength and speed of the individual athlete and momentum also affect the outcome of the competition. There are several other factors that affect stability. If balance is an important objective of a particular sport, then the vertical alignment of the parts of the body must be considered. **A body is more stable when its parts are vertically aligned (P. 6. 0.).** In lifting weights for example, it is much easier to balance the weight if the weight is kept in alignment with the vertical line through the center of gravity and the center of the base of support. This would explain then why it is so difficult to perform a front scale in gymnastics (there is no vertical alignment of the body segments). Yet, performing a head stand is relatively easy. See Figure 5-2.

Figure 5-2. Hand-Head Stand

54

When teaching gymnastic stunts, or diving, or trampoline stunts, one of the constant things we hear coaches say is 'keep the eyes open.' A gymnast who is performing on the balance beam can have a very difficult time of it if other activity is taking place within the visual field. A trampoline performer tries to find a constant focal point to help maintain balance. **Obstruction of visual stimuli may cause loss of balance (P. 7. 0.).**

Additionally, increasing the friction between two surfaces in contact with each other can improve stability. Therefore, athletes wear spiked shoes in baseball, golf, track, football and soccer. This greatly enhances the athletes' ability to regain stability after movement. Rubber soled shoes in basketball, volleyball and racquetball perform the same function. It is difficult to keep one's balance when playing on a dirty gym floor.

The greater the friction between the supporting surface and the parts of the body in contact with it, the greater the body's stability will be (P. 8. 0.).

The supreme test of stability in sport comes when control of the center of gravity is needed for starting and stopping. Figure 5-3 shows some guidelines for starting quickly.

TO START QUICKLY

1. Raise center of gravity
2. Place center of gravity over forward edge of base in direction of movement
3. Have a small base
4. Be in a position to create force in direction of movement
5. Increase friction between feet and surface

Figure 5-3 To Start Quickly

To start quickly in one direction, create friction between the supporting surface and base, keep the center of gravity as high as possible and as near the edge of the base in the direction of movement as possible, and be in a position to create force (P. 9. 0.).

Nearly the opposite set of guidelines applies when attempting to stop quickly. The guidelines are seen in Figure 5-4.

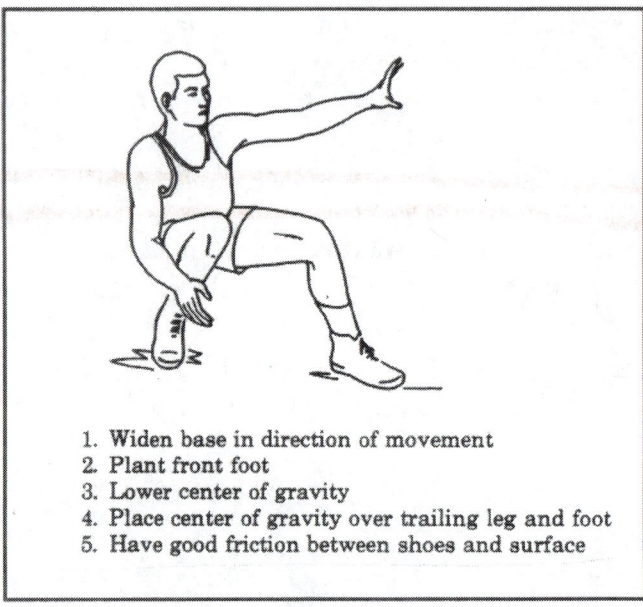

1. Widen base in direction of movement
2. Plant front foot
3. Lower center of gravity
4. Place center of gravity over trailing leg and foot
5. Have good friction between shoes and surface

Figure 5-4. To Stop Quickly

To stop quickly when in rapid movement, widen the base in the direction, plant the forward foot to create friction, lower the center of gravity, and place the center of gravity over the rear foot (P. 10. 0.).

In most activities involving movement, **stability must be compromised in order for optimal performance to occur (P.11.0).** The relatively simple activity of walking is seen as simply losing and then regaining equilibrium. The more skilled we become at regaining equilibrium, the more coordinated that skill becomes. Also, it is obvious that stability in the extreme is not conducive to efficient running. Frequently the most stable position does not allow for performance of the skill being attempted. A rower in a canoe must maintain a stable position in order to stay upright. The most stable position in the canoe is lying flat in the bottom of the boat! This position is not at all practical for rowing. So, some compromises must be reached. The rower will most likely assume a position on the knees in rapid water and seated higher when there is no external threat to stability.

Humans (and cats) appear to possess an innate ability to regain stability after losing balance. The vestibular system provides constant feedback to the brain regarding the state of equilibrium of the body. When a person momentarily loses his or her balance, that person will instantly make adjustments to regain balance. **The principles of stability also apply to regaining equilibrium after a fall, jump, run, vault, etc. (P.12.0.).**

A gymnast who has executed a dismount from an apparatus will initially lower the center of gravity above the base of support and, if necessary, widen the base of support in the direction of the movement in order to regain balance. Additional movements, such as moving a body segment in the direction opposite the overall movement, may also prove beneficial. A person who attempts to walk on an icy sidewalk will also find it necessary to apply the principles of stability.

In all support activities, the center of gravity should be in line with the base of support (P.13.0.). This principle plays a major role in gymnastics. A performer on the pommel horse shifts his feet in the opposite direction of the movement of his head and shoulders in order to keep the center of gravity over the pommels. When executing a handstand on the rings, a gymnast must keep his center of mass over his hands in as nearly a vertical alignment as possible.

Determination of the relative stability of a body is fairly simple to do. If knowledge of the dimensions of the base of support, the height of the center of gravity, the weight of the body and the distance of the center of gravity of the body from the edge of the base are known, simple calculations can be made to determine the amount of force needed to move the center of mass outside the base of support. **The degree of equilibrium or the stability of a body is determined by multiplying the weight of the body by the distance the center of gravity is raised in order to move it outside the base in the direction of movement (P.14.0.).**

Example

A football lineman weighing 200 pounds takes a four-point stance with a base of support 20 inches wide by 36 inches long. His center of gravity is located 24 inches above the center of his base. How many inch-pounds of force will be required to move his center of gravity outside his base?

By using the Pythagorean Theorem, the distance of the center of gravity from the forward edge of the base can easily be determined. That distance is the length of the hypotenuse of the right triangle formed by the scalars representing the height of the center of gravity and the horizontal distance of the center of gravity from the edge of the base. Stability is determined by multiplying the weight of the body by the height that the center of gravity must be raised to move it outside its base. That height is the mathematical difference between the vertical height above the base and the true distance of the center of gravity from the edge of the base, or the hypotenuse. Figure 5-5 shows a schematic representation of the problem.

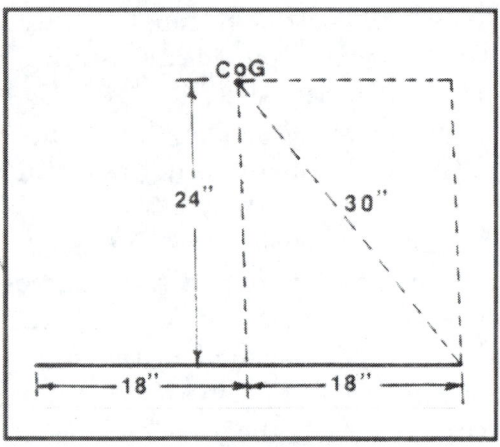

Figure 5–5

$$H^2 = 18^2 + 24^2 \qquad S = (30 - 24) \, 200$$
$$H^2 = 324 + 576 \qquad S = 6 \times 200$$
$$H = 30 \qquad S = 1200 \text{ inch-pounds}$$

Previously, it was mentioned that the center of gravity of a body could be located outside the actual body. The center of gravity of a body can also be moved to a different location *within* the body, as well. By moving the arms upward a person can shift the center of gravity upward; or by moving one of the arms away from the body can shift the center of gravity in that direction. The manipulation of the center of gravity's location within the body plays a major role in the performance of sport skills. Not only does the movement of a body segment change the location of the cog, but the movement of the center of mass provides force to help overcome inertia in many movements. This helps to explain why jumpers use their arms to aid in the production of force at takeoff.

If a performer is in the air free of support, the position of the center of gravity within the body can be changed and the body may be lowered or raised above the floor by the movement or change in position of a member of the body (P.15.0.).

The overall performance of a movement can be greatly influenced by the shifting of the position of the center of gravity within the body. However, **if a performer is in the air free of support, the height to which the center of gravity can be raised above the ground cannot be affected by body movement (P.16.0.).**

Although P.15.0. and P.16.0 appear to be in conflict with each other, this is not the case. By relocation of the center of gravity within the body after leaving the ground, an athlete can actually enhance the height that can be reached. By lowering the center of gravity within the body the ultimate height reached is increased. Therefore, the basketball player at the time of a tip reaches as high as possible with the tipping hand, but forcefully lowers the other hand, straightens the legs, and points the toes. These actions effectively lower the center of gravity within the body as much as possible. By creating as great a distance as possible between the tipping hand and the center of gravity, the athlete maximizes the height at which the ball can be tipped.

A body in the air free of support cannot change the path the center of gravity will take (P.17.0.). It may appear, for example, that the use of poor landing technique in the long jump causes the center of gravity to land prematurely. But, in actuality the center of gravity continues on it path as the long jumper falls or stumbles forward.

Gravity and the Coriolis Effect

Gravity or gravitational force refers to the attraction of the earth for objects or persons on its surface. All objects on the earth exert gravitational force, but the total mass of the earth is so great and is so close in proximity to objects on its surface, its gravity acts upon every mass particle of an object or person and is applied in one direction only, towards the center of the earth. It is as if all the individual's mass were concentrated at a single central focal point, which we commonly refer to as the center of gravity of that person. This hypothetical concept suggests that the **center of gravity** of an object or individual is the point at which the weight of the body is considered to be concentrated. The mathematical construct is essential to the computation and understanding of problems in the analysis of human motion.

Gravity demonstrates three (3) unique characteristics:

1. it is constant, without interruption;

2. it is applied in only one direction, towards the center of the earth; and'

3. it acts upon every mass particle of objects or persons on the earth.

However, Heiskanen (2,3) suggested that the attraction of the planet for objects on its surface varies with geographic location and could cause discrepancies in athletic records. Tables were calculated to determine correction factors which could be used to equalize track and field athletic performances at different latitudes. See Table 5-2

Table 5-2

Latitude Degrees	Correction Factor	High Jump 245 cm. Salamanca Spain	Long Jump 895 cm. Tokyo Japan	Triple Jump 1829 cm. Gothenburg Sweden	Pole Vault 614 cm. Sestriere Italy	Shot Put 2312 cm. Westwood California	Discus 7407 cm. Neubrandenburg Germany	Javelin 9566 cm. Sheffield England
90 (Pole	+.003045	+0.75	+2.72	+5.57	+1.87	+7.05	+22.54	+29.11
70	+.002463	+0.60	+2.20	+4.50	+1.51	+5.69	+18.24	+23.56
65	+.002117	+0.52	+1.89	+3.87	+1.30	+4.89	+15.68	+20.25
60.2 (Helsinki)	+.001760	+0.43	+1.58	+3.22	+1.08	+4.07	+13.04	+16.84
60	+.001747	+0.43	+1.56	+3.20	+1.07	+4.04	+12.94	+16.71
57 (Cape Horn)	+.001501	+0.37	+1.34	+2.77	+0.92	+3.47	+11.12	+14.36
55.8 (Moscow)	+.001403	+0.34	+1.26	+2.57	+0.86	+3.24	+10.39	+13.42
55	+.001337	+0.33	+1.20	+2.45	+0.82	+3.09	+9.90	+12.79
52.3 (Berlin, London)	+.001119	+0.27	+1.00	+2.05	+0.69	+2.59	+8.29	+10.70
50	+.000901	+0.22	+0.81	+1.65	+0.55	+2.08	+6.67	+8.62
48.8	+.000796	+0.20	+0.71	+1.46	+0.49	+1.84	+5.90	+7.61
45	+.000450	+0.11	+0.40	+0.82	+0.28	+1.04	+3.33	+4.30
42.2 (Barcelona)	+.000198	+0.05	+0.18	+0.36	+0.12	+0.46	+1.47	+1.89
42 (Rome)	+.000180	+0.04	+0.16	+0.33	+0.11	+0.42	+1.33	+1.72
40 (Columbus)	0	0	0	0	0	0	0	0
38 (Seoul)	-.000180	-0.04	-0.16	-0.33	-0.11	-0.42	-1.33	-1.72
37.7 (Melbourne)	-.000199	-0.05	-0.18	-0.36	-0.12	-0.46	-1.47	-1.89
35 (Tokyo)	-.000436	-0.11	-0.39	-0.80	-0.27	-1.01	-3.23	-4.17
34.3 (Atlanta)	-.000501	-0.12	-0.45	-0.92	-0.31	-1.16	-3.71	-4.79
34.1 (Los Angeles)	-.000514	-0.13	-0.46	-0.94	-0.32	-1.19	-3.81	-4.92
34 (Sydney)	-.000523	-0.13	-0.47	-0.96	-0.32	-1.21	-3.87	-5.00
30	-.000846	-0.21	-0.76	-1.55	-0.52	-1.96	-6.27	-8.09
26.5 (Johannesburg)	-.001076	-0.26	-0.96	-1.97	-0.66	-2.49	-7.97	-10.29
25	-.001216	-0.30	-1.09	-2.22	-0.75	-2.81	-9.01	-11.63
20	-.001536	-0.38	-1.37	-2.81	-0.94	-3.55	-11.38	-14.69
19 (Mexico City)	-.001625	-0.40	-1.45	-2.97	-1.00	-3.76	-12.04	-15.54
15	-.001795	-0.44	-1.61	-3.28	-1.10	-4.15	-13.30	-17.17
10	-.001986	-0.49	-1.78	-3.63	-1.22	-4.59	-14.71	-19.00
5	-.002103	-0.52	-1.88	-3.85	-1.29	-4.86	-15.58	-20.12
0	-.112143	-0.53	-1.92	-3.92	-1.32	-4.95	-15.87	-20.50

Olympic and other international competitions should consider that track and field records differ at different latitudes. The adjustments above will correct record heights and distances to the gravity value at 40 degrees latitude Each correction is obtained by multiplying the existing record, listed at the top of each of the seven track and field events, by the correction factor in the second column. Above 40 degrees latitude, the corrections should be added to the actual performance figure; below 40 degrees should be subtracted. The site where these records were established is also given for each.

Gravity is slightly greater at the poles than at the equator and this causes differences in gravitational force at different latitudes. Objects in flight appear to be affected by the earth's rotation causing a point nearer the poles to travel at a slower speed than one at the equator. This rotation seems to cause a deflection towards the east in the northern hemisphere and towards the west in the southern hemisphere known as the **Coriolis Effect.** Figure 5-6 illustrates the Coriolis Effect.

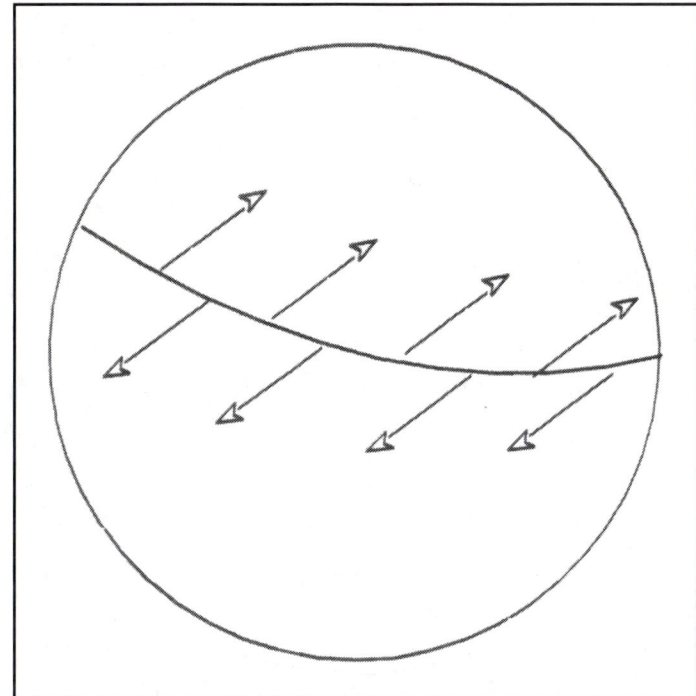

**Figure 5-6. The rotation of the earth causes a deflection
towards the east in the Northern Hemisphere
and a deflection towards the west in the Southern Hemisphere.
This is referred to as the Coriolis Effect.**

The deflection appears to be at its maximum at the poles and is non-existent at the equator. It would appear that high jumpers could jump higher and javelin throwers could throw farther in Sydney, Australia for the 2000 Olympics than they did in the 1991 Olympic Games in Barcelona, Spain. Making corrections for the smaller force of gravity at Sydney because of its closer location to the equator, the current world record for the javelin throw which was set in Sheffield, England is equivalent to 15.7 centimeters or almost six inches farther at Sydney than at Sheffield. For the same reason, a quarterback in the northern hemisphere passing a football towards the east throws slightly farther than he can when facing west. A naturally occurring example of this phenomenon is demonstrated by the direction of rotation of storm systems. Tornadoes and hurricanes rotate counter-clockwise in the northern hemisphere; clock-wise in the southern hemisphere. Many students have heard this story and relate it to water going down the drain. However, Salzseider (5) states that "it is a common misconception that water spirals down a bathtub drain clockwise in one hemisphere (southern) and clockwise in the other (northern). In the United States, it would rotate counter-clockwise while in Australia, it would rotate clockwise. See Figures 5-7 and 5-8. Salzseider concluded that the Coriolis force exerted on water in a bathtub is much too small to be observed. The residual momentum of the water is what really causes water to spiral down a drain. Water going down a drain will almost always have some net angular momentum in one direction or the other.

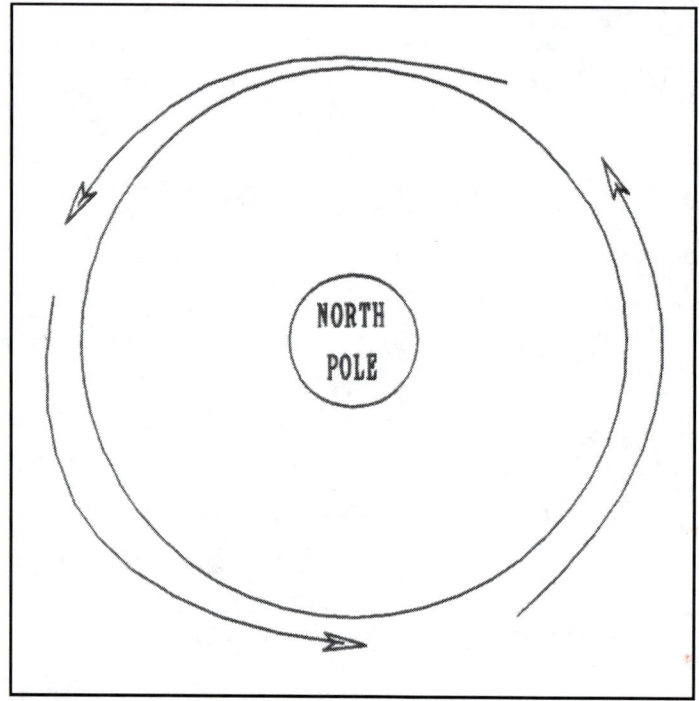

Figure 5 7. From the perspective of the North Pole,
objects in flight rotate or spiral in a counter-clockwise direction.
Water spiraling down the drain in the Northern Hemisphere
rotates counter-clockwise. Storm systems also spin in this direction,
i.e. tornadoes and hurricanes.

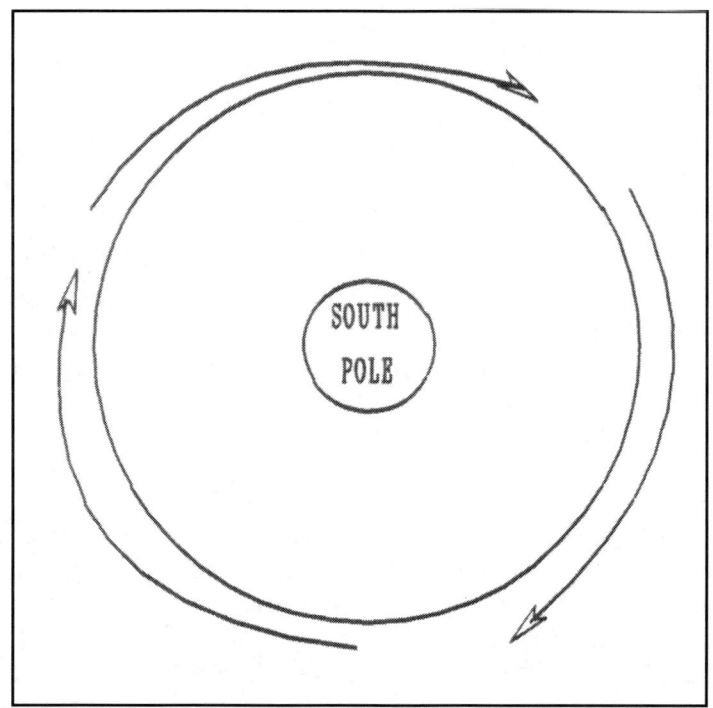

**Figure 5-8. From the perspective of the South Pole,
objects in flight rotate or spiral in a clockwise direction.
Water spiraling down the drain in the Southern Hemisphere
rotates clockwise. Storm systems also spin in a clockwise direction,
i.e. tornadoes and hurricanes.**

References

1. Bauman, Robert P. (1992) Physics that textbook writers usually get wrong: III. forces and vectors. *The Physics Teacher*, October, 30: 402-407.

2. Grombach, John V. (1960) The gravity factor in world athletics. *Amateur Athlete*, April, 31: 24-25.

3. Heiskanen, Weikko A. (1955) The earth's gravity. *Scientific American*, September, 193: 164-174.

4. Levi, F.A. (1988) A new look for coriolis. *The Physics Teacher.* November, 26: 508-509.

5. Salzseider, John C. (1994) Exposing the bathtub coriolis myth. *The Physics Teacher*, February, 32: 107.

Problems

1. Peter assumes a stance with a base of support of 30 × 30 inches and he weighs 150 lbs. His center of gravity is located 20 inches above the center of his base. Peter weights 235 lbs. How much force will it take for him to move his center of gravity outside his base of support to upset equilibrium?

2. Joe weighs 150 lbs. and takes a four-point stance with a base of support of 24 × 42 inches. His center of gravity is located 28 inches above the center of his base. How much force will it take for him to move his center of gravity outside his base of support to start movement forward? How much force will it take for him to move sideways?

3. Susan weighs 120 lbs and takes a track starting position with her center of gravity 6 inches back of the forward edge of her base of support in the direction of movement and 20 inches high. Jill weighs 120 lbs and takes a starting position with her center of gravity 3 inches back of the forward edge of her base of support and 16 inches high. Which athlete is in the best starting position? By how much?

4. Jim weighs 200 lbs and takes a four-point stance with a base of support that is 30 × 48 inches with his center of gravity 20 inches back of the forward edge and 18 inches above the base. How stable is Jim in the forward direction? How stable is Jim backwards?

5. A swimmer weighing 130 lbs. takes a starting position with a base of support of 9 × 9 inches. In which of the following positions would it take the least force to start her toward the water? By how much?

   a. A position in which her center of gravity was 6 inches back of the forward edge and 3 feet above the base.

   b. A position in which the center of gravity was 3 inches back of the forward edge and 3et above the base.

6. Two wrestlers each weighing 175 lbs. take the referee's position on the mat. A takes a position with a base of 18 × 18 inches with his center of gravity directly over the center of his base of support and 12 inches high. How much force must **B** use to move **A** outside his base of support? If **B** takes a position with a base of 36 × 36 with his center of gravity 24 inches high and directly over the center of his base, will he be more or less stable than **A** ? By how much?

7. A football lineman weighing 260 lbs. takes a position with his center of mass over the center of his base. In one case, his base is 18" × 18" and his center of mass is 16'" above his base of support. In another scenario, his base is 24" ×

24" and his center of mass is 20 inches above his base of support. In which position is he the most stable? By how much?

8. A football lineman weighing 250 lbs. takes a staggered defensive stance with a base that is 24 inches wide. The up foot in his stance is 24 inches from the hand and the back foot is 36 inches back of the hand. His center of gravity is 12 inches back of the forward edge and 24 inches above the base of support. How stable is he backwards?

Exercises

Observe the following activities and report your observations.

1. Have a person run and stop as quickly as possible. Describe the action he/she took to accomplish the movement. Note the action/reaction of the person's center of gravity

2. Try to take real life measurements (or estimates) of the dimensions of at least three human pyramids built in a tumbling class. List them from most stable to least stable. Does this correspond to difficulty of the pyramid?

3. Watch a college or professional football game. Note the stances used by the offensive and defensive linemen in different situations. Are they different? Explain.

4. Evaluate the need for stability in the following situations based upon the basic techniques of each:

   a. a track start versus a defensive lineman in football

   b. a swimming start versus a wrestler's down position

   c. a tennis ready position and a basketball defensive position

   d. a golf swing versus a baseball swing

   e. a handstand versus a hand spring

5. Walk on a balance beam, climb a rope and take an arm support position on the parallel bars. Describe the relationship of your center of gravity to your point of support in each case.

Study Questions

1. What is the center of gravity of a body? What is equilibrium? How are the two related?

2. Is a moving body in equilibrium? Discuss.

3. What is stability? Are there different degrees of stability? How is stability related to equilibrium?

4. What are the principles of stability?

5. What should an athlete do to start quickly? To stop quickly?

6. What are some examples of the Coriolis Effect?

EXPERIMENT 5.1

Purpose

The purposes of this experiment are to:

1. Calculate the stability of a body.
2. Compare stability of one's own body in various athletic positions.
3. Relate the principles employed that dominate each position.

Procedures

Secure a partner and take each of the positions described in the conditions listed below. At each position have your partner determine the dimensions of your base, height of center of gravity, and distance of center of gravity is back from forward edge. Record findings in results section of the report along with your weight.

Condition 1. Get into a wrestler's down position.

Condition 2. Maintain a 4 point linesman defensive football stance.

Condition 3 . Take a 4 point fast start position with toes on same line.

Condition 4 . Stand at military attention.

Results

Record the following: Weight _____

| | **Base** | | **Center of Gravity** | |
	Length	Width	Height	Distance to forward edge
Condition 1	_____	_____	_____	_____
Condition 2	_____	_____	_____	_____
Condition 3	_____	_____	_____	_____
Condition 4	_____	_____	_____	_____

How much force is required to start you moving in a forward direction in each condition?

Condition 1 _____

Condition 2 _____

Condition 3 _____

Condition 4 _____

How much force is required to knock you off balance to the rear in each condition?

Condition 1 _____

Condition 2 _____

Condition 3 _____

Condition 4 _____

State the principles that are the major contributors to each condition.

Key Terms from Chapter Five

Balance—To control movement, to keep the center of gravity of a body within its base of support

Center of Gravity—The center of mass of a body, the weight center of a body

Equilibrium —State of rest of a body

Foot-pound—Work done when a body is moved one foot against an opposing force of one pound

Gravity—The attraction or pull of the earth upon an object

Mass—The quotient obtained by dividing the weight of a body by the acceleration due to gravity

Pythagorean Theorem—The square of the hypotenuse is equal to the sum of the squares of the other two sides of a right triangle

Stability—Degree of equilibrium

Weight—The force the earth exerts on a body, gravitational pull

6

ROTARY OR ANGULAR MOTION

Angular motion occurs when a body or object rotates around a fixed axis. If the body or object is a lever, the distal end creates an arc or possibly, a complete circle. This axis of rotation lies at right angles to the plane of motion. Rarely does the human body as a whole exhibit angular motion. An example is when the entire body rotates around a fixed axis, such as, performing a giant swing on the horizontal bar in gymnastics.

Some athletic performances demonstrate both angular and linear motion. Angular motion occurs at most diarthrodial joints when the distal end of the articulating bone describes an arc and the proximal end is the axis of rotation. A jack-knife dive incorporates both angular and linear motion. Flexing into the jack-knife position demonstrates angular motion, while the path of the diver's body as a whole describes curvilinear motion. Most sports and physical education activities are combinations of several of these two motions. When several linear and angular motions are combined, they are referred to as general motion. The angular motion of the arms and legs of a runner impart linear motion to the body as a whole.

Rotation is angular movement of an object that occurs around an axis of motion. Rotation or spin may be imparted to almost any object, including the human body. The most common method of inducing rotation to objects in sports is **eccentric thrust**. Eccentric thrust is caused by striking an object, such as a ball, off center. A batted ball that is hit below its center of gravity tends to be popped up. A tennis ball that is contacted with a low to high swing tends to produce top spin. A golf ball struck by a golfer swinging outside-in tends to slice or fade. The same golfer swinging inside-out will hook or draw the ball.

Another means of imparting rotation is the application of the principle of **transfer of momentum**. An athlete wishing to induce rotation to the entire body transfers momentum from part of the body to the total body. The high jumper leaning back at takeoff transfers the momentum of his flexed back to his entire body and the result is forward rotation over the bar.

A third method of inducing rotation is to **check linear velocity at an extremity**. A runner attempting to clear a hurdle in track trips on the hurdle. When the hurdle is struck, linear velocity is checked at an extremity and the runner rotates forward and downward towards the ground.

The **principles** in this chapter are descriptive of a somewhat simplified view of rotary motion. To fully describe rotary motion, one must understand a much more complicated calculus-based approach to biomechanics. This description is beyond the scope of this text.

As previously suggested, rotary motion is defined as movement of a body, a segment, or an object in a circle or arc of a circle about a center of rotation (**P.1.0**). The relationship between the properties of the rotary movement play a very important role in the quality of the rotary movement. These movements can be described in terms of rotary, or angular velocity. Angular velocity is generally expressed in terms of radians as the chief units of measurement. Because the movement about an arc is not linear in nature (it is curvilinear), ft/sec is inadequate to describe the motion. We, therefore, use degrees/sec, or radians/ sec as the unit, with preference given to radians/sec.

Understanding of the basic principles for describing curves is essential to solving problems regarding rotary motion. Basic facts are as follows:

A. There are 360 degrees in one revolution around a circle.

B. There are 6.28 (or 2π) radians in a circle.

C. The diameter of a circle is the distance from one point on the circle through the center to another point on the circle.

D. The radius of the circle is one-half of the diameter.

E. The radian represents a 57.3-degree arc.

The rotary motion of a body is characterized by two factors, angular speed and length of radius of rotation (**P.2.0**). If one increases the length of a radius of rotation while maintaining angular speed, a much greater linear velocity will result. A shortening of the radius of rotation has the opposite effect on linear velocity, but will increase angular velocity. This phenomenon is very obvious in running and walking. The bending of the knee during the drive phase of the non-support leg in running provides for a rapid acceleration of the thigh in preparation for the foot strike phase.

In order to calculate the linear velocity of a point on a rotating body, we must know two quantities: the rotary velocity in radians/sec., and the length of the radius of rotation. The linear velocity is equal to the rotary velocity multiplied by the length of the radius (**P.3.0**).

$$V_L = V_R(r)$$

Where:　　　　　　　　V_L = Linear Velocity in feet per second

V_R = Rotary velocity in radians per second

r = Radius in rotation in feet

Examples

A diver in a layout position is spinning at one revolution per second with a radius of rotation of 3 feet assumes a tuck position with an effective radius of 1.5 feet. What happens to the diver's rate of rotation?

$$V_L = 6.28\ (3)$$

$$V_L = 18.84\ \text{ft/sec}$$

$$18.84 = V_r\ (1.5)$$

$$V_r = \frac{18.84}{1.5}$$

$$V_r = 12.56\ \text{radians/sec or 2 rev/sec}$$

A discus thrower is spinning as he releases the discus at 25 radians per second with a radius of rotation of 4 feet. What was the linear velocity of the discus at release?

$$V_L = 25\ (4)$$

$$V_L = 100\ \text{feet/second}$$

Figure 6-1 The Discus Throw: Application of transferring rotary velocity into linear velocity.

The example of the discus thrower suggests an important principle related to rotary motion. That is, rotary motion may be transferred into linear motion (**P.4.0**).

The relationship can be clearly seen in the example of the slingshot. The velocity of the projectile from a short slingshot will not be nearly as great as from a longer slingshot. When a batter in baseball gets "jammed," the arms must be shortened in order to get the barrel of the bat on the ball. This shortening results in a weaker hit. In a similar manner, the design of golf clubs is such that each club is of different length in order to change the amount of force (related to club head speed) each can impart.

When angular velocity is held constant, as it should be in the golf swing, the linear velocity of a point (the club head) about the center of rotation is directly proportional to the radius (length of the shaft) (**P.5.0**). Two discus throwers of different heights may spin at the same rate, but when they release the discus at the same angle, the taller of the two will have a better result. Very often, taller, leaner discus throwers are more successful than their typically shorter, more muscular counterparts. Technically, a discus thrower should be fully extended in the throwing arm at release in order to optimize release velocity. A shortening of the radius of rotation has a negative effect, as suggested by P.5.0. A diver who wishes to slow down the rate of rotation need only to extend the body from the tuck or pike position to do so.

When linear velocity of a point about a center of rotation is held constant, the angular velocity is inversely proportional to the length of the radius of rotation (**P.6.0**). Figure 6-2 shows the effect of lengthening the radius of rotation on a diver. Conversely, if the diver discovered that the dive was going to come up short of vertical, a shortening of the radius would increase the rotary velocity enough to bring the dive to vertical. This could be accomplished by piking at the hips slightly or by bending the knees. A graphic example of this principle can be seen when a figure skater in a spin pulls in the arms to increase the rotary velocity to almost a blur!

There are situations in which the shortening of the radius of rotation can actually result in increased linear velocity. In many throwing or striking activities, additional velocity may be gained by bending a joint (**P.7.0**). The involvement of the wrist in the golf swing or in a badminton stroke all produce the effect of the transfer of a small amount of rotary velocity into a much larger amount of linear velocity (i.e., release velocity racket head speed or club head speed). The relaxation of the wrist joint in these movements provides for more freedom in swinging movements and greater velocity.

The following principles are also related to the relationship between the length of the radius of rotation and rotary velocity:

(**P.8.0**): In swinging activities on the bar, speed of rotation is directly proportional to the length of the radius of rotation on the downswing. When performing a giant swing on the horizontal bar, the gymnast performs subtle changes in the length of his body, in order to effectively shorten (upswing) and lengthen (downswing) the radius of rotation.

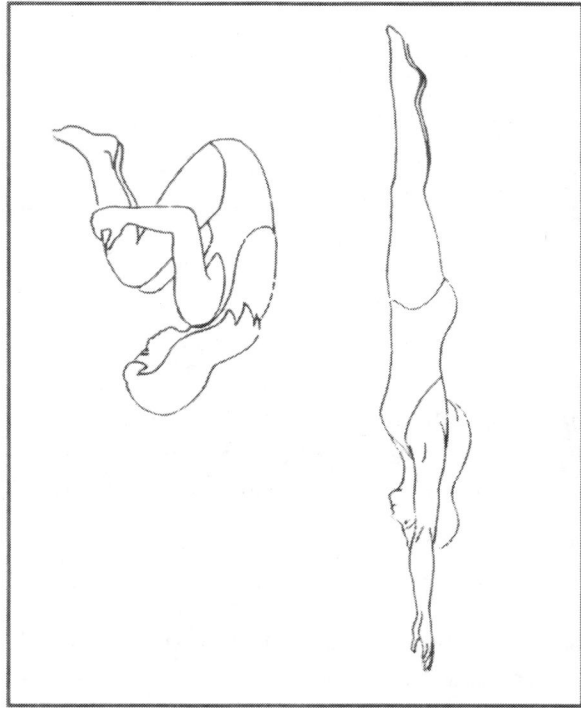

Figure 6-2

(**P.9.0**): When rotary motion is converted to linear motion, the greatest velocity is gained when the linear direction is a right angle to the radius of rotation. The discus thrower has much better results when the release in at 90 degrees to the angle of the throw.

(**P.10.0**): A long lever has greater velocity at the end than does a short lever. This principle can be especially evident when one observes a tumbling pass in gymnastics. The feet have much greater velocity than the hands during the back handspring when the hands are on the floor.

Another useful rotary measure is the conversion from rotary distance to linear distance. It is often problematic to achieve accurate measures around a curve. However, with accurate knowledge of the radius of the curve, it is possible to calculate the distance in linear feet around that curve. In fact, this is the very principle upon which running tracks are designed. Linear distance is equal to rotary distance in radians multiplied by the radius of the circle. (**P.11.0**).

$$D_L = D_R(r)$$

Where:
D_L - Linear distance in feet
D_R - Rotary distance in radians
r - Radius of rotation in feet

Example:

On an indoor track the radius of the inside lane is 40 feet. The curve of the track subtends a 180 degree angle. What is the length of the curve for the inside lane?

$$D_L = 3.14(40)$$
$$D_L - 125.6 \text{ feet}$$

With knowledge of the width of the lanes of the track, the engineer also is able to determine where the spacing for staggers should be relative to the inside lane starting position. This is done by simply increasing (r) by the width in feet for each lane.

As alluded to earlier, movements such as walking and running are related to rotary motion. In fact, all human motion results for rotary movements of the limb segments about joints in the body (**P.12.0**). When kicking a ball, the kicker attempts to keep the knee bent until just before contact in order to get maximal velocity of the foot at contact. In order to optimize performance in many activities, there should be an integration of forward linear motion and rotary motion (**P.13.0**).

Examples

Although the discus event appears at first to be a completely rotary event, it is, in reality a combination of rotary and linear movements.

A javelin thrower should integrate the initial run up with the cross over step and rotary movement of the arm. The value of the initial run up is lost when the thrower stops before the rotary action takes place.

A baseball player steps forward and should integrate that movement with the rotary motion of the arm in throwing.

In running, there is an integration of the rotary motion of the legs to obtain linear motion of the body.

In activities involving swinging, the upward and downward momentum is determined generally by the height from which the downward movement is initiated. This pendulum type motion is a product of the momentum generated by the down movement (**P.13.0**). In general, the longer the radius of rotation in these swinging activities, the longer it takes for a round trip to occur. These round trips, by the way, are not affected by the weight of the swinging body as far as velocity is concerned. Many swinging activities, especially those in gymnastics, involve performance of a stunt (i.e., a release move, or a flip) during the swing. The optimal time for execution of these stunts is at the peak of the swing when velocity has decreased to zero.

Seemingly natural activities like walking and running are very dependent upon rotary movement for the coordination of the movements. The efficient movement of the arms to counterbalance angular movements created by the lower limbs takes place naturally to a certain degree and must be present for skilled performance (P.14.0). An exaggeration of the effect of counterbalance by the arms can be seen when observing a person go over a hurdle. Balance in this event is critical and is partly accomplished by using the arms to counterbalance the actions of the legs.

Two general effects can be seen related to the arm movements used to initiate twisting movements that are often seen in diving and gymnastics. Body movements that are away from the longitudinal axis of the body after the body is air-borne will be in the opposite direction from the direction of rotation (P.15.0). In other words, a wide circular sweep of the arms counter-clockwise while in the air will result in rotation of the body in the clockwise direction. On the other hand, body movements that are executed close to the longitudinal axis of a body that is air-borne will be in the same direction as the rotation (P.16.0). A tight wrapping action of the arms will enhance twisting movements. Both of these principles apply to actions taken when the body is in the air and free of support. However, if the twisting action is initiated while the body is supported, both wide and tight actions of the arms will result in rotation in the direction of the arm movements.

In a sea of air, the role of rotation becomes very important to the trajectory characteristics of projectiles. It is quite amazing to see the effects that changing the exposure surface of projectiles to air has upon the flight characteristics. Variations of the distance across which an air current must pass over a surface creates pressure differentials that create upward or downward movement on the projectile. The magnus force on an airplane wing, for example can cause lift that is sufficient to overcome gravity; even for a very large jumbo jet. In sports, this effect can be seen dramatically in the flight of a baseball or softball. The magnus force on a spinning ball is at right angles to the trajectory, thus affecting the ball differently at different points along its trajectory (P.17.0). This effect is seen in Figure 6-3.

As a ball travels through the air, the resistance of the air creates drag that is tangent to the trajectory in the opposite direction. This drag force is what causes the trajectory of a ball to be a skewed parabola. It is this combination of spin, drag, and gravity that gives spinning balls certain predictable trajectories; so that:

(P.18.0): A ball traveling along a trajectory with topspin will curve downward toward the ground. Examples: a tennis ball with topspin, a topped golf shot, or a sinker ball thrown by a pitcher.

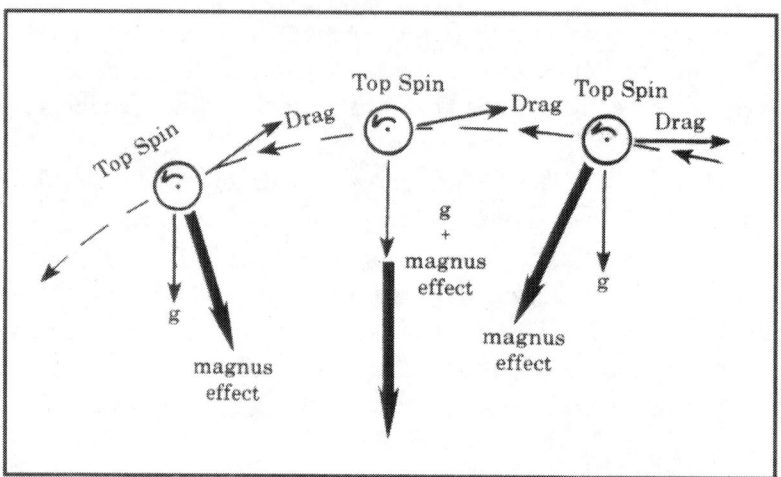

Figure 6-3. The magnus effect of a tennis ball with top spin.

(**P.19.0**): A ball traveling along a trajectory with backspin will tend to rise. Examples: a hard driven golf ball will tend to rise, a tennis ball with backspin will stay in the air longer, a softball pitched with backspin will rise before it reaches the plate.

(**P.20.0**): A ball with clockwise spin will curve to the right, and a ball with counter-clockwise spin will curve to the left.

These principles related to spin prove to be very useful in all types of activities. On important factor that must be considered when discussing the effects of spin is the velocity of the projectile. A ball with high velocity is affected little by the magnus force, but as it slows, the magnus force will cause the ball to curve more (**P.21.0**).

Examples

The path of a baseball pitched with spin curves all the way to the plate but curves more as it approaches the plate. The reason for this phenomenon is that the ball slows more horizontally than it does in revolution around its axis. So, as it nears the plate, it is revolving more each linear foot. Therefore, it deviates more from its original path. A pitcher who is able to impart a rapid, tight spin on a ball will often be successful.

A bowling ball with a lot of spin and good initial velocity will tend to travel a trajectory that hooks into the one-three pocket. The reason for the hook rather than the curve is that it is slowing down more horizontally than spin around its axis and thus, is spinning more revolutions per linear foot as it approaches the pins. (Friction also plays a role in this particular situation).

Research Report
(Kinematic Laboratory Results)
The Effect of Rotating about the Transverse Axis (somersault)
on the Ability to Rotate about the Longitudinal Axis (twist)

Variable Dive	Test 1 Straight	Test 2 Pike	Test 3 Front	Test 4 1	Test 5 $1^1/_2$	Units
Landing Distance from Tower	6.55	6.82	8.41	7.34	6.56	feet
Maximum Velocity for Transverse Rotation	0	0	203.15	462.16	491.30	degrees/sec.
Average Velocity of Transverse Rotation	0	0	101.25	234.17	390.03	degrees/sec.
Total Transverse Rotation	0	0	178	367.66	540	degrees
Initial Twisting Velocity	156.28	361.99	452.37	498.27	649.13	degrees/sec.
Average Twisting Velocity	121.0	242.92	263.03	390.02	574.28	degrees/sec.
Total Twist	180	246	366	358.6	450	degrees

Problems

1. An ice skater is spinning at 3 radians per second with an effective radius of 2' shortens the effective radius of rotation to one foot. How fast is the skater now spinning?

2. An outdoor track has a curve radius of 100 feet and is a perfect half circle. How far is it around the curve?

3. A diver is executing a somersault from a tuck position and is turning at a rate of 2 revolutions/sec. The radius of rotation is 12 inches. Before entering the water, he opens to a layout position with a radius of rotation at the same point of 3 feet. What is his angular velocity when hitting the water?

4. A gymnast is executing a somersault from a layout position, radius of rotation 2.5 feet, and is turning at the rate of 360°/sec. He assumes a tuck position so that the radius of rotation is reduced to 1.5 feet. What would be his new angular velocity?

5. Two discus throwers get set to throw a discus. John spins at a rate of 15 radians/sec. at the moment of release and the center of the discus is 3 feet

from the center of rotation. Jack spins at a rate of 12 radians/sec. at the moment of release and the center of his discus is 3.5 feet from the center of rotation. Both released the discus at an angle of 35°. Who threw the discus farthest? What was the release velocity of the discus in each case?

6. A discus thrower at the moment of release is spinning at a rate of 10 radians/second with a radius of rotation of 3 feet, 6 inches. What was the velocity of the discus at release?

7. An indoor track has a radius of 40 feet at each end that is a perfect half circle. The straight-a-way on each side is 110 feet. How far is it around the track?

8. A diver is in a layout position turning at 171.87°/second with a radius of rotation of 3.5 feet. He tucks to where his radius of rotation is 1.5 feet. What is his new rotary velocity?

9. A discus thrower is spinning at release of a discus at a rate of 18 radians/second with a radius of rotation of 3 feet. He has potential radius of rotation of 3 feet 3 inches. What difference in release velocity of the discus will the 3 inches make?

10. If the discus thrower in the above problem released the discus at an angle that would get the same distance as one thrown at a 45 degree angle in a vacuum, what would be the range of each throw? What difference would the 3 inches make?

Exercises

1. Describe uses the body makes of rotary motion to bring about linear distance of an object such as a ball, shot, discus, javelin, etc.

2. State two principles describing rotary motion.

3. Try a back pull-over to feet on the trampoline. What did you do to make it all the way to your feet? Now try a back pull-over to a front drop. What did you do different than before?

4. Throw a baseball at a target. Describe the action of the throwing arm. What types of movements went into the linear path of the ball? Explain the movements you made.

5. Describe the uses a diver makes of the principles of rotary motion.

Table 6-1
The Effect of Air Resistance on Linear and Rotary Velocity
of a Pitched Baseball Resulting in a Magnus Effect

Ten foot intervals	Feet					
	0-10	10-20	20-30	30-40	40-50	50-60
Velocity (ft/sec)	90	82	77	74	71	68
Revolutions	5.3	6.6	7.0	7.2	7.4	7.9
Change in Feet (Deviation from a straight line)		.228	.336	.537	.641	.736

Study Questions

1. What is meant by rotary motion? What is another name for rotary motion?

2. Rotary motion is characterized by what factors?

3. What uses do athletes make of rotary motion in competition?

4. What characteristics would you look for in selecting a discus thrower?

5. How do we use rotary motion to walk? How does a gymnast complete the giant swing?

6. Complete the following table by filling in on the dotted lines, the three (3) methods of inducing rotation. Then on the line corresponding to each of the listed events, place a check (x) beneath the correct cause of rotation.

Event	(1) eccentric	(2) transfer	(3) check
Underspin on volleyball serve	X		
Runner trips on curb			X
Topped golf ball	X		
Javelin thrower arches back to throw		X	
Rise ball in softball	X		
Batter steps into pitched ball		X	
Double back flip on trampoline		X	
Popped up fly ball in baseball	X		
Hooked bowling ball	X		
Pole vaulter bends pole on takeoff		X	X

EXPERIMENT 6.1

Purpose

The purposes of this experiment are to:

1. Experience rotary motion of the human body under various conditions.

2. Compare the effect of various movement on rotary motion of the body.

3. Relate the mechanical principles employed to the techniques used to obtain rotary motion.

Procedures

Execute the following conditions several times using different body movements. Record the method used to obtain the maximum turning motion for each condition in the results section of the report.

Condition 1. Stand flat footed on the floor, jump into the air and twist as far as possible before landing. (Each athlete should be able to turn at least 180°) twisting may begin before leaving the floor.

Condition 2. Stand flat footed on the floor, jump into the air and twist as far as possible before landing. Do not begin twisting action until after leaving floor.

Condition 3. Stand on turn table with weight equally distributed over center of table. Experiment with various movements to initiate a twist.

Results

Describe the movement used in twisting for each of the three conditions. Give direction in relation to twist as you describe each body movement.

Condition 1

Condition 2

Condition 3

For each of the movements described above relate the mechanical principles in operation.

EXPERIMENT 6.2

Purpose:

The purposes of this experiment are to:

1. Experience various velocities of rotary motion of the human body under various conditions.

2. Compare the effect of various movements on the rotary motion of the body.

3. Relate the mechanical principles employed to the techniques used in rotary motion.

Procedures

With the help of a partner and a turntable execute the following conditions several times. Record the results under each condition in the results section of this report. Relate the results to principles of mechanical kinesiology in the space provided in the results section.

Condition 1. Stand on the turntable feet as wide as table permits. Stretch arms out sideward with 4 pounds of weight in each hand. With weights held outstretched have your partner turn you on the turntable and move out of the way. *Bring weights into chest.*

Condition 2. Same as Condition 1 with 2 ½ pound weights.

Condition 3. Same as Condition 1 with no weights.

Results

Describe the results under each condition of the experiment and relate the mechanical principles present. Compare the results of each condition and explain the results with a concluding principle.

Condition 1:

Why?

Principle

Condition 2:

Why?

Principle

Condition 3:

Why?

Principle

Comparison of Conditions:

Describe:

Why?

Concluding Principles:

Key Terms from Chapter 6

Angular Speed—Velocity in terms of revolutions, radians, or degrees and seconds.

Center of Rotation—That point about which a body rotates while in rotary motion.

Degree—1/360 of the circumference of a circle.

Pi—(∏)—The ratio of the circumference of a circle to its diameter or 3.1459 to 5 decimal places.

Radian—The angle subtended by the arc of a circle that is equal to the radius of the circle. (57.3 degrees)

Radius—The distance from the arc of rotation of an object to the center of rotation.

Revolution—A complete rotation about an axis. (6.28 Radians) (360 degrees)

Rotary Motion—Movement of a body in a circle or arc of a circle.

Rotary Speed—Velocity in terms of radians per second.

Rotation—To turn on an axis.

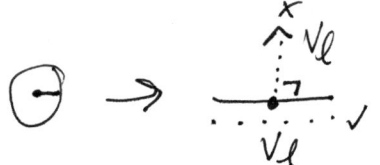

7
FORCE AND FACTORS AFFECTING FORCE

Force is absolutely necessary for the production of any type of movement or physical activity. We need force not only to create motion, but to resist motion and to maintain posture. It is possible in some situations for there to be force without motion; there can never, however, be motion without force. One can see this concept in action by simply pushing as hard as possible against a brick wall. Force is a quantifiable factor in all movement. Force is a function of mass of the body to which the force is applied and acceleration (**P.1.0.**). The familiar equation used long ago by Sir Isaac Newton to quantify force is:

$$\Delta F = ma \text{ or } \Delta F = mv/t$$

Where:

$$\left[\begin{array}{l} m = w/32 \text{ and } a = v/t \\ \Delta F = \text{change in force} \\ m = \text{mass} \\ a = \text{acceleration} \end{array} \right]$$

Example

A baseball weighing 5 ounces (5/16 of a lb.) is thrown with an initial velocity of 90 fps. If the acceleration was uniform and the initial velocity of the baseball was developed in 0.1 sec., what would have been the force generated?

$$\Delta F = m(a) \qquad m = 5/16 \div 32 \qquad a = 90 \div 0.1$$
$$\Delta F = 450/51.2 \qquad = \qquad 8.79 \text{ lbs.}$$

Additionally, force is inversely proportional to the time it takes to develop it. In other words, if the velocity is developed in a very short time, the force is greater than if it is developed over a longer duration. If the initial velocity of the baseball in the above situation had been developed in 0.01 sec. instead of 0.1 sec., the force would have been 87.9 lbs.

Newton's Second Law of Motion says that the acceleration of any object is directly proportional to the magnitude of the force that caused the acceleration. If mass is held constant, greater force will produce greater acceleration and conversely. The more rapidly a muscle can contract, the greater the force that muscle is able to produce. The importance of this idea is obvious in activities involving the need for explosive power. A great deal of training time in these sports is spent in developing explosion.

Often the application of force takes on greater importance than the development of sheer brute force. There are situations that arise in sport in which a small player is required to match-up physically against a larger, stronger opponent. The larger player does not always win in these situations. Why? **The application of force and the direction the force is applied is sometimes more important than brute force (P.2.0.).** By applying forces at the optimal angle, athletes are better able to optimize performance. If one desires to maximize horizontal force, for example, one should apply force as nearly as is practical in the horizontal direction. The desire here is to create as much **effective force** as possible.

Figure 7-1 Football Punt: Application of explosive power

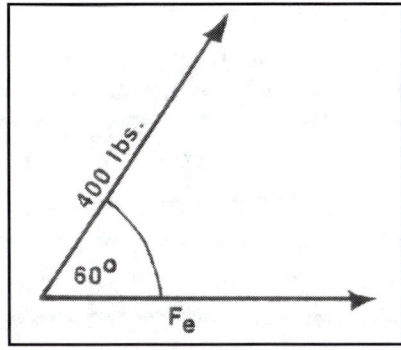

Figure 7–2

$$\text{Cos } 60° = \frac{F_e}{400}$$

$$F_e = \text{Cos } 60° \ (400)$$

$$F_e = (.5) \ (400)$$

$$F_e = 200 \text{ lbs.}$$

Figure 7-2 is a schematic of a situation in which a sprinter is exerting 400 lbs. of force against a starting block at an angle of 60 degrees to the horizontal. The goal of the sprinter should be to optimize effective force in the direction of the finish. In this case, the effective force is diminished due to the high angle of takeoff, as is shown in the solution.

If, however the sprinter had created the same amount of force at a 30-degree angle, more of the force would have been effective force. (See Fig. 7-3)

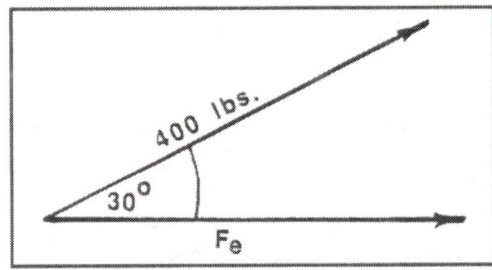

Figure 7–3

$$\text{Cos } 30° = \frac{F_e}{400}$$

$$F_e = \text{Cos } 30° \ (400)$$

$$F_e = (.866) \ (400)$$

$$F_e = 346.4 \text{ lbs}$$

By comparison it is easy to see that the sprinter in the second scenario was much more efficient in the use of force. In fact, that sprinter was able to apply 146.4 lbs. more force in the desired direction. **When horizontal velocity is desired, force should be applied as close to the horizontal as possible so that as much of the total force applied is effective force (P.3.0.).** In general, **force should be applied as directly as possible in the direction of the intended motion so that as much of the force as possible can be utilized as effective force (P.4.0.).** If a small football player has to take on a larger player, the smaller player must work against the center of gravity of the larger player at a lower angle to have a chance.

Forces can frequently be produced as a result of collisions between bodies. For example, when two football players meet at an angle, the resultant force of the collision is generally greater than the individual force of either. **An object acted upon by two forces moves in the direction of the resultant of the two forces. This is the Principle of the Parallelogram of Force (P.5.0.).** The resultant force vector is defined as the diagonal of the parallelogram created when lines are drawn parallel to the original force vectors of the two bodies.

Example

Two players hit at right angles. Player A hits with 200 lbs. of force and Player B hits with 100 lbs. of force. What is the resultant force and at what angle is player B displaced from his initial path?

A schematic of the above situation is shown in Fig. 7-4.

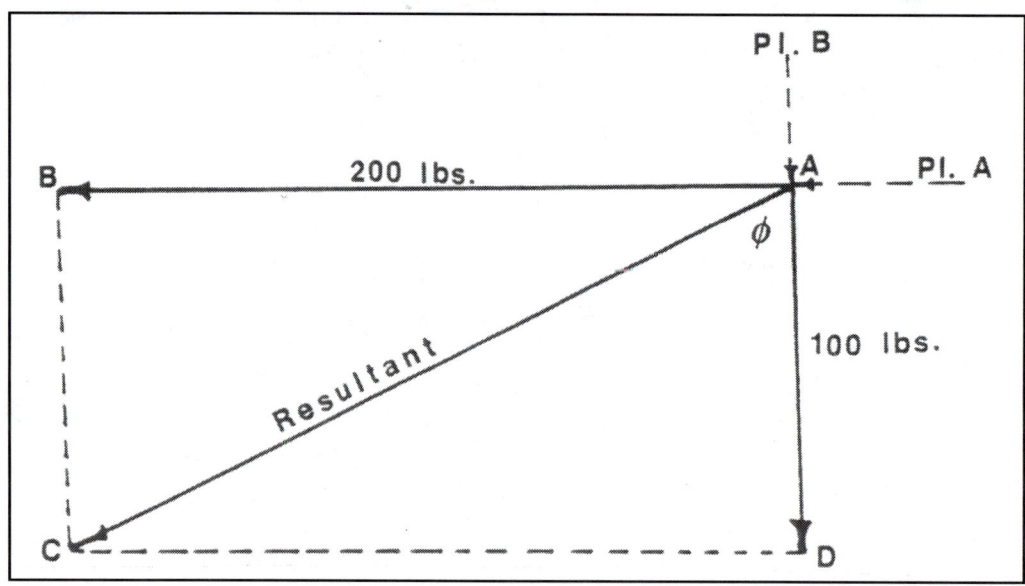

Figure 7–4

The resultant force and direction is the diagonal of the parallelogram of force. Player A and B collide at point A. Player A creating a force vector AB equal to 200 lbs and player B creating a force vector AD equal to 100 lbs. at right angle to each other. The resultant force is the diagonal AC of the rectangle ABCD. The solution to the resultant is found by simple use of the **Pythagorean Theorem**. Player A and player B increase their force after contact to 223.61 lbs. in the new direction AC.

ø is the angle player B is displaced from his initial path.

$$\text{Tan } ø = 200/100 = 2$$

$$ø = 63.43 \text{ degrees}$$

Player B is displaced from his original path over 63 degrees.

Unfortunately, not all collisions are at right angles. Although at first it appears much more complicated to deal with non-right angle collisions, mathematically, it really is quite simple. The following equation is used for <u>non-right angle collisions</u>:

$$R^2 = A^2 + B^2 - 2AB \cos a$$

Where: R = resultant force

A = force of contact of A

B = force of contact of B

a = angle of contact

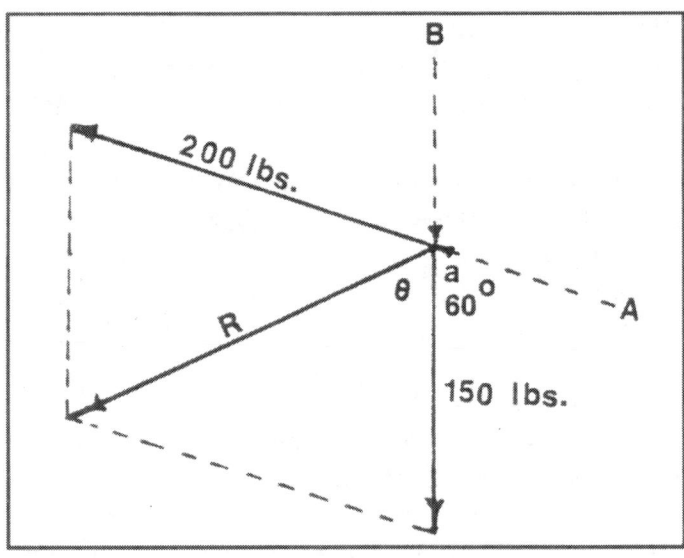

Figure 7–5

$$R^2 = (200)^2 + (150)^2 - (2)(200)(150)(\text{Cos } 60°)$$

$$R^2 = 40,000 + 22,500 - (60,000)(.5)$$

$$R^2 = 62,500 - 30,000$$

$$R^2 = 32,500$$

$$R = 180.28 \text{ pounds}$$

In order to find θ use the formula:

$$A^2 = R^2 + B^2 - 2RB \text{ Cos } \theta$$

$$(200)^2 = (180.18)^2 + (150)^2 - (2)(180.28)(150) \text{ Cos } \theta$$

$$40,000 = 32,500 + 22,500 - 54,084 \text{ Cos } \theta$$

$$54,084 \text{ Cos } \theta = 55,000 - 40,000$$

$$\text{Cos } \theta = \frac{15,000}{54,084} = .2773$$

$$\theta = 73.9 \text{ degrees}$$

Forces that result in movement are themselves the result of a chain of forces. Forces in general are summed up as they are produced in series. A long jumper, for example, runs down the runway to build up speed and then applies subsequent forces to lift into the air. **Total effective force may be the sum of the forces applies in a single direction and in proper sequence (P.6.0.).** The limitation of forces in a series is the weakest force in that series. Sometimes extremely strong individuals may be hampered by weaknesses in some area of their sport. A weight lifter when executing the clean and jerk may be easily strong enough to execute the move, but have weak wrists, and be unable to hold the weight in the clean position. Forces that are generated in series are also very dependent upon proper timing of muscular contractions.

When generating force in a series, each successive force should be started at the point of greatest velocity and least acceleration of the previous movement (P.7.0.). The javelin thrower utilizes the run-up, the crossover steps, the leg drive, and the throw in proper order to achieve the greatest possible velocity of the javelin at release. The proper sequence of these forces is critical to performance of the javelin throw, as well as to other sports. If the throw occurs before the leg drive is at maximum, the result is a weak throw.

The application of forces to objects by using other objects, as in striking activities, is dependent upon the velocity of the striking implement. In order for maximum effectiveness to be achieved, the wrists must be as relaxed as possible, so as to not inhibit the swinging action. However, to get maximum effective force at contact, the grip must be firm at contact. This firming up of the grip at contact is a significant problem in golf, tennis, and baseball. Usually, the grip is firmed up too much, thus, causing tension in the forearms. This frequently leads to poor results and even to injury. In activities involving striking without an implement, such as in karate or boxing, it is also important for the member of the body being used to be as rigid as possible at contact.

Sport often requires that forces be absorbed rather than directed at another. Many sports have techniques that are specifically designed to lessen the effects of absorbing external forces. **In order to lessen the shock of a blow, fall, throw, or kick, the shock should be spread over as large an area as possible and/or through as long a distance as possible (P.8.0.).** When a football player falls on a loose ball, or a base runner slides into base it is important for the player to gradually absorb the shock. The negative consequence of not doing so in these situations often include injury to the player. The baseball player, by spreading the slide over as large an area as possible, avoids the painful abrasions on the lower leg and hip that frequently occur. This is why many experts feel that the headfirst slide is actually easier on the body. Increasing the distance over which a blow is absorbed can considerably lessen the effects of the blow. When a catcher gives with a pitch as it enters the mitt, the force of the ball on the hand is greatly reduced. The judo performer tries to spread out the landing when thrown as does the gymnast when landing on a dismount. An excellent example of this principle in action can be seen in the dreaded egg toss competition, however. Unless the catcher properly times the absorption of the force of the incoming egg, there will usually be messy results! Mathematically, the absorption of force and the subsequent dissipation of that force is:

$$\left[\quad Fd = 1/2 \ mV^2 \middle| \begin{array}{l} \text{Since } a = V^2/2d \text{ and } F = ma \\ \text{Then, } F = mV^2/2d \end{array} \right]$$

dissipation of force

It then follows that as distance increases, then force would decrease.

Figure 7–6. Absorbing Shock

During the performance of sports there are often actions taken that reduce the level of performance. For example, throwers in track and field often attempt the jump into the air as they throw. Force cannot be applied while in the air. A shot putter who dips down in the middle of the ring creates specific problems with inertia. Thus, he/she creates a shot that is relatively heavier than it should be.

Newton's Third Law states, 'For every action there is an equal and opposite reaction.' **In order to obtain maximal effective force** when **throwing or pushing, one or both feet should be in contact** with the **ground or a hard surface (P.9.0.).** Pushing a car in the mud is nearly impossible, because there is not a hard surface to push against. Several other important principles regarding the application of force exist.

Additional force may be gained by bending a joint (P.10.0.). Immediately before the swimming starts, the swimmer may drop her heels in order to provide for additional force application. It is virtually impossible to hit a strong badminton shot without utilizing the wrist. Likewise, increasing the distance over which acceleration can be developed will help generate greater force. When a batter keeps the hands back as he strides forward, the distance over which force can be developed can be greatly enhanced. Not only is the distance increased, but the muscles involved are placed in a stretched state, which causes a more powerful contraction.

The greater the distance over which acceleration can be developed, the greater the force developed (P.11.0.).

The more fully a muscle is stretched the greater the force it can exert **(P.12.0.).**

For every action there is an equal
and opposite reaction.

For greatest distance keep in contact with ground

Figure 7–7

An old wise person once said, 'the bigger they are, the harder they fall." This sounds like a reasonable saying and has a small ring of truth to it. However, in sport it may be more proper to say, "the bigger they are, the harder they hit." **The greater the mass of the object imparting force and the faster it is moving, the greater the force imparted (P.13.0.).** If a player makes contact with another player and they are both moving at the same velocity, the heavier of the two players will usually come out best in the collision. And, if the players weigh the same, the faster of the two will come out best.

Another type of force results from movement around a curve is centrifugal force. This force causes bodies moving on a curve to fly off of the circle at a tangent to the circle. The weight of the body on the curve and its velocity are the components of centrifugal force. **Centrifugal force varies directly as the weight and velocity squared of a body and inversely as the pull of gravity and radius of the circle (P.14.0.).**

$$CF = wV^2 / gr$$

Where:

CF = centrifugal force

w = weight of the body

V = velocity of the body

g = force of gravity 32 ft/sec/sec

r = radius of the curve

Example

If an indoor track has a radius of 50 feet, what is the centrifugal force on the center of gravity of a 200-lb. sprinter on the curve running at 30 fps?

$$CF = \frac{200(30)^2}{(32)(50)} = \frac{200(900)}{1600}$$

$$CF = \frac{180,000}{1,600} = 112.5 \text{ lbs.}$$

The force pulling the runner out of his lane is 112.5 lbs. This is far too much for him to handle and still be able to stay in his lane. The runner can compensate for the effects of centrifugal force in three ways. He can: a) lean; b) slow down; or c) increase the radius of the curve. Since he is in a race and must stay in his lane, b and c are not good alternatives. So, he must lean. The amount of lean necessary to compensate for this situation is calculated using the following formula:

$$Tan\ ø = V^2 / gr$$

ø = the angle of lean with the vertical or the slope of the track.

The **greater the centrifugal force, the greater the lean or banking necessary to balance the force** (P.15.0.) A baseball player who is rounding first base may have to compensate for the turn by increasing the radius of his curve. This is why players typically run an elliptical path around the base on the way to second.

A runner may counteract centrifugal force in any combination of the following ways: a) lean; b) slow down; c) increase radius of curve (P.16.0.).

There are a number of factors which affect the response that projectiles will have when forces are applied and, usually, they are quite predictable. The first of these important factors is the relationship between the spin of a ball and its surface as it relates to the angle of rebound. If we know the nature of the surface upon which a sport is played, we can generally make fairly accurate predictions regarding how the ball will bounce on that surface. **The angle of rebound is greater than the angle of incidence for compressible balls hitting a smooth surface with no spin (P.17.0.).** The deviation of the angle of rebound of a compressible ball from the angle of incidence tends to increase from 0 to 45 degrees and decrease from 45 to 90 degrees. It will, however, always be greater than the angle of incidence. When the element of spin is added to the mix, this is no longer true. **Topspin on a ball causes a lower angle of rebound, a longer bounce and more roll (P.18.0.).** Although in this situation, the ball appears to pick up speed, we know that in all cases it does not do so. **Backspin on a ball causes a higher angle of rebound, a shorter bounce and less roll (P.19.0.).** It should be pointed out here that if a ball is non-compressible the reaction to the surface depends upon the nature of the surface. However, in general, with no spin, angle of incidence more nearly approximates angle of rebound. Such is the case in billiards, but the addition of spin to the ball often results in some seemingly unpredictable results.

Another key factor in the reaction of force application is the resistance. The advantages or disadvantages of wind conditions in certain sports are dependent on the nature of the sport itself. A slight headwind may be actually desirable in some sports (discus). Yet, it may be undesirable in others (cycling). **The reaction of air on an object in flight is dependent upon the active surface area of the body over which the air stream passes and the velocity of the air stream with respect to the body (P.20.0.).** The active surface area plays an important role in this prin-

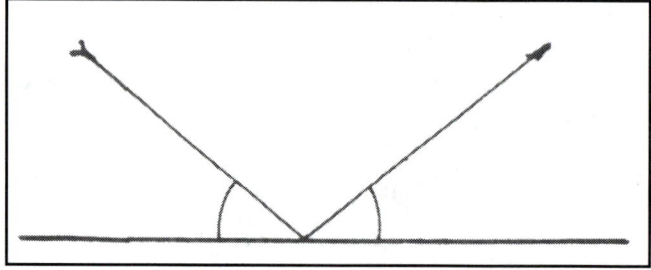

Figure 7–8 Pool ball rebound

ciple. Golf ball manufacturers spend a great amount of their research dollars to develop golf balls that will fly farther and straighter. The general variations that takes place in golf ball design are in the dimple and cover design. It is known that a smooth golf ball will not go as far as a dimpled one.

Another interesting phenomenon that occurs in sport is the curving of different balls during flight. A pitched baseball with side spin will curve all the way to the plate but will curve more at the end because it has lost linear velocity at a greater rate than rotary velocity. The relationship between spin and forward velocity is such that, as linear velocity decreases, the effects of spin are greater. Objects thrown into the air with no spin will be erratic in flight. A football thrown with no spin will not go very far or be very accurate. A discus with no spin will tumble in flight. Spin acts to aid in stabilizing the flight of a projectile in air. A football thrown with a tight spiral will have better flight characteristics.

Collisions and striking force are somewhat affected by the elasticity and the restitution properties of the ball and implement. The speed of flight of a struck ball depends upon the weight and striking force of the ball and bat and the coefficient of restitution of the ball and bat. In softball, the trend has been toward lighter and lighter bats. The thinking behind this trend is that lighter bats provide for greater bat speed; but, as the weight of the bat becomes closer to the weight of the incoming ball, there could be a point of diminishing return.

The coefficient of elasticity of a ball is a function of height bounced and height dropped (P.21.0.). The higher the bounce in relation to the height dropped, the greater the coefficient of elasticity. An official basketball when properly inflated must rebound to a height of between 49 and 54 inches when dropped from a height of 72 inches. This is why the basketball referee tosses the ball and watches how high it bounces before using it in a game.

Example

A basketball dropped from a height of 6 feet rebounds to 50 inches. What is its coefficient of elasticity?

$$e = (hb/hd)^{.5} \quad = \quad (50/72)^{.5} \quad = \quad .833$$

The coefficient of elasticity of the basketball is .833, well within the acceptable range. (Note any number raised to the .5 power is the same as the square root of that number).

A good many sports would be nearly impossible or even dangerous to play without the presence of friction. Friction plays a major role in the characteristics of the bounces of various balls and in the way many balls roll. Additionally, players of same sports rely upon friction in many cases and curse it in others. It would be a nightmare to play basketball without the friction between the shoes of the players and the court. Tennis takes on different qualities if played on grass than if played on clay. These qualities are directly related to friction. How important friction is to the performance of bowling is evident in the development of materials for bowling balls. **The coefficient of friction is dependent upon the composition of the two surfaces, the compression weight of the surfaces, the action between the two surfaces and the irregularity of the surfaces, but is independent of the area of contact of the two surfaces (P.22.0).** The coefficient of friction is determined by the formula:

$$C = P/W$$

where:

C = coefficient of friction

P = horizontal force necessary to start slipping

W = the weight of the body

If a certain basketball shoe worn by a player weighing 150 lbs. takes 225 lbs. of horizontal force to start slippage, what is the coefficient of friction of the shoe?

$$C = 225/150 = 1.5$$

The coefficient of friction of this basketball shoe on the playing surface was 1.5. This is not uncommon for a good shoe on a good surface. It so happens that this coefficient is also used to determine the angle a player may lean before slippage begins.

$$\text{Tan } \phi = P/W$$

In the above case:

$$\text{Tan } \phi = 225/150 \text{ or } 1.5$$

$$\phi = 56 \text{ degrees}$$

This is more than enough to allow basketball players to lean.

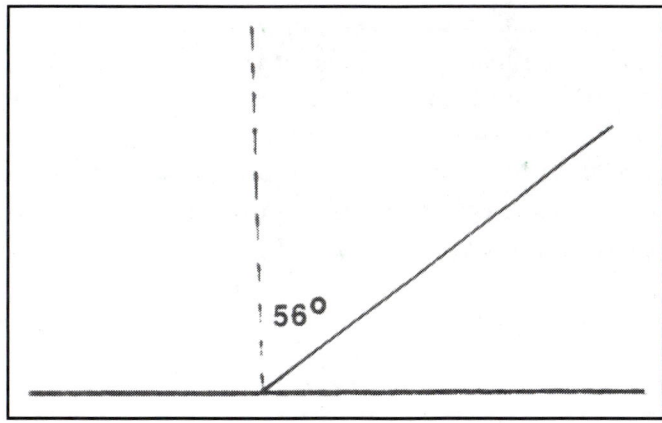

Figure 7–9

The problems caused by air resistance to movement are small compared to those caused by water. In swimming, there are several factors that affect performance. These are shown in Fig. 7-10.

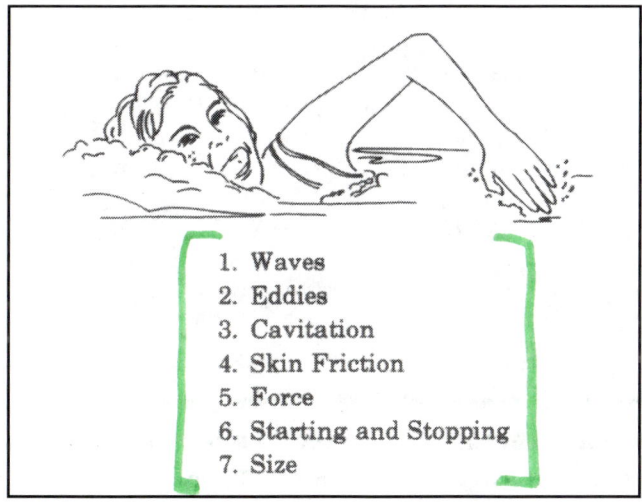

1. Waves
2. Eddies
3. Cavitation
4. Skin Friction
5. Force
6. Starting and Stopping
7. Size

Figure 7-10

Because water is 40 times denser than air, efficiency of force becomes even more dramatically important than brute force.

Finally, a component of force that is vital for our production of movement is the relationship between speed of contraction and the force available for contraction. **In the human body, available force varies inversely with the speed of movement (within limits) (P. 23.0.).**

If a muscle is contracting at its maximum speed; nothing is left for it to create additional force. During the last three steps of the long jump, the jumper ceases his efforts to accelerate and maintains near maximum speed without maximal effort (momentum) so that he will have force available for the takeoff. If the maximum speed of a particular muscle is known and maximum strength of that muscle is known, then the following formula may be used to determine the external force that can be applied at any speed of contraction:

$$Fa = Fm\ (1 - Va/Vm)$$

Where:
Fa = applied force
Fm = maximum force
Va = applied velocity
Vm = maximum velocity

If a muscle is capable of a maximum contractile velocity of 50 mm/sec. and can exert 500 lbs. of force it may be seen that maximum force is available at a contractile velocity of zero.

$$Fa = 500\ (1 - 0/50) = 500(1) = 500\ \text{lbs.}$$

In fact, when:

$Va = 0$	$Fa = 500$
$Va = 10$	$Fa = 400$
$Va = 20$	$Fa = 300$
$Va = 30$	$Fa = 200$
$Va = 40$	$Fa = 100$
$Va = 50$	$Fa = 0$

In order to increase the amount of force that can be exerted at a specified speed, the development of strength is vital. As strength requirements become greater the optimal force-speed relationship becomes more critical. In the long jump, the conservation of horizontal velocity is of paramount importance. Thus, the long jumper approaches at a greater speed and places less emphasis upon the actual jumping action. In sports that require vertical jumping, such as, basketball and volleyball, approach velocities must be slower. These velocities are usually around 60 to 70 percent of maximum for one-foot takeoffs and 50 to 60 percent for two-foot takeoffs. Additionally, **in jumping activities the depth of the gather is directly proportional to the strength of the muscles. That is, the stronger the muscles, the greater the gather for optimal height (P.24.0.).**

Whenever physical or mechanical work is done, there is some force acting to move a body or object over a distance or through space. Work is equal to force applied times the distance through which the force acts. It is defined by the formula:

$$W = F \times d$$

Example

If a high jumper in the Fosbury flop technique lifts her center of gravity from the lowest point at takeoff to the point of toe-off a distance of 2 feet, and is able to exert 300 lbs. of force, the amount of work done is simply 600 ft. – lbs.

Closely related to work is power. This is one of the important qualities that most athletes work very hard to develop. Power is the force applied times the velocity of the movement. It is defined by the equation: $P = FV$.

Movements and changes of position always create energy in addition to the need for energy to produce them. The energy created by these movements is called kinetic energy. Kinetic energy is equal to one-half the mass of the body divided by the gravity of the body being moved times the velocity of movement squared.

$$KE = 1/2mV^2 = Fd = W$$

Finally, potential energy is the energy of position. The calculation of potential energy is done by multiplying the weight of the body times the height of the center of gravity.

The techniques performed in sport are best accomplished when executed according to the laws of physics. When the principles of movement are adhered to the end result is efficient use of energy and optimal force production.

Problems

1. A 16 lb. shot leaves the putter's hand at a velocity of 30 fps. If this velocity is obtained in 0.2 sec., how much force is applied to the shot?

   How fast is the shot accelerating?

2. A long jumper weighing 100 lbs. develops a force through a distance of 2 feet in 0.1 sec. Find the amount of force she developed in her jump.

3. Lineman A develops a thrust in his legs of 1000 lbs. leaning at angle of 60 degrees. Lineman B blocking him head-on can develop a thrust of 600 lbs. with his legs. At what angle must lineman B contact at lineman A's center of mass in order to stop him?

4. A runner comes off of her mark at an angle of 60 degrees and can exert 400 lbs. against the block. How much of this force is effective force?

5. An offensive lineman A makes contact with a defensive lineman B at right angles. Lineman A on his charge is leaning at an angle of 45 degrees and developing a thrust against the ground of 600 lbs. Lineman B is developing a thrust of 1000 lbs and leaning at angle of 60 degrees. What is the resultant force and at what angle has lineman B been displaced from his original path?

6. A football fullback weighing 200 pounds hits the line with his body inclined at an angle of 30 degrees with the ground. His force in this direction is 600 pounds. What would be the force directed toward the goal line? If his angle of lean were 45 degrees, what force would be exerted toward the goal line?

7. By actual measurement it has been found that a track man pushed with both feet at the start of a race with a force of 500 pounds. In the start, the direction of force was at an angle of 50 degrees with the horizontal. How much of this force was effective in starting down the track?

8. Outdoor tracks usually have a radius of about 100 feet. Assume that a runner is traveling at 20 ft/sec and that he weighs 180 pounds. How much force tends to pull him out of his lane at the turn?

9. What angle of lean is necessary to compensate for the conditions described in problem 8?

10. A 12-pound shot leaves the putter's hand at a velocity of 40/ft/sec. If this velocity is attained in 3/10 of a second, how much force is applied to the shot? How fast is the shot accelerating?

11. A high jumper weighing 150 pounds develops a force through a distance of 1 foot in .5 seconds. Find the amount of force developed in the jump.

12. A runner comes off his mark at an angle of 60 degrees. The force exerted against the starting blocks is 325 pounds. How much of this force is effective force? If the angle is 30 degrees, what are the results?

13. A ball carrier hits the line with his body inclined at an angle of 80 degrees with the ground. His force in this direction is 400 pounds. What would be the force directed toward the goal line? If his angle of lean were 45 degrees, what force would be exerted toward the goal line?

14. A back running with a force of 300 pounds toward the goal line is hit by a linebacker at a right angle with a force of 500 pounds. At what angle is his new direction changed from is original path?

15. On a quarterback sneak, the quarterback drives at an angle of 30 degrees with the ground at a force of 500 pounds. What is the force toward the goal line? A lineman hits the quarterback at a right angle to his path at his center of gravity with a force of 300 pounds. At what angle has the quarterback changed his direction from the goal line? What is the resultant force?

16. An indoor track has a 25-foot radius at the ends. It is built to accommodate a runner at the rate of 25 ft/sec. What is the angle at which the track must be banked so that the runner may run perpendicular to the track?

17. A sprinter running the curve of a track with a radius of 50 feet at 30 ft/sec weighs 200 pounds. How much force tends to pull him out of his lane? What angle must he lean to counter this force?

18. A baseball is caught traveling at 90 ft/sec and the force is dissipated over a distance of 2 feet. What magnitude of force was needed to stop the ball? What would have been the force if dissipated over .5 feet?

19. A baseball is caught traveling at 80 feet per second and the force is dissipated over a distance of 2 feet. What magnitude of force would the ball have hit if the glove had given only 1/2 foot?

20. The maximum strength of a muscle is 400 pounds and its maximum speed of contraction is 30 mm per second. If the muscle is called on to exert 150 pounds of force what velocity could be applied to the movement?

21. The official basketball is standardized in accordance with the length of its rebound. When dropped from a distance of 6 feet, measured from the bottom of the ball, it must be inflated so that it will rebound to a height of from 49 to 54 inches, measured to the top of the ball. What is the minimum elasticity of an official basketball?

22. The coefficient of friction of a pair of rubber soled shoes with a certain floor is .80. The player weighs 200 pounds. What angle of lean is possible before he will slip?

23. A football player must move to a position to make a block contracting major movement muscles at 80% of maximum velocity. If the maximum strength of the muscles is 1000 lbs., what force will be available to block?

24. The maximum strength of a muscle is 300 lbs. and its maximum contractile velocity is 40 mm/sec. If the muscle is called on to exert 175 lbs. of force what velocity could be applied to the movement?

25. A football player must move to a position to make a block contracting major muscles at 70% of maximum velocity. If the maximum strength of the muscle is 1000 lbs., what force will be available to block?

Exercises

1. Throw a baseball with as much force as you can. Describe how you created this force.

2. Catch a basketball. Describe the principles you used in dissipating the force.

3. Run as fast as you can around the center circle of a basketball court. How do you combat centrifugal force?

4. Explain the statement, "the available force varies inversely with the velocity of movement."

5. Describe the use of the principle "the angle of incidence equals the angle of reflection." List some examples.

6. Throw a ball that hits a smooth surface such as a tennis ball hitting the court: with topspin, spinning counter clockwise, spinning clockwise, and with backspin. How does each affect its flight and rebound?

EXPERIMENT 7.1

Purpose

The purposes of this experiment are to:

1. Experience the effects of force under various conditions.

2. Compare the effect of various force production on effective force.

3. Relate the principles of force employed under the conditions described below.

Procedures

Condition 1. Spin a weight attached to a string around your finger. Describe the principles of force involved in the results section of the report.

Condition 2. Push a desk across the floor applying force at different angles to the path of movement. Describe the force exerted under each application.

Condition 3. Perform a curl with a set of weights under the following conditions (1) curl weight very slowly, (2) curl weight as fast as possible. Which condition requires the greatest force?

Results

Describe the application of the principles of force in each condition of the experiment. Relate the principle to the movement involved.

Condition 1:

Condition 2:

Condition 3:

EXPERIMENT 7.2

Purpose

The purposes of this experiment are to:

1. Determine the effect of running speed on jumping ability (available force).
2. Compare various running speeds on jumping performance.
3. Determine optimum running speed for maximum height in jumping.

Procedures

Tape a yardstick to a basketball backboard. Have a partner on a step ladder measure height of jump. Jump three times under the following conditions and measure highest jump for each condition.

Condition 1.   Standing jump

Condition 2.   Step and jump

Condition 3.   1/4 maximum speed

Condition 4.   1/2 maximum speed

Condition 5.   3/4 maximum speed

Condition 6.   Maximum speed

Results

Enter maximum jump under each condition.

Condition	Height Jumped
1	_____
2	_____
3	_____
4	_____
5	_____
6	_____

1. Which horizontal speed resulted in the highest jump?

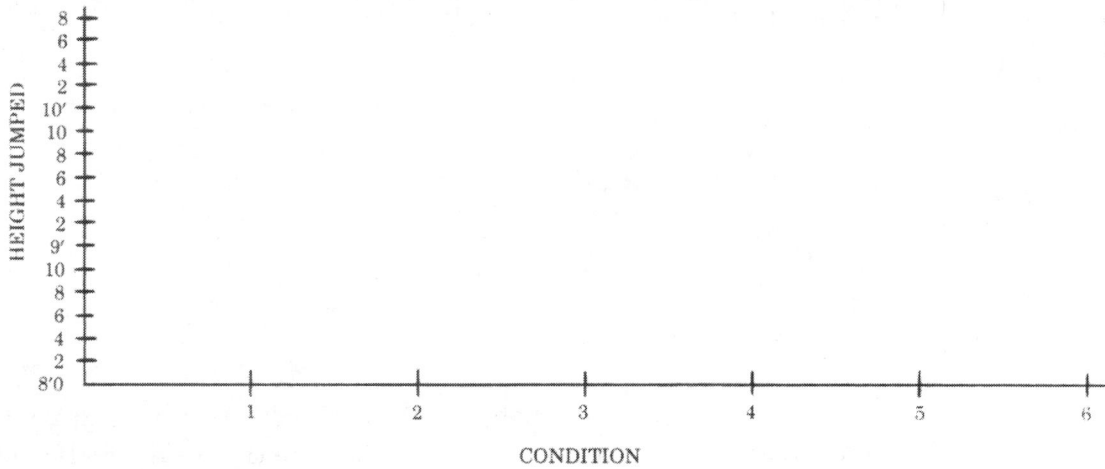

2. What principles do you feel were the major contributors to your jump under each condition?

EXPERIMENT 7.3

Purpose

The purposes of the experiment are to:

1. Determine the effect of factors affecting force on the trajectory of an object.
2. Compare conditions that affect force.
3. Relate the principles of factors affecting force to each condition below.

Procedures

Condition 1. Throw a softball, plastic ball, and shuttlecock. Draw a diagram of the trajectory of each in the space provided in the results section of this report.

Condition 2. Throw a baseball into a pool of water. Note the direction of the throw and the position where the ball hit the bottom. Draw a diagram of the path of the ball hitting the surface of the water and place where ball hit bottom in the space provided in the results section of this report.

Condition 3. Stand and execute the Sargent jump. Execute the sargent jump stepping as you jump. Now perform the Sargent jump at half speed. Repeat the jump running at full speed. Record your results and state the principles involved.

Results

State the results and relate to principle involved for each condition listed below.

Condition 1:

softball
plastic ball
shuttlecock

Trajectory

Principle:

Condition 2:

Trajectory

Principle:

Condition 3:

	Height Jumped	Principle
standing	_____	_____
step	_____	_____
1/2 speed	_____	_____
full speed	_____	_____

EXPERIMENT 7.4

Purpose:

The purposes of this experiment are to:

1. Determining the elasticity of a racquetball, handball, and tennis ball.

2. Compare the elasticity of a racquetball, handball, and tennis ball.

3. Determine the effect of backspin, topspin, and side spin on a basketball as it contacts the playing surfaces

Condition 1. Drop a racquetball, handball, and tennis ball from a height of 6 feet (top of ball) onto a basketball wood surface. Measure the height of the rebound (top of ball) and place in results section of this experiment.

Condition 2. Pass a basketball down a line on the basketball floor with (1) no spin (2) top spin (3) back spin (4) clockwise spin (5) counterclockwise spin. Describe the results in the results section for each condition.

Results

State the results and relate the principle involved for each condition listed below.

Condition 1

	height bounced	height dropped	elasticity
racquetball	_____	72 inches	_____
handball	_____	72 inches	_____
tennis ball	_____	72 inches	_____

Comparison:

Principle:

Condition 2
Results

1. No spin _____

2. Top spin _____

3. Back spin _____

4. Clockwise spin _____

5. Counter-clockwise spin _____

Principles:

1. _____

2. _____

3. _____

4. _____

5. _____

Key Terms from Chapter Seven

Applied force—amount of force exerted against an object.

Available force—that force within the human body that may be used for external work.

Centrifugal force—that force which tends to cause a rotating body to fly off at a tangent to its circle of movement or that pulls away from the center of rotation.

Centripetal force—the force that tends to pull a rotating body inward toward the center of rotation.

Effective force—force resulting in the desired direction.

Elasticity—that property of a body that causes it to resist deformation and thereby recover its original work.

Energy—capacity for doing work.

Force—that quantity that creates motion or prevents motion.

Gyroscopic action—a rotating-stabilizing action, e.g., passing a football.

Kinetic energy—energy of a body due to its motion.

Magnitude of force—that quantity of numerical value that may be compared to other quantities of the same class.

Moment of force—applied force multiplied by the perpendicular distance of that force from the axis of rotation.

Parallelogram of force—the quadrilateral formed by drawing two sides parallel to two force vectors.

Potential energy—energy stored in a body due to its relative position in space.

Restitution—that characteristic which causes a body to resume its original shape after some force has deformed it.

Resultant force—the combined effect of two or more force vectors.

Vector—a quantity that has both magnitude and direction.

Work—that phenomenon that takes place when force causes displacement of an object.

8

QUALITATIVE—VISUAL ANALYSIS

In sports, approximately ninety percent of the information that we receive is visual in nature. Nonvisual forms of feedback are also often helpful in movement analysis. Sound and kinesthetic feel or touch are also valuable forms of information. The sound of the baseball hitting the bat allows the outfielder to anticipate the proper response and movement of the ball. Football linemen and wrestlers depend upon their tactile sense to determine how and where their opponents are moving and/or their attempts to gain an advantage on them. Kinesthetic feel tells the performer if the shot was good or bad, successful or unsuccessful.

The quality of movement refers to the process, form, coordination, or technique displayed by the student during class or the athlete during competition. It is necessary to assess or evaluate individual physical skills by observing the performance and analyzing whether the movement characteristics desired are present. Qualitative analysis refers to a description of quality without the use of numbers. The trained observer learns from experience to recognize faulty or unskilled movement However, it is virtually impossible to accurately observe ballistic motion.

Explosive muscular contraction is not visible to the normal eye. Years of experience, training, practice and repetition does provide some basis for judging performance outcomes.

In order for qualitative analysis to be objective and reliable, several parameters or guidelines must be considered. An acceptable qualitative analysis procedure might include the following considerations:

Select the Optimal Vantage Point

The proper observational distance may be closer to the performer if smaller, more precise body movements are to be analyzed, or at a greater distance if an entire sequence of movements is to be evaluated. Observe the movement from different vantage points or angles. If examples of situations in competition do not occur frequently, then observe the performance from a carefully selected angle. The observation of an elite or highly skilled performer as a model can be helpful in establishing a criterion or basis for evaluating other, lesser skilled performers.

Simplify the Movement

Most skills in sports and physical education occur so rapidly that they are difficult to analyze. The speed of movement is generally a summation of many forces. Movement is initiated by the larger joints towards the smaller ones, from the shoulders and torso out to the arms and legs and finally the hands and feet. Break the movement down into separate parts or phases. An example might be the baseball pitching act broken down into five phases: (1) wind-up; (2) cocking; (3) acceleration and ball release; (4) deceleration; and (5) follow-through.

Observe the subject to see if he or she demonstrates the good timing and proper sequence of action. Proper technique eliminates problems, such as, "opening up" or committing yourself too soon.

Establish and Maintain the Correct Body Position

Balance, control and stability are essential in obtaining the proper body position. Establishing a proper starting and finishing position should provide a good base to insure stability and control throughout the movement. Lowering the center of gravity by bending the knees, widening your base of support and keeping your center of gravity over your base of support enhances stability and balance.

Look for unnecessary or undesired movement that may cause inefficiency in movement. Coordinated movements require that the arms and legs work in opposition to each other and serve to counterbalance. For example, the non-dominant arm often is held up for balance or assists in speeding up rotation of the upper body in throwing activities.

Momentum developed from the angular motion of the arms and legs can be transferred to the entire body. In this manner, the arms greatly assist the legs in propelling the body in a vertical jump.

Flexibility should be Maintained throughout the Motion

A full range of movement is necessary to generate one's maximum force and speed. Placing the muscles on stretch greatly increases the force available for movement. The preliminary wind-up or the backswing places muscles on stretch prior to their contraction. Other preparatory movements, such as, flexing the knee, cocking the wrist or arching the back prior to release or propulsion take advantage of this mechanical principle.

Mechanical Analysis of Sport Skills

1. Swing arms forward and upward in the take-off in the standing broad jump—Transfer momentum from the part (the arms) to the whole (body) for greater lift and distance.

2. Flick your wrist at the moment of release in pitching a baseball—When angular velocity is constant, greater speed is attained by adding a short radius of rotation.

3. The development of explosive power is important in getting distance from a punt—Force is inversely proportional to time, the faster the muscles contract, the greater the force created.

4. A heavier football player meets the ball carrier head on, the lighter player might do better at an angle—A light player possibly could not develop the force necessary to stop the heavier player but by hitting at an angle could slow him down and displace his intended direction following the law of the parallelogram of forces.

5. On the start of a race one should reduce the angle of projection—So that as much of the force as possible will be in the desired direction (horizontal) rather than in an undesired direction (vertical). Result—As much of the force as possible becomes effective force.

6. The human body is built for speed rather than strength—The human body is made up mainly of third class levers which develop speed at the expense of strength. Third class levers sacrifice mechanical advantage for speed.

7. In executing hanging activities in gymnastics the moment arm should be as short as possible—The moment of force is equal to the weight times the moment arm, the longer the moment arm, the more force required.

8. Elevate your hips in the track start—Elevating the hips in the track start moves the center of gravity upward and toward the forward edge of the base in the direction of movement which enables the runner to start movement forward with least amount of force, since stability is indirectly proportional to the height of the center of gravity above the base and directly proportional to the horizontal distance of the center of gravity from the forward edge of the base in the direction of movement.

9. Swing arms while running—Swinging arms counters the rotation of the legs in running and allows the runner to move in a straight line. Left arm is forward while right leg is forward and vice-versa.

10. Chop stride while starting—To accelerate, the foot must push against the ground (for every action there is an equal and opposite reaction.) While the foot is in the air the body will not accelerate.

11. In running, keep center of gravity on a straight line—A body reacts to force as if it were applied to the center of gravity, thus, since the shortest distance between two points is a straight line, less force is needed if the center of gravity travels a straight line.

12. Bend the knee after the foot leaves the ground in the push-off while running —Speed of rotation is increased by shortening the radius allowing quicker recovery time for the foot.

13. Reduce acceleration before hitting the take-off board in the long jump—In the human body, available force varies inversely with the velocity of movement and if the body is moving as fast as it can then there is nothing left to develop force.

14. In the pole vault, the center of gravity of the body should be directly below the hands as the pull-up is made—With the center of gravity directly below the point of support the total force exerted will be effective force, (moment of force is least). Moment of force equals weight times moment arm.

15. On clearing the bar a pole vaulter should use the jackknife movement— (Principles of the ends and the middle), when the head and feet are brought down the hips move up and vice-versa.

16. Warm-up vaults and total vaults should be limited—A muscle loses its elasticity quickly if put under stretch too often or for too long a period of time.

17. The velocity of the shot should continually increase from the start, across the circle, until release—In developing greatest final velocity there should be a continuous acceleration from the beginning of the movement to the finish.

18. A runner on the indoor track should lean to the inside as rounding the curve —Leaning will counteract the centrifugal force created at the curve and allow the runner to maintain balance in his lane.

19. Keep arm extended when throwing the discus—When angular velocity is constant the longer the radius of rotation the greater the linear velocity of the discus.

20. Impart spin to the discus—Spin produces a stabilizing effect allowing the discus to maintain a steady course and not tumble such that the retarding effect of the air flow is kept to a minimum.

21. Throw into a slight wind with the discus when possible—Since the reaction of the discus to the air flow is such that a lifting effect is created, the discus will remain in the air longer and obtain a greater distance when throwing into a slight head wind.

22. Baseball pitchers should start their pitch with striding foot back of the pitcher's rubber—The greater the distance through which force can be developed the greater the force imparted.

23. Do not palm the ball while throwing—Fingers allow for better control of the ball and additional distance is gained by having a longer radius of rotation with the same angular velocity.

24. Recoil when catching the ball—To absorb force, the force should be absorbed over as great a distance as possible.

25. Flatten body out on ground when sliding into a base—To absorb shock, the force should be spread out over as great an area as possible to prevent injury.

26. Do not hop when taking a lead off base—In order to change direction and move on to the next base or move back to base, one must be in contact with the ground. If you are in the air you return to earth only as a free falling body at the rate of 32 feet per second, per second.

27. A bunted ball will more likely deviate from its angle of incidence than will hard hit ball—Spin on the ball has a longer time on the bat on a bunted ball than on a hard hit ball and thus has a chance to take effect.

28. Swing the leg across the median line of the body in punting a football—This imparts spin to the football giving it stability, preventing it from tumbling through the air.

29. A football charge should be more vertical than horizontal—when the charge is more vertical more of the applied force is effective force making it easier to move a man.

30. In stopping quickly, lower the center of gravity, spread the base in the direction of movement and keep the center of gravity over the trailing leg—A low center of gravity and a greater distance within which to keep the center of gravity the more stable a body becomes.

31. Keep the head between the arms when entering the water—water resistance is proportional to the cross-sectional area of the body entering it.

32. Drop the heels as the push-off starts in swimming—This gives a greater distance through which to develop force.

33. Arch of a basketball can compensate for inaccuracies in shooting—The higher the arch the larger area of the basket is available for the basketball to enter.

34. In basketball jumping, extend the legs downward and swing the arm downward sharply just before the maximum height of the jump is attained—This lowers the center of gravity in the body as much as is possible and makes a greater distance from the center of gravity to the tipping fingers allowing height for tipping.

35. The golf club used determines the distance obtained—As the angle of incidence changes, the angle of rebound changes, allowing club heads with different angles to get different distances.

36. In hitting a baseball the grip should be firm on impact—For every action there is an equal and opposite reaction. A firm grip prevents recoil and allows more force to be effective force.

37. In returning a tennis ball the racquet should be held at arms length—The longer the power arm or lever, the greater the force.

38. Snap the wrists before impact in baseball, golf, etc—By shortening the radius of rotation the more immediate the action, and the greater the force imparted to the ball.

39. In rope climbing the center of gravity should be as nearly below the hands as possible—The shorter the power arm the less force needed to create movement.

40. In throwing a baseball for distance throw at an angle of about 30° in order to get the greatest distance—At an angle of 30° more of the force is effective force and air resistance is less than throwing at a higher angle as time of flight is reduced, thus reducing total air resistance.

Contributions of Research in the Kinemechanics Laboratory at Texas A & M University to Principles of Mechanics

Falling Objects Principle (Velocity)

(The velocity of a falling ball increases at the rate of 32 feet/second each second it falls)*

Question: Does a falling ball continue to increase in velocity at the rate of 32 feet/second each second it falls?

1. Balls fall at different velocities. (13, 14, 29)
2. A ball's initial velocity is least. (13, 14, 29)
3. A ball's final velocity is greatest. (13, 14, 29)
4. A falling ball's velocity increases to a maximum. (13, 14, 29)
5. The heavier the ball, the faster its velocity. (13, 29)
6. The lighter the ball, the slower its velocity. (13,29)
7. The larger the cross-sectional area of a ball , the slower it will fall. (14,29)
8. The smaller the cross sectional area of a ball, the faster it will fall. (14, 29)
9. If a ball falls far enough, it will reach a terminal velocity. (13, 14, 29)
10. The heavier the falling ball, the faster the terminal velocity. (13,29)
11. The lighter the falling ball, the slower the terminal velocity. (13,29)
12. The less the cross-sectional area of a falling ball, the faster the terminal velocity. (14,29)
13. The greater the cross-sectional area of a falling ball, the slower the terminal velocity. (14,29)

---

* Principle as stated in majority of biomechanics textbooks when research was conducted.

Falling Objects Principle
(Acceleration)

(The acceleration of a falling ball is 32 ft./sec./sec.)*

Question: Do balls in physical education fall at a constant acceleration of 32 ft./sec./ sec.?

1. A ball's initial acceleration is greatest. (13, 14, 29)
2. A ball's final acceleration is least. (13, 14, 29)
3. A falling ball's acceleration decreases to zero. (13, 14, 29)
4. Balls fall at different accelerations (13, 14, 29)
5. The heavier ball decreases in acceleration slower than a lighter ball. (13, 29).
6. The lighter ball decreases in acceleration faster than a heavier ball. (13, 29)
7. The larger the cross-sectional area of a ball, the faster the deceleration. (14,29)
8. The smaller the cross-sectional area of a ball, the slower the deceleration. (14, 29)

Falling Object Principles

(All balls regardless of weight or cross-sectional area fall at 32 ft./sec./sec.)*

Question: Do all balls fall at 32 ft./ sec./sec. regardless of weight or cross-sectional area?

1. The larger the cross-sectional area of a ball and the lighter the ball, the slower it will fall. (13, 14, 29)
2. The smaller the cross-sectional area of a ball and the heavier the ball, the faster it will fall. (13,14,29)
3. The larger the cross-sectional area of a ball and lighter the ball, the faster it decreases in acceleration. (13,14,29)
4. The smaller the cross-sectional area of a ball and the heavier the ball, the slower it decreases in acceleration. (13, 14, 29)
5. The heavier the ball and the less the cross-sectional area, the faster the terminal velocity. (13, 14, 29)
6. The lighter the ball and the greater the cross-sectional area, the less the terminal velocity. (13, 14, 29)

7. Due to air resistance, objects that are dropped accelerate at varying rates toward the earth. As velocity increases acceleration decreases in proportion to the cross-sectional area and mass of the object. (47, 49, 50)

Time of Flight Principle
(Vertical)

(The time of flight up of a projectile is equal to the time of flight down)*

Question: Is the time of flight of a ball thrown vertically equal to the time of flight down when distance up and distance down are the same?

1. A ball thrown vertically has a time of flight going up that is less than the time of flight coming down. (29, 50, 59)

Velocity of Flight Principle
(Vertical)

(The velocity of an object projected up is equal to its velocity down measured at the same horizontal plane.)*

Question: Is the velocity up of a projected ball equal to its velocity down measured at the same horizontal plane?

1. Upward velocity of a thrown ball is greater than the downward velocity (29, 51)

Angle of Projection Principle

(The angle of projection for maximum distance is 45 degrees.)*

Question: In order to obtain greatest distance should a ball be projected at an angle of 45 degrees with the horizontal?

1. The angle of release of a thrown or kicked object is less than the angle at contact or return to the same plane as released. (3, 4, 5, 6, 10, 11, 12, 30, 31)
2. The optimum angle for greatest distance for a thrown or kicked ball is approximately 30 degrees with the horizontal. (5, 6, 11, 13, 30)

Range Formula Principle

(The range of a projected object is determined by the formula

$$R = \frac{V^2 Sin 2\theta}{g}$$

Question: Does the formula $\quad R = \dfrac{V^2 Sin 2\theta}{g}$

accurately determine the range of projected balls used in physical education?

1. Formulas that are to be used to accurately predict time of flight, final velocity or acceleration must take into account the weight and cross-sectional area of the ball as well as the effect of gravity, initial velocity, and angle of projection. (29, 30)

2. The formula for determining the range of a punted football is

$$R = (V^2 Sin 2\theta, g) \tag{3,4}$$

3. The formula for determining the range of a thrown baseball or softball is

$$
\begin{aligned}
R\ &= (2WV, r\,) \\
W\ &= \text{Weight in pounds} \\
V\ &= \text{Velocity 90 ft/sec or greater} \\
r\ &= \text{Radius in inches} \\
0\ &= 30 \text{ degrees} \tag{34}
\end{aligned}
$$

Time of Flight Principle
(Trajectory)

(The time of flight up is equal to the time of flight down of a projected ball.)*

Question: Is the time of flight up of a projected ball equal to the time of flight down to the same horizontal plane as released?

1. When a ball is thrown for distance, the time of flight from release to apex is less than the time of flight from apex to the same plane from which the ball was thrown. (29, 51).

2. A ball or implement thrown or kicked for distance has a longer upward limb than a downward limb but the time of flight to the apex is less than the time of flight down to the level from which it was thrown. (48).

3. The difference between time of flight up and time of flight down is due to air resistance and is dependent upon the mass, initial velocity, and cross-sectional area of the object projected. (47, 48, 50, 51)

4. The downward flight of a thrown ball to the same horizontal plane from which it was released is greater than the time on the upward flight. (48, 49, 51)

Velocity of Flight Principle
(Trajectory)

(The velocity of an object projected up is equal to its velocity down measured at the same horizontal plane.)*

Question: Is the velocity of flight up equal to the velocity of flight down of a projected ball?

1. When a ball is thrown for distance, the velocity of the ball on its upward flight is greater than the velocity on the downward flight. (29)

2. For any projected object, upward velocity is greater than downward velocity if measured at same height above the ground. (48, 50, 51)

Air Resistance Principle

(Air resistance has little effect on the flight of the ball.)*

Question: Does air resistance affect the flight of a ball?

1. The heavier the ball, the less the effect of air resistance on velocity and acceleration. (13, 29)

2. The lighter the ball, the greater the effect of air resistance on velocity and acceleration. (13, 29)

3. The larger the cross-sectional area of a ball, the greater the effect of air resistance on velocity and acceleration. (14, 29)

4. The smaller the cross-sectional area of a ball, the less the effect of air resistance on velocity and acceleration. (14, 29)

5. The heavier a ball and the less the cross-sectional area, the less the effect of air resistance on velocity and acceleration. (13, 29)

6. The lighter a ball and the larger the cross-sectional area, the greater the effect of air resistance on velocity and acceleration. (13,29)

7. Air resistance has a significant effect on the range a ball will travel if thrown for distance. (30)

8. Air resistance affects the optimum angle of release of a ball thrown for distance. (The lighter the ball, the greater the initial velocity, and the greater the cross-sectional area, the less the angle of projection in order to obtain maximum distance.) (30)

9. Air resistance produces a substantial effect on the angle of projection, range and trajectory of balls thrown for distance. (30)

10. Air resistance produces a substantial effect on the upward and downward acceleration, velocity and time of flight of balls used in sports. (29)

11. Air resistance retards the range of balls thrown for distance up to 50 percent depending on initial velocity, cross-sectional area, mass, and shape. (4,10, 11, 12, 15, 17, 18, 19, 34, 91, 98, 99)

Parabolic Trajectory Principle

(The path of the flight of an object is a parabola.)*

Question: Do projected balls used in physical education travel a trajectory that is a parabola?

1. The trajectory of a ball in flight is not a parabola, but the upward limb has a longer horizontal value than the downward limb and angle of release is less than angle on return to same plane. (3, 4, 5, 6, 10, 12, 17, 18, 19, 98)

2. The angle with the horizontal of a thrown ball is less on the upward flight than on the downward flight. (30)

3. The range of the upward limb of the trajectory of a ball thrown for distance is greater than the range of the downward limb. (31)

4. The angle of the trajectory at release of a ball thrown for distance is less than the angle of the trajectory when returning to the same plane. The trajectory of a ball in flight is a skewed curve with the descent of the ball steeper than the ascent. (30)

5. Air resistance is a significant factor in determining the trajectory of a ball. (The greater the velocity, the greater the cross-sectional area and the less the

weight of the ball, the greater the effect and the more the trajectory deviates from a parabola.) (11, 17, 47, 48, 49)

Angle of Rebound Principle
(No Spin)

(Angle of incidence is equal to angle of rebound)*

Question: Does the angle of incidence equal the angle of rebound for a compressible ball striking a smooth surface with no spin?

1. When compressible balls used in physical education activities contact a smooth surface with no spin, the angle of rebound is *greater* than the angle of incidence. (21, 22, 28, 37, 44, 46)

2. The deviation of the angle of rebound from the angle of incidence is positive and increases as the angle of incidence increases up to 35 degrees and then the deviation decreases to zero as the angle of incidence increases to 90 degrees. (21, 22, 37)

3. When compressible balls used in physical education contact a smooth surface with top spin, they will rebound at a lower angle than one with no spin. (45)

4. When compressible balls used in physical education contact a smooth surface with back spin, they will rebound at a higher angle than one with no spin. (45)

5. As velocity increases for compressible balls contacting a smooth surface, the angle of rebound decreases. (37, 44, 46)

6. The deviation between the angle of incidence and the angle of rebound of a tennis ball contacting a smooth surface with no spin is greatest at 35°. (28)

7. Tennis balls projected at a slow incidence velocity will exhibit greater deviation in their angle of rebound than balls projected similarly, but at a faster velocity. (46)

Angle of Rebound Principle
(Top Spin)

(Angle of rebound is less than angle of incidence)*

Question: Is the angle of rebound of a compressible ball used in physical education, that strikes a smooth surface with top spin less than the angle of incidence?

1. A ball projected with top spin will have a lesser angle of rebound than a ball projected similarly, but without spin. However, its angle of rebound may still be greater than its angle of incidence. (45)

2. A ball projected with back spin will have a greater angle of rebound than that of a ball projected similarly, but without spin. (45)

3. The angle of rebound of a tennis ball with top spin is greater than the angle of incidence. (26)

Velocity of Rebound Principle

(The rebound velocity of a ball is less than the incidence velocity.)*

Question: Can a ball pick up horizontal velocity after rebound?

1. When compressible balls used in physical education contact a smooth surface with no spin, the velocity of rebound is less than velocity at contact. (21, 22, 37, 44, 45)

2. When compressible balls used in physical education contact a smooth surface with back spin, they will rebound at a slower forward velocity than one with no spin. (45)

3. When baseballs contact an artificial surface with backspin, the velocity of rebound is less than velocity of incidence. (35)

4. When baseballs contact an artificial surface with back spin, the forward velocity of rebound is less than the forward velocity of incidence. (35)

Velocity of Rebound Principle
Topspin

(A ball striking a smooth surface will have a velocity of rebound that is slower than the velocity of incidence.)*

Question: Can a ball striking a smooth surface with topspin pick up horizontal velocity?

1. The nature of spin upon incidence has a significant effect upon the magnitude of velocity deviation. Backspin causes the ball to deviate more in velocity; topspin causes the ball to deviate less. (45)

2. When baseballs contact an artificial surface with top spin, the velocity of rebound is less than the velocity of incidence. (36)

3. When baseballs contact an artificial surface with top spin, the forward velocity of rebound is less than the forward velocity of incidence. (36)

4. When baseballs with top spin contact a wet artificial surface, the velocity of rebound is less than the velocity of rebound of baseballs contacting a dry artificial surface. (36)

5. When baseballs with top spin contact a wet artificial surface, the forward velocity of rebound is less than the forward rebound velocity of baseballs contacting a dry artificial surface. (36)

6. When compressible balls used in physical education contact a smooth surface with top spin, they will rebound with a greater forward velocity than one with no spin. (45)

Spin of Rebound Principle

(A ball will pick up topspin after rebounding from the surface.)*

Question: Does a ball pick up topspin after rebounding from a surface?

1. When compressible balls used in physical education contact a smooth surface with no spin, they will rebound with top spin. (44)

2. When compressible balls used in physical education contact a smooth surface with top spin, they will rebound with faster top spin. (45)

3. When compressible balls used in physical education contact a smooth surface with back spin, they will rebound with top spin. (45)

4. As velocity increases for compressible balls contacting a smooth surface, the velocity of top spin increases on rebound. (44)

5. The less the angle of incidence at contact and the greater the velocity at contact, the greater will be the velocity of top spin on rebound. (44, 45)

6. The incidence angle and incidence velocity have a significant effect on the amount of topspin acquired. (45)

7. When balls contact a smooth surface with clockwise spin, they will continue to spin clockwise on rebound. (45)

8. When balls contact a smooth surface with counterclockwise spin they will continue to spin clockwise on rebound. (46)

Curve Ball Principle

(A ball curves, a ball breaks, a ball cannot curve.)*

Question: Does a pitched "curve" ball curve, break at the plate or is it an optical illusion?

1. A curve ball pitched to the plate curves all the way but is curving more each linear foot as it approaches the plate. This gives the batter the illusion that a curve ball breaks at the plate. (38)

Conservation of Momentum Principle

(Movement in one direction is equal to movement in the opposite direction)*

Question: Is it possible to create rotary motion once free of support?

1. When free of support, the faster one is spinning around the transverse axis (somersaulting), the greater the ability to twist about the longitudinal axis. (1, 2)

2. Once free of support, skilled athletes twist in a given direction by throwing body parts in the direction of the twist close to the axis of rotation and away from the axis or rotation in the opposite direction from the twist. (1, 2)

Force Production Principle

(Force equals mass times acceleration)*

Question: Does total force produced equal mass times acceleration?

1. For those situations where change in movement is involved, change in force is equal to mass times acceleration. (23)

$$\Delta F = ma$$

Center of Gravity Movement Principles

(The center of gravity may be changed within the body by segmental movement.)*

Question: Is there a difference between men and women in movement of the center of gravity by segmental movement?

1. The center of gravity of men is higher than the center of gravity of women. (7)

2. Men can move their center of gravity by arm movement more than women. (7)

3. Women can move their center of gravity by leg movement more than men. (7)

Force of Impact Principle

(Force equals mass times acceleration)*

Question: How can force be determined without acceleration?

1. For any moving object, there is a linear relationship between force of impact and velocity at impact. (25, 32)

2. Force of impact varies directly with the weight of an object and velocity at impact. (25)

3. The formula for determining the force of impact of a falling (moving) ball contacting an immovable surface is

$$Fi = (1.5 + 16.60W - 2.433W^2) Vi$$

Fi = Force at impact

W = Weight

Vi = Velocity at impact   (25)

4. The maximum force that can be exerted at impact using leg techniques is about twice that of arm techniques. (32)

Available Force Principle

(Available force is inversely proportional to speed of movement.)*

Question: Is there an available force—effective-force trade-off?

1. Skilled athletes may increase their jumping height by running at speeds between 50 and 70 percent of their maximum velocity. (27, 39, 40)

2. Jumping height increases as horizontal velocity increases to between 50 and 70 percent of maximum horizontal velocity and then decreases as horizontal velocity increases to maximum. (27, 39, 40)

3. As one approaches maximum horizontal velocity (such as the approach in the long jump), the maximum angle of projection approaches zero. (27, 33)

4. The angle of take-off with the horizontal is inversely proportional to horizontal velocity when horizontal velocity is between 80 and 100 percent of maximum. (33)

5. In the long jump, the optimum angle at take-off is about 20 degrees with the horizontal and optimum forward velocity (effective force) is about 95 percent of maximum. (33)

Stability and Effective Force Principle

(To start quickly assume a position of instability and be in a position to apply effective force; i.e., the Bunch start.)[*]

Question: Is the Bunch start or the standing start the best for a quick start?

1. The standing track start produces a faster elapsed time over the first ten yards than the crouch track start. (9, 16)

Principle of Running

(Run on your toes)[*]

Question: Do runners run on their toes, i.e., contact the surface with their toes first?

1. A runner contacts the surface with the outside of the heel (contact phase), rolls forward on the outer component of the foot and across the ball of the foot to the greater toe (support phase) and drives forward off the inside of the greater toe (thrust phase). (8, 20)

2. One usually accelerates on the toes (toes make first contact with the surface) and runs on the heels (heels make contact first). (24)

3. Generally, a sprinter's *toe* makes contact with the surface first, while middle distance runners contact the surface with *foot flat*, and distance runners contact the surface *heel* first. (20)

Principle of the Ends and Middle

(When the ends move up, the middle moves down and vice versa.)[*]

Question: Is the principle of the ends and middle in operation in the Fosbury Flop style high jump?

1. The center of gravity goes below the bar in the Fosbury Flop style high jump, so the principle of the ends and the middle is in operation in this style jump. (43)

Research Report
(Kinematic Laboratory Results)
The Effect of Horizontal Velocity on Vertical Jumping Ability
(available Force) of Volleyball Players

Percent of Maximum Horizontal Velocity	Mean Maximum Vertical Ft.	Mean Maximum Vertical Force Lbs.
0	2.732	388.316
20-29	2.918	899.294
30-39	2.920	908.096
40-49	3.039	949.798
50-59	3.254	1268.178
60-69	2.932	915.365
(100)	(0.000)	(0.000)

Study Questions

1. What is meant by qualitative or visual analysis? Mechanical analysis?

2. What is meant by the term, ballistic motion?

3. In sports approximately how much of the information that we receive is visual?

4. Why does a track man elevate his hips in the start? Throw one arm forward in starting? Chop stride while starting? Swing arms while running?

5. Why does a swimmer drop his heels at the start? Throw arms upward and forward when starting?

6. Why does a basketball player when stopping quickly lower his center of gravity widen his base in the direction of movement, plant his feet and placer his center of gravity over trailing leg?

Selected References of Research Studies Completed in the Kinemechanics Laboratory at Texas A&M University

Bartee, H. A, cinematographical analysis of twisting about the longitudinal axis when performers are free of support. Doctoral dissertation, Texas A&M University, 1977.

Bartee, H. and Dowell, L.J., A cinematographical analysis of twisting about the longitudinal axis when performers are free of support. *Journal of Human Movement Studies,* 8, (1), 1982, pp. 41-54.

Cunnigman, J.E., A cinematographical analysis of three selected types of football punts. Doctoral dissertation, Texas A&M University, 1976.

Cunningham, J.E. and Dowell, L.J., The effect of air resistance on three types of football trajectories. *Research Quarterly,* December, 1976, 47, 852-854.

Colfer, G., A cinematographical comparison of three selected field goal place kicking styles. Doctoral dissertation, Texas A&M University, 1977.

Colfer, G. and Dowell, L.J., Effect of air resistance on the angle of projection and range of a place-kicked football. *Texas Association for Health, Physical Education and Recreation Journal,* 1980, p. 70.

Dowell, L.J., A comparison of changes in height of center of gravity by manipulation of body parts. Research Council Proceedings, *Southern District American Alliance for Health, Physical Education, Recreation and Dance,* February 1981, p. 12.

Dowell, L.J., Biomechanical aspects of running. *Proceedings, 1st Annual Symposium on Aerobic Running,* Texas A&M University, Department of health and Physical Education, Fall, 1977.

Dowell, L.J., Comparison of the standing and crouch sprint starts. *Abstracts American Association for Health, Physical Education and Recreation,* 1976.

Dowell, L.J., The effect of air resistance on angle of projection and range of a place-kicked football, *Abstracts, Research Papers 1977 AAHPER Convention,* Seattle, March, 1977.

Dowell, L.J., The Effect of air resistance on the angle of projection and range of balls thrown for distance. *Proceedings, SDAAHPER Research Council,* Atlanta, 1977.

Dowell, L.J., The effect of air resistance on three types of football trajectories. *Proceedings, SDAAHPER Research Council,* 1976.

Dowell, L.J., The effect of air resistance on falling spherical balls with equal cross-sectional areas and different weight. Unpublished research paper, Kinemechanics Laboratory, Texas A&M University.

Dowell, L.J., The effect of air resistance on falling spherical balls with equal weight and different cross-sectional areas. Unpublished research paper, Kinemechanics Laboratory, Texas A&M University.

Dowell, L.J., Throwing for Distance: Air resistance, angle of projection and ball size and weight. *Motor Skills: Theory into Practice,* 1978, 3, 11-14.

Dowell, L.J., Track and Gield—Getting out of the blocks, what starting position works best? *Coach and Athlete,* April 1981, 43, 6, 48-49.

Dowell, L.J., Trajectory of a ball in flight: The parabolic myth? *Texas Association for Health, Physical Education and Recreation Journal,* October 1981, *50,* . 14, 15, 62, 63.

Dowell, L.J. & Colfer, G., The effect of air resistance on the angle of projection and range of a football place kicked for distance. A research paper presented to the Research Section of American Alliance for health, Physical Education and Recreation, Seattle, March 1976.

Dowell, L.J. and Cunningham, J.E., The effect of air resistance on three types of football trajectories. Southern District American Alliance for health, Physical Education and Recreation, Mobile, March 1976.

Dowell, L.J. Jessup, G., Lambert, J. and Mamaliga, E., A cinematographical comparison of body alignment from foot contact to ascension of sprinters and distance runners at optimum velocity-acceleration zero. *The Foil,* Fall, 1976, 14-16.

Dowell, L.J. and Lisk, J., A comparison of angle of incidence and angle of rebound of selected balls contacting a wood surface without spin. *Human Performance Monograph,* Texas A&M University, 1987.

Dowell, L.J. & List, J., A comparison of angle of Incidence and Angle of Refraction of selected balls. A research paper presented to the research section, Texas Association for Health, Physical Education and Recreation, Fort Worth, December, 1979.

Dowell, L.J. Lisk, J. and Saunders, L., The relationship between available force and resistance. Abstracts, Research Papers, *American Alliance for Health, Physical Education and Recreation Convention,* 1978, 62.

Dowell, L.J., Mamaliga, E. and Jubela, R., A cinematographical analysis of the 100-yard dash during acceleration and at optimum velocity acceleration zero. *Journal of Sports Medicine and Physical Fitness,* March 1976, 15, 20-25.

Dowell, L.J. Mamaliga, E. and Weeks, D., Development of a formula to predict force of impact (Fi) when velocity and weight of an object are known. Unpublished research paper, Kinemechanics Laboratory, Texas A&M University.

Dowell, L.J., Middlebrook, J.W., and Krebs, G., The effect of topspin on rebound angle deviation and horizontal velocity deviation of tennis balls. Unpublished research paper, Kinemechanics Laboratory, Texas A&M University.

Dowell, L.J., Saunders, L. & Lisk, J., The effects of changes in velocity on the application of available force. *Proceedings of the Research Council of the Southern District, American Alliance of Health, Physical Education and Recreation,* 1978, 141.

Dowell, L.J., Smith, F., Miller, G., Hope, A., and Krebs, G., The effect of angle of incidence on rebound deviation of a tennis ball. *Journal of Human Movement Studies,* 1987.

Dowell, L.J., Smith, F., Thiebaud, R., and Thigpen, K., The effect of air resistance on the upward and downward acceleration velocity and time of flight on selected spherical balls. *Human Performance Monograph,* Texas A&M University, 1987.

Dowell, L.J., Smith, F., Thiebaud, R., and Thigpen, K., A comparison of range, time of flight and trajectory of the upward and downward limbs of selected spherical balls thrown for distance. *Journal of Human Movement Studies,* 11(4), October 1985, 209-221.

Jordan, C.D., A cinematographical analysis of selected karate arm and leg techniques. Doctoral dissertation, Texas A&M University, 1973.

Jubela, R.,Angle of projection and available force in the long jump. Doctoral dissertation, Texas A&M University, 1981.

Kelly, R.L., Determination of a range formula for a spherical ball under environmental conditions. Doctoral dissertation, Texas A&M University, 1979.

Krebs, G., Dowell, L.J. and Brown, J.D., The effect of backspin and artificial surface on the rebound velocity of a baseball. Unpublished research paper. Kinemechanics Laboratory, Texas A&M University, 1986.

Krebs. G., Dowell, L.J., Middlebrook, J. and Sadler, W., The effect of top spin on the rebound velocity of a baseball projected on a wet and dry artificial surface. Unpublished research paper, Kinemechanics Laboratory, Texas A&M University, 1986.

Lisk, J.W., Effects of speed, surface and angle of incidence on angle of the rebound of tennis balls. Doctoral dissertation, Texas A&M University, 1980.

Montgomery, S.B., Factors effecting the lateral deflection of a curving baseball. Doctoral dissertation, Texas A&M University, 1980

Saunders, H.L., II. A cinematographical study of the relationship between speed of movement and available force. Doctoral dissertation, Texas A&M University, 1980.

Saunders, L., and Dowell, L.J., Relationships between speed of movement and available force in the volleyball spike. *Journal of the National Volleyball Coaches Association,* 3(1), 1982, 41-49.

Saunders, L. Dowell, L.J. and Johnson, S., Construction of an inexpensive internal timing device for film speed determination. *Research Quarterly for Exercise and Sport,* October 1980, 5-6.

Seidel, H.S. ,A comparative analysis of the layout back somersault and full twisting back somersault in tumbling. Master's thesis, Texas A&M University, 1976.

Smith, C., A cinematographical analysis of the action of the lead leg in the flop high jump. Master's thesis, Texas A&M University, 1984.

Smith, F., Dowell, L. and Smith, C., A comparison of angle, velocity and rotary velocity at incidence and rebound of selected balls contacting a smooth surface with no spin at various angles and velocities. Unpublished research paper, Kinemechanics Laboratory, Texas A&M University, 1984.

Smith, F., Dowell, L.J. and Smith, C., A comparison of angle, velocity and rotary velocity at incidence and rebound of selected balls contacting a smooth surface with top spin and back spin at various velocities. Unpublished research paper, Kinemechanics Laboratory, Texas A&M University, 1984.

Smith, F. Dowell, L.J., Miller, G. and Smith, C., Rebound behavior of compressible balls. *Human Performance Monograph,* Texas A&M University, 1987.

Smith, F., Thiebaud, R., Thigpen, K. and Dowell, L.J., The effect of mass and cross-sectional area on acceleration of falling balls. Unpublished research paper, Kinemechanics Laboratory, Texas A&M University.

Thiebaud, R., Thigpen, K., Smith, F. and Dowell, L.J., A comparison of time of flight and trajectory of the upward and downward limbs of selected spherical balls thrown for distance. Unpublished research paper, Kinemechanics Laboratory, Texas A&M University, 1982.

Thiebaud, R., Thigpen, K. and Dowell, L.J., The effects of air resistance on spherical balls. A research paper presented to the Research Section, Texas Association for Health, Physical Education and Recreation, Dallas/Fort Worth, December 1979.

Thigpen, K., Thiebaud, R. and Dowell, L.J., The effect of air resistance on velocity of a ball in flight. Unpublished research paper, Kinemechanics Laboratory, Texas A&M University, 1983.

Thigpen, K., Thiebaud, R., Smith, F. and Dowell, L.J., A comparison of upward and downward time of flight on selected spherical balls. Unpublished research paper, Kinemechanics Laboratory, Texas A&M University, 1983.

9
QUANTITATIVE MOVEMENT ANALYSIS

History

Studies of human motion began in the late 1800's. Edward Muybridge took the first analytical photographs of animals and people. At first, only frozen movement could be photographed. The first moving pictures were a series of still photographs which could be mechanically animated by moving the pictures fast enough to simulate actual movement. Since our understanding of motion depends upon our ability to view the action, advances in photographic devices to provide permanent images of movement was necessary. In the 1890's, the first genuine motion picture camera was developed. Frenchman, Jules Marey, discovered that by running his cameras at fast speed and then projecting the film back at normal speed, slow motion could be produced.

During the 1930's, the next stage in motion analysis was accomplished by drawing a line describing the path of motion. This tracing of the patterns of motion in space was the forerunner of the science of Biomechanics. Today, these lines are drawn by computers. Photography has become much more sophisticated with video cameras capable of operating at rates more than fifty times faster than the human eye can detect.

During the last two decades, enormous progress has been made in the field of biomechanical analysis. The first electronic digitizer constituted a significant improvement and replaced the traditional tracing technique. Prior to 1968, manual processes involved in biomechanical analysis were slow, tedious, and frequently included arithmetic error. However, the computerization of many of these steps has accelerated the development and improvement in analyzing biomechanical applications.

One of the first applications of these computerized innovations occurred during the recording of Olympic athletic competition. The electronic digitizer decreased the time needed for locating and storing joint center coordinates and also reduced many of the tracing and measurement errors. In addition, computers allowed data collection and the analysis of biomechanical data in different locations. The digitizing process could thus be conducted at one location and the digitized points transferred on-line to a main frame computer for further processing. Despite these advances, access to the mainframe computer severely limited the public's access to this new form of technology.

However, computers have been developed with new forms, capacities and applications. Mainframe-based data processing has evolved to computing over a variety of formats. The Internet and the development of the World Wide Web have provided new options in many high tech areas involving science, business and engineering. Rapid advances in video and multimedia technology have also made possible the presentation of information in three-dimensional and virtual reality images.

Newer, faster and more advanced computers along with the Internet have created opportunities for research in the field of Biomechanics. Biomechanical analysis has progressed from athletics to space exploration to sports medicine and further extended its impact into industrial design and general medical practice. Rapid advances in networking, communications, and presentation technology make the benefits of biomechanical analysis much more accessible to a wider audience and a greater range of applications. The use of the Internet and multimedia promises to greatly facilitate biomechanical research.

The technology for using the Internet requires video sequences from one computer being sent to another site through on-line processing. The video sequence which was captured originally on a Video Camera Recorder (VCR) now uses a Digital Video Device (DVD). The first step is the selection of the performance for subsequent analysis. A researcher examines the specified sequence of the video performance, frame by frame. The size of the pixels at the digitized site (maximum 72 dots per inch) determine the resolution at each site. After determining the performance for analysis, the researcher is required to define the joints to be digitized. Specialized instructions are presented for defining the specific joints, such as the foot, ankle, knee, hip, as well as the implement being used, i.e., golf club, bat, ball, et cetera. Following the naming and labeling of files, the actual digitization can began. As each of the selected points is digitized, the X,Y coordinates for each point is determined and can be stored in the appropriate file on the computer. The digitized points create a matrix of X,Y coordinates for further analysis. If only the two-dimensional analysis is desired, analysis of the data can be performed at this point. However, because two cameras are used to record the event, it is also possible to obtain the preferred three-dimensional analysis. Thus, the digitization process can be repeated for the second camera view.

Biomechanical Analysis of Movement

Ballistic motion in sports is very difficult to observe with the normal eye. Over the years, observations have been made by physical education teachers and coaches who have watched various sports activities and have formed opinions in their minds as to exactly what happens during human movement. Many of these impressions were erroneous and led in many instances to misconceptions and misinformation in the analysis of the mechanics of motion.

The speed with which the body segments move during a ballistic motion, such as, overhand baseball pitching, is phenomenal. The time frame from the cocking position during wind-up where the pitcher starts forward to the release point is approximately 80-90 milliseconds. This is too brief of a time for the human eye to precisely see what is occurring.

High-Speed Imaging Equipment

Mechanical analysis of motion requires high-speed imaging equipment. The basic choices are sixteen millimeter film and videotape. Sixteen-millimeter film analysis has been available for several years but are rarely used today. The maximum speed that can be run with Lo-cam cameras is approximately 500 frames per second (fps). Some motion analysis cameras with rotating prisms have much higher capabilities; however, 500 fps is fast enough to record the moments and torque that exist during ballistic movement.

Cinematography or Film Analysis

One of the major drawbacks in using 16 mm film is the time lag required to process the film. Occasionally, a great deal of time and effort is spent recording the film only to lose the film during processing.

An additional constraint in film and video analysis is the necessity to determine the magnitude of the forces that act upon the body during the actual movement. In order to measure or reproduce the behavior of the body in three dimensions, a minimum of two cameras are needed to film the motion. Two Lo-cam 16 mm cameras are routinely used filming at 400 fps. They must be phase-locked to ensure synchronization of the film. This is accomplished with a Phase-Lock loop. Without this system in place, perspective and/or photographic errors may occur. A scaling device should also be placed within the frame of reference.

The film can then be digitized and placed into a computer which calculates the three dimensional positions of each point. This technology is well developed and comes from the three dimensional photographic techniques used to create topographical maps from airplanes. Once the action has been reduced to numbers in three dimensions, then the process of evaluating the movement in stick figures (stick-men projection) or observing the deceleration moments that exist is quite possible.

It is not necessary to use the conventional lateral view, front view and overhead view to have three-dimensional reproduction. In fact, an exact three-dimensional reproduction cannot be obtained when the three cameras are placed orthoginal to one another. The main reason is that two cameras must be able to record exactly the same location on the subject to be able to resolve the three-dimensional coordinates of that point. The mathematical method used to obtain this coordinate depends upon the location of only two cameras, located approximately twenty degrees apart.

Videography or Video Analysis

The preferred alternative to 16 mm film is television or videotape. The video camera also has the added benefit of immediate playback of the recorded picture. Video with a shuttered lens allows video to be stopped in motion and looks different from the normal television image. This is an excellent method of visual analysis for coaches and teachers. Television captures data at a rate of sixty frames (fields) or images per second (fps) and is unable to record the precise details, mechanisms of release/contact or the acceleration and deceleration of body segments. However, television can split the screen and take successive images that can increase the speed up to 240 fps. However, shuttered video requires television cameras with a very high, light sensitivity in order to be able to record the action. Also, because ambient light is most often the only available light, image retention may be a problem if the camera is run with the lens wide open. Refraction errors may also occur.

Current video systems are now well enough developed to give relatively high quality pictures in low light conditions. Modern video camera systems are interfaced with computers that automatically perform digitizing and calculation of various angular and linear velocities for interpretation.

Spin Physics, a division of Kodak, has a system that can record video images up to 2000 fps. This is a complete system that has an especially manufactured tape deck to run at these higher speeds. The resolution on these cameras seems to be very good. However, they are still dependent upon ambient light to provide illumination.

Peak Performance Technologies, Inc. introduced the PEAK 2D Video/Computer Motion Measurement System in 1986 and remains one of the premier biomechanical analysis systems available. The Peak Performance motion analysis system generates computer graphic representation of human movement and its kinematic elements from video. This system can provide detailed information regarding the stresses placed on the musculoskeletal system along with dynamic biomechanical modeling. Biomechanics uses the laws of physics and engineering concepts to describe motion of the various body segments and the forces acting on these body segments during normal, daily activities or athletic events. PEAK provides a motion analysis computer system that can be interfaced with devices, such as, force platforms, EMG, and EKG, as well as, kinematic calculation software to provide displacements, velocities, angles and accelerations along with segmental and total body centers of mass. The PEAK High-Speed Video System records at twice the normal video speed, thus, doubling the sampling rate and providing twice as much information per trial. By recording at 120 fields per second, it increases the accuracy of locating ball contact or foot strike, along with, calculating velocities and accelerations. Once recorded, it can be viewed on normal television at one-half of real time speed for qualitative motion analysis.

The Peak5 System is a new upgrade that allows the tracking of unavailable 2D and 3D points by interpreting data from other coordinates for faster and more accurate digitizing. The Peak 2D Core Module is a stand-alone product that provides a wide variety of graphic and data analysis capabilities. The Peak 3D Module can be added to the 2D Core Module and can be used with up to six cameras. Two cameras are sufficient to conduct 3D studies. However, for more detailed studies, such as gait, it is recommended that a four-camera configuration be used. The strength of the Peak 2D/3D System is its ability to digitize in difficult conditions without the need for body markers. However, to digitize more quickly, reflective markers can be used with the Peak Automatic Tracking Module.

For conversion of analog to digital data, the Peak Analog Sampling Module consists of an acquisition board (16 channels or 32 channels) and software. The Peak Analog Sampling Module can collect raw data signals from electromyography (EMG) and electrocardiography (EKG) electrodes, force platform and other analog sources. The Peak Analog Sampling Module is designed to be synchronous with the video analysis from the Peak 2D and 3D systems. The analysis of EMG analog data may require an EMG analysis software package. The use of software packages from Run Technologies Inc. or from Noraxon Inc. is suggested. These software packages are compatible with data collected by the Peak Analog Sampling Module.

The Peak Force Platform Analysis Module provides computations, graphics and reports unique to force platforms. The software is compatible with Kistler, AMTI or Bertec platforms. This software is included with the purchases of the Peak 3D Gait Analysis Module or can be purchased separately. The PEAK 3D Motion Measurement Module permits the collection, computation, display and analysis of movements in three-dimensional space when two or more cameras are used. No specific camera placements, special lenses, or leveling procedures are needed. The only requirement is that a portable calibration frame be videotaped prior to or after, data collection. With this 3D Module, accelerations, angles, velocities, et cetera can be computed. All of the calculated parameters can be graphed against other parameters over time. The digitized, spatial model can be rotated to allow viewing from virtually any angle. Stick figure graphs, as shown in Figure 9-1, can be displayed alone or with other computed quantitative parameters for study.

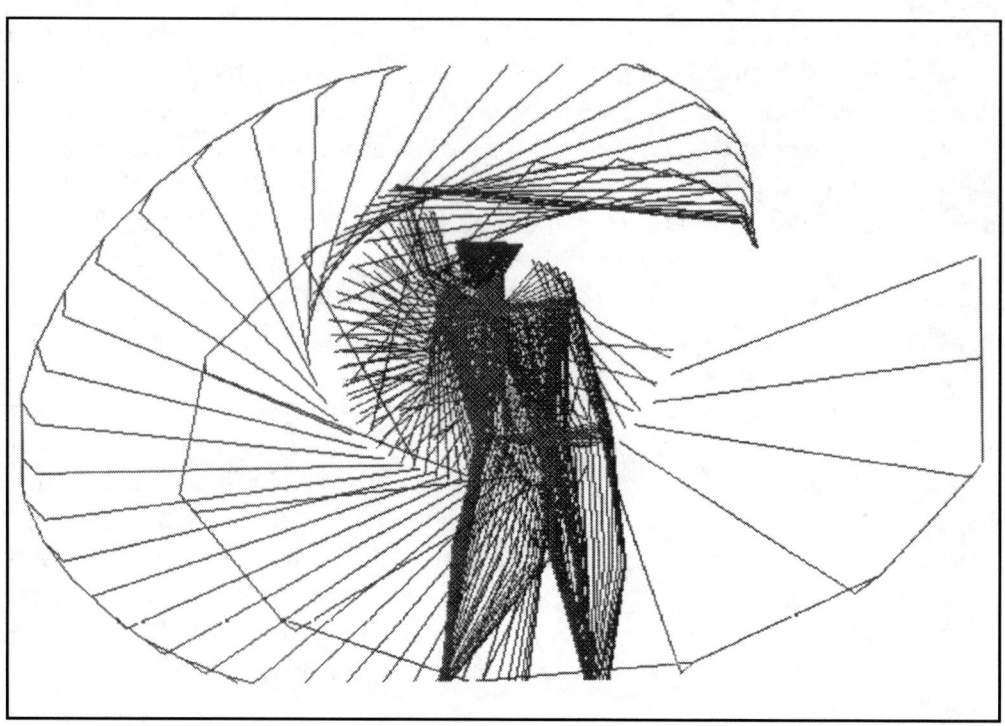

**Figure 9-1. PEAK 2D Video/Computer Motion Measurement System
by Peak Performance Technologies.**

PEAK also offers an Event Synchronization Unit (ESU 4000) that uses an interval event marker placed directly on the video image. The Peak Event Sync Unit reduces cumbersome and extraneous interconnecting cables and avoids using external light emitting diodes. Photocells may also be used to capture linear and angular velocities throughout the skill performance.

The Ariel High Performance System (APAS) is a high-speed, video-computer interfaced analysis system developed by Dr. Gideon Ariel. The APAS is an interactive computer system which automatically digitizes the points of reference. It measures, analyzes, and presents movement characteristics for the biomechanical analysis of human motion. The APAS provides a means to quantify motion utilizing input information from any or all of the following media: visual (video or film), EMG, and force platforms. The APAS Core Module is a 3D System which includes a 2D System. The 2D System is a subset of the 3D System where the "Z" coordinate equals zero. More hardware is not needed to perform a 3D analysis as compared with a 2D analysis. The Ariel System includes two cameras for 3D/2D analysis. However, the APAS System can combine data from as many as nine cameras. During the digitizing process, the joint centers or points can be selected visually or can be chosen by the automatic identification option. The APAS System utilizes fractal technology to locate markers automatically. The Automatic Tracking system is included in the Core Module.

The APAS System can compare from one trial to another or from one athlete to another and provides views from all sides and can stop the action at any time. Digitizing and Viewing Modules provides additional information beyond the video images. The APAS System includes force plate software to support all available plates. There is no need to purchase any additional Gait software since everything is included in the Core Module. Ariel Dynamics was the first company in the world to integrate the Force Plate by Kistler to the computer in 1972.

Force Platforms, Force Plates and Force Insoles

During recent years, there has been considerable interest in measuring the distribution of pressures under the foot. Cavanaugh, et al (1982) developed a pressure plate which measures a thousand pressure sensitive points that can display data on a three-dimensional grid. During ground contact, 300 or more of these points are activated and can be displayed graphically and continuously by a computer. A series of these pictorial displays permits the collection and study of a pressure distribution pattern. The PEAK Force Platform Analysis Module collects data, such as, forces and moments, centers of pressure, and vertical force vectors. It may be used with one or two force platforms.

A force insole also permits the determination of the center of pressure underneath the sole of a shoe. Forces equivalent to approximately 3.5 times the body weight can be generated under the foot. Software allows the center of pressure path and the ground reaction forces to be melded together into a single, graphic display as shown in Figure 9-2. The Pedar System by NOVEL is an accurate and reliable pressure distribution measuring system for monitoring loading of the foot inside the shoe. The Parotec System by PAROMED evaluates in-shoe plantar pressure by using hydrocell sensors that capture both vertical and shear pressures in each shoe. Applications may include gait analysis, rehabilitation assessment, shoe research and design, shoe prescription and orthotic design. Both systems can be synchronized to video and EMG systems to measure the kinetic analysis of free gait. The Pedar Mobile and the Paromed Data Logger can collect data while walking, running, climbing stairs, carrying loads, riding a bicycle or playing badminton without being connected to a computer.

PEAK also offers an Event Synchronization Unit (ESU 4000) that uses an interval event marker placed directly on the video image. The Peak Event Sync Unit reduces cumbersome and extraneous interconnecting cables and avoids using external light emitting diodes. Photocells may also be used to capture linear and angular velocities throughout the skill performance.

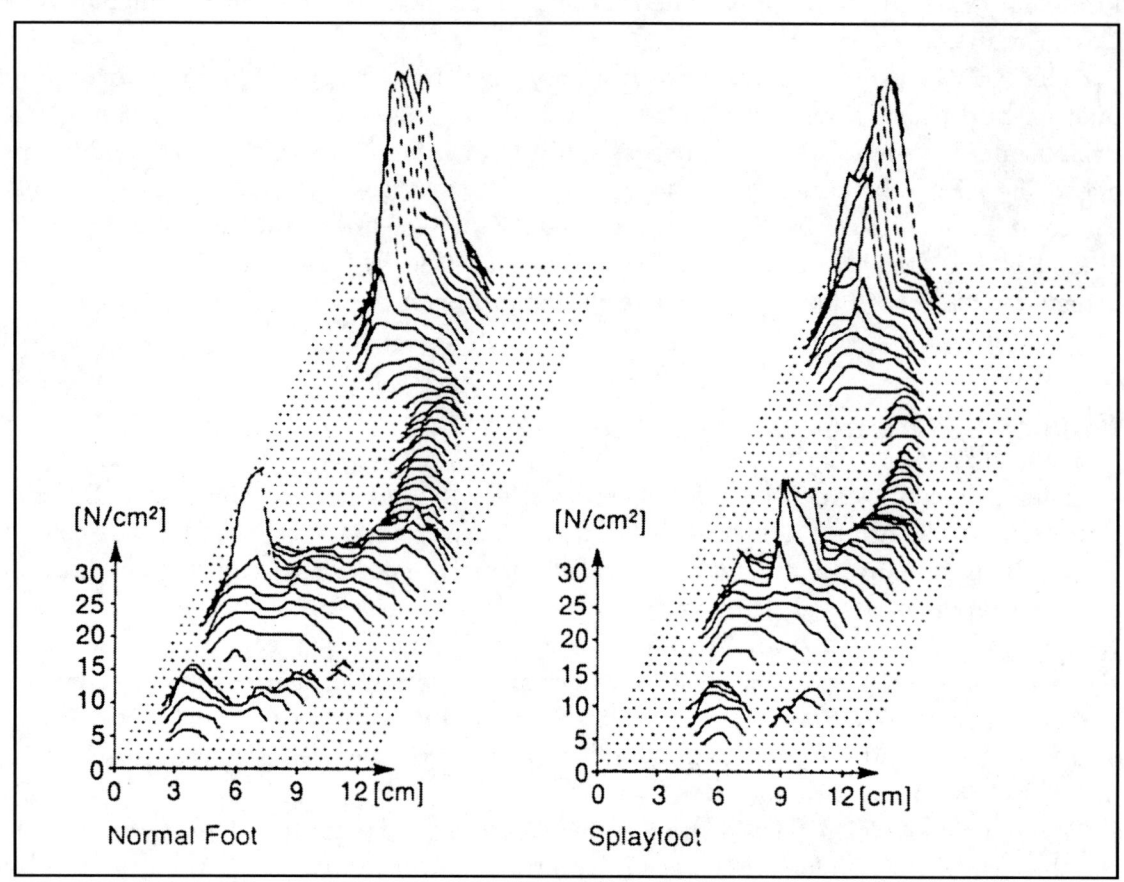

Figure 9-2. Three-dimensional representation (standing) of a normal foot (left) and a splayfoot (right).

Study Questions

1. What is meant by Cinematography? Videography?

2. Describe how the first "moving pictures" were generated.

3. How was "slow motion" filming discovered?

4. Historically, why has film been more accurate for high-speed motion analysis than video?

5. How many cameras are needed to film motion in three dimensions? Why?

6. Approximately how much force or impact does each foot exert when striking the ground while running?

Key Terms from Chapter 9

Cinematographic analysis—Scientific study of motion by use of motion pictures.

F.P.S., Frames or Fields Per Second—Speed with which a camera records images of motion.

Line Graph—A graph that connects points of two variables e.g., angle or rotation and time.

Mechanical Analysis—Analysis of the coaching and teaching points based upon the laws of physics.

Perspective Error—Errors found in measurement due to objects varying in distance from the camera.

Photographic Errors—Errors due to camera, lens, photographer, etc.

Refraction Errors—Errors due to refracted light through different mediums, such as water, etc.

Scaling—Converting measurements on film to actual distances.

Skill Analysis—Breakdown of a skill into its basic teaching or coaching points.

Stick-men Projection—Plotting the center of joints of subjects on paper from motion picture film and connecting adjacent points.

10
HUMAN GAIT ANALYSIS

One of the earliest uses of mechanical analysis was to study the gait patterns of various animals and humans. Muybridge did early studies on human and animal patterns by animating still photographs and creating the appearance of motion. It was this technique that allowed the discovery of the airborne phase of running in the gait cycle of horses, for example. Subsequent discoveries followed. Among those were the invention of slow motion filming by Marey and animation of film. The advent of personal computers and video cameras has allowed tremendous progress to be made in the area of gait analysis.

Traditionally, human gait analysis has placed emphasis upon the walking and running cycles. Though the two have similarities there are major differences between them. In walking, for example, there is a period of double support that disappears as the cadence increases to approximately 112 steps per minute. It is at this point that running commences. Peculiar to running is a period of non-support in which the entire body has no contact with the surface. Several key terms must be dealt with in addition to those mentioned.

Boiled down to its simplest description, what is walking? **Walking is the act of upsetting equilibrium in the forward direction by causing the center of gravity to pass outside the forward edge of the base of support (i.e., the feet)(P1.0).** Then, the legs are instinctively moved in order to regain equilibrium. Certain terminology has been used to describe the phases and stages of walking. Some of this terminology has been misused, however.

One of the most common mistakes in terminology made among coaches and teachers is the reference to "stride length." It is not uncommon to hear a coach comment about the length of a runner's **stride** when, in fact, the coach means the length of a runner's **step**. **A stride is the term used to describe the distance from contact of a reference extremity until subsequent contact of the same extremity (P 2.0).** One the other hand, **a step is defined as that distance from contact of a reference extremity until contact by the contra-lateral (on the opposite side) extremity (P 3.0)**. Taking a long stride is usually not counterproductive to sprinting; however, taking a step that is too long will definitely hinder the production of speed.

The Stance Phase

A rhythmic process that is cyclical in nature characterizes the human walking pattern. That is, the events are repeated in a definite pattern. Therefore, we refer to analysis of walking as gait cycle analysis. There are several events that are evident in this pattern. Heel contact is often referred to by several other terms (i.e., initial contact, heel strike, foot on). Heel contact marks the beginning of the stance or support phase of walking. This is that period of time during which the body's weight is supported by one or both feet being in contact with the surface. Conversely, toe off (also, foot off, terminal stance) marks the end of the stance phase.

The transition from heel contact, to foot flat (mid-stride), to toe off, results from the motion created by the momentum of the center of gravity of the body passing over the supporting foot. In reality, the act of walking is but the process of loosing and regaining control of the momentum of the center of gravity. One need but observe a toddler learning to walk to see this phenomenon in action. The toddler appears to be running because of the need to keep up with the center of gravity, which is unusually high in toddlers. The mass of the head in an infant or toddler is relatively greater than the body causing a very high center of gravity. As we learned earlier, stability is compromised when the center of gravity is raised.

The stance phase consists of several events that are defined by the relative positions of the foot and the tibia. The following chart (Table 10-1) describes these relationships.

Table 10-1
Stance Phase

Event	Foot/Tibia Position	Description
Heel Strike	Foot leading tibia	Beginning of stance
Foot Flat	Tibia moving to vertical	c.o.g. passing over foot
Mid-stance	Vertical tibia	c.o.g. perpendicular to foot
Heel Off	Tibia leading foot	c.o.g. ahead of foot
Toe Off	Foot leaving surface	End of stance

As Table 10-1 shows, the center of gravity (c.o.g.) continues to travel over the supporting foot during the stance phase. It is at the point of mid-stance that the single foot supports all of the body's weight. The stance phase is punctuated by heel contact of the leading leg and toe-off of the contra-lateral leg. This, of course, defines the all important double support stage of walking (a defining characteristic of walking). Figure 10-1 graphically demonstrates these relationships (the reference extremity is the right).

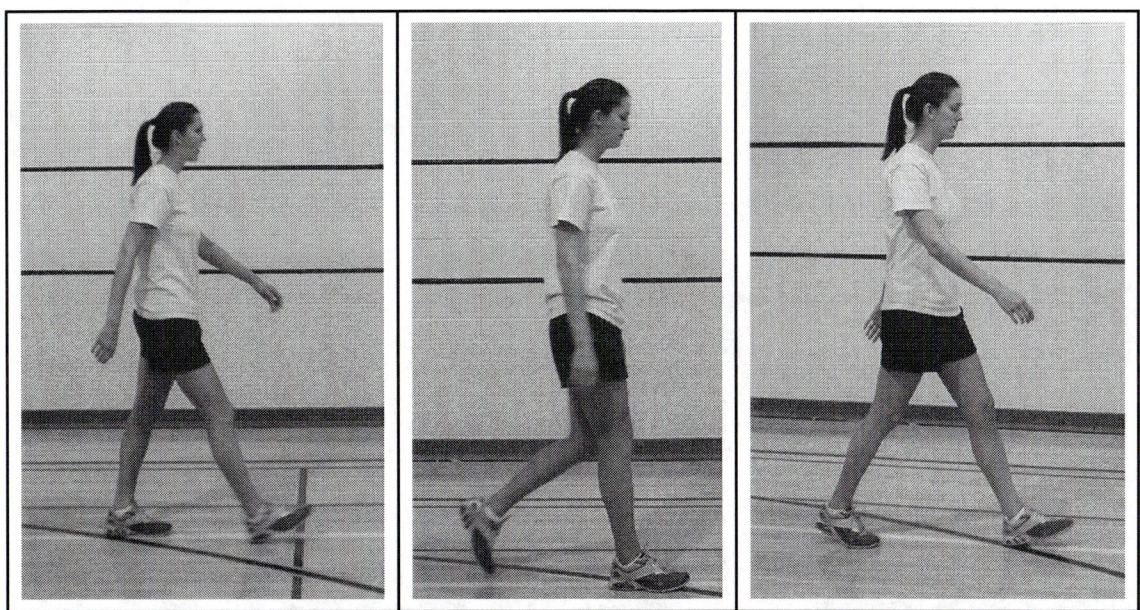

Figure 10-1. The support phase of walking (Ref. extremity is the right leg).

Note in figure 10-1 that the heel strike of the reference corresponds with the toe-off of the contra-lateral extremity. This is indicative of the double-support phase of walking.

The Swing Phase

So, how does the process of walking occur? Most experts in motor development agree that the action of walking is reflexive in nature. With further stimulation, the pattern becomes myelinated and a motor program for walking is established in the brain. Ideally, the process of walking is controlled subconsciously for the non-handicapped individual, the process actually involves the brain only on a very limited basis.

Previous information concerning levers (Ch. 3 and Ch. 6) sheds some important light of the process of walking, as well. Variations in the length of the swinging leg bring about the **acceleration** and **deceleration** stages of the swing phase. The shortening of the swinging extremity at the point of toe off shortens the overall radius of rotation of that extremity at the hip. The natural result of a shortened lever is, of course, increased rotary velocity. Conversely, the lengthening of the radius of rotation brings about marked angular deceleration. The advantage of this decreased angular velocity is the controlled placement of the leading heel and a significant reduction of the angular momentum of the foot. Thus, the ground reaction forces of the foot strike are diminished. The swing phase of the right extremity is shown in Figure 10-2.

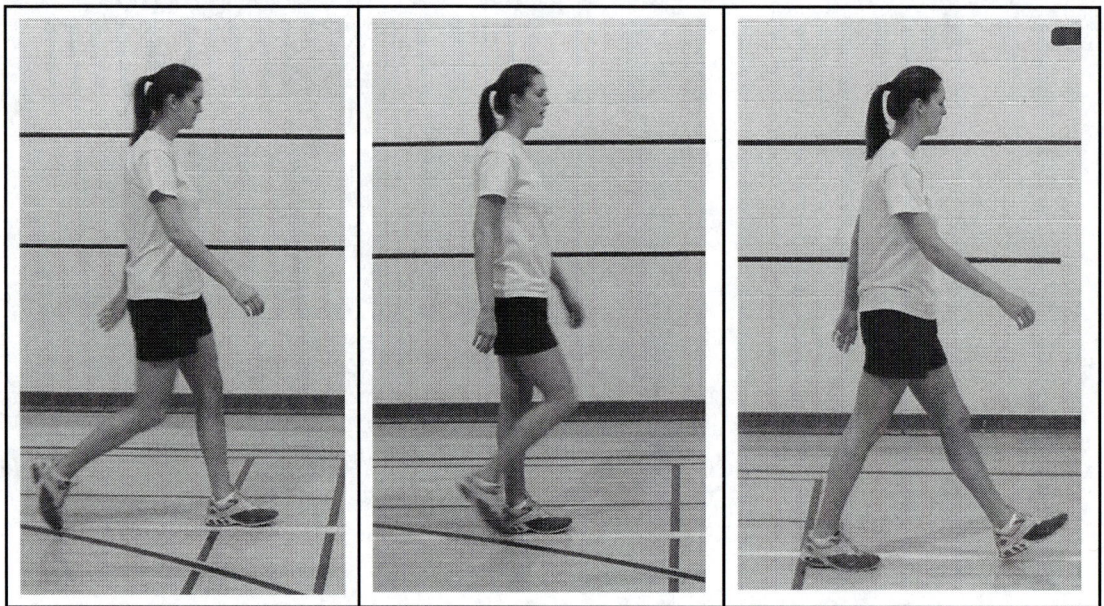

Figure 10-2. The stages of the swing phase.

A summary description of the swing phase is shown in Table 10-2 and begins at the moment of **toe off** of the swinging extremity. As the foot breaks contact with the surface, the swinging knee bends to allow space for the leg to swing. This shortens the radius of rotation and causes rotary acceleration to occur. At **mid-swing**, the knee is at its greatest flexion and the leg passes directly under the body. This is also the point at which the tibia of the contra-lateral leg is perpendicular to the surface. Once the leg passes the mid-swing stage, extension occurs. The result of this extension is the **angular deceleration** of the entire leg.

Table 10-2
Swing Phase

Event	Foot/Tibia Position	Description
Acceleration	Foot leaves surface	Shortened Radius
Mid Swing	Swing leg c.o.g. in line with body c.o.g.	Vertical Alignment
Deceleration	Ahead of Base of Support	Lengthened Radius

Kinematics

The speed of gait is determined somewhat by the location of the foot strike relative to the center of gravity. This is determined by two factors: the angular velocity of the femur and the range of motion of the entire leg. As the foot is placed further ahead of the center of gravity, a slowing down of the walking velocity is evident. As one attempts to increase walking velocity, a more active landing action of the leading foot occurs. This is accomplished by pulling the foot toward the center of gravity as foot strike occurs; this is more commonly observed in running than in walking. Changes in step length and frequency interact to increase walking velocity. Key kinematic variables are shown in Table 10-3.

Table 10-3
Important Kinematic Variables of Walking

Distance	Temporal	Duration
Stride/Step Length	Stride/Step Duration	Stance Time
Base Width	Stride/Step Cadence	Swing Time
Toe In/Out	Stride/Step Speed	Single Support time
	Walking Velocity	Double Support Time
	Walking Speed	Stride Duration

There are several factors that affect the kinematics of walking. Each of these may affect the quality of walking behavior and efficiency, as well as, the actual ability to perform the skill.

The first element that must be considered is **age.** There are obvious differences in the performance of walking across the lifespan. Most prominent is the width of the base of support. The pattern across the lifespan is wide to narrow to wide from young to mature to old age. This change in base of support is related to changes in the vestibular system (balance control) and visual acuity.

Next on the list of factors is **gender**. There are subtle differences between men and women in their mature walking patterns. Typically females at normal walking speeds (free walking) tend to take short strides, but have a higher stride frequency than males. Additionally, the relative heights of the centers of gravity affect the efficiency of the movement in general. The types of footwear that women wear may provide some artificial differences, as well.

Morphology may also play a role in the pattern of walking. The constraints present because of segment length, **Q–angle**, height of the center of gravity and obesity, for example require the walker to adapt. Decreases in joint range of motion through injury and or genetic peculiarities may cause abnormalities to be present

155

during walking. Walking velocity and sometimes step length may be affected by psychological factors, too.

It is not within the scope of this chapter to discuss abnormal walking gait. Many crippling diseases and injuries may result in particularly unusual gait patterns. These are often associated with loss to joint range of motion or muscular control.

Exercises

1. Observe the gait characteristics of several people wearing different types of footwear. Make notes of different patterns and correlate them with the type of shoes.

2. Try to observe some individuals who have obvious gait irregularities. Note the changes in the gait pattern compared to the "normal pattern."

Experiment 10.1

Dartfish Analysis of Human Gait

Instructions: Using a video camera, video the walking patterns of the following:

    1) Male – Athletic Build   2) Female Athletic Build

    3) Male – Non-Athletic   4) Female Non-Athletic

Produce a Simulcast overlay for comparisons of Male to Female, and Athletic to Non-Athletic.

Complete the Charts below:

	Male	Female
Step Length		
Step Width		
Toe Out/In		
Notes:		

	Athlete (M)	Non-Athlete (M)
Step Length		
Step Width		
Toe Out/In		
Notes:		

	Athlete (F)	Non-Athlete (F)
Step Length		
Step Width		
Toe Out/In		
Notes:		

Conclusions

1)

2)

3)

Key Terms from Chapter 10

Contralateral—on the opposite side

Double support—period when both feet are in contact with the supporting surface

Foot flat—period when weight is supported by the entire foot

Heel contact—also, heel or foot strike; beginning of the stance phase

Ipsilateralon—the same side

Mid-stance—point where center of gravity is directly over the supporting foot

Mid-swing—point at which the center of gravity of the swinging leg is aligned with the center of gravity of the body

Myelinated—indicator of maturity of motor neurons

Q-angle—angle of the intersection of the femur and the tibia

Step—heel contact of reference foot to heel contact of the contra-lateral foot

Strideone gait cycle; heel contact of reference foot to the next contact of the same foot

Toe off—marks the end of the support phase

Vestibular system—system of balance and spatial awareness

11
OTHER FACTORS
THAT AFFECT PERFORMANCE

Several other factors may also affect your athletic performance. They include the following:

1. Clothing
2. Equipment
3. Fear/Anxiety
4. Strategy/Tactics
5. Motivation
6. Readiness
7. Talent Identification

Clothing

Clothing in light or pastel colors are most recommended along with white, primarily because white reflects heat better than darker colors and is cooler. The cost and quality of what you wear, what you play with and where you play varies greatly. Most sports incorporate shorts, shirt, tennis shoes or court shoes and socks with possibly a warm-up suit in cooler weather. Many tennis and/or racquetball players wear nylon, cycling shorts or a cotton pant liner under their shorts for support and comfort. A blouse and skirt or a tennis dress may be preferred by some women. In addition, headbands, wristbands and towels may be needed to help keep perspiration from the face, eyes, and hands. A soft, leather glove is often used to provide a better grip and cushion the hand in most racquet sports, golf, baseball and softball.

Some of the latest technological advances in athletic clothing are designed to boost the performance of Olympic athletes. Swimmers were recently introduced to a new, reduced friction swim suit. The latest polyester and polyurethane fabric has a heat-rolled finish that gives it less resistance. Research indicates that it might be even faster in the water than bare skin. It is porous and dissipates heat quickly. To get the maximum benefit, men may wear a long or full body suit, similar to the woman's suit. Flo Jo Griffith Joyner set the current 100 meter dash world record of 10.47 seconds in a similar track suit. Olympic down-hill snow skiing has also taken advantage of the newest, elastic synthetics to produce a slicker, less air resistant ski suit which is also tougher and offers more protection in a fall.

Equipment

Innovations and changes in equipment, from shoes to implements to facilities, has revolutionized the manner in which various sports are played. Perhaps, more than any other piece of equipment, the improvement in comfort and quality of sports shoes has been a boon to all forms of athletic participation. Recreational running has possibly benefited the most. The athletic shoe provides traction(friction) and support; it acts as a shock absorber and as a means of propulsion. The traction of a shoe can be calculated as the coefficient of friction. Soles may be of polyurethane or rubber. Some shoes are smooth soled or ribbed while others have treads, spikes, or cleats designed to increase friction.

Sports implements of all kinds have greatly affected the way that several games are played. Golf clubs now have medal woods and square grooves. Tennis rackets have gone from spaghetti stringing to giant, economy sizes. Aluminum alloy baseball and softball bats now ping instead of crack. The shape and length of the javelin has been altered to prevent it from traveling as far. The pole-vault pole has evolved from a cane pole to aluminum to fiberglass to graphite/carbon composites. The action of the pole makes the event more closely resemble a catapult rather than a vault.

Badminton, tennis and racquetball rackets have gone from wood to metal to newer, lighter rackets of boron/carbon and graphite. These are often one piece in design and can be made of varying degrees of stiffness. There are also wide-body and over-size rackets for less air resistance and less torque. Strings are usually nylon, gut, or synthetic gut. Nylon is much less expensive, more durable and is often strung tighter than gut. Gut is more resilient, pliable and offers greater "touch", but is generally more costly and less durable due primarily to changes in the weather. Synthetic gut offers most of the positive attributes of regular gut, is more durable and slightly less expensive. Nylon and synthetic gut seem to be more practical choices for the average player. String tension is also an important consideration in determining how well your racket is going to perform. The newer composite rackets are lighter and yet stronger. It is not uncommon for today's tennis rackets to be strung at over 90 pounds per square inch tension. Research indicates that this more tightly strung racket gives you better control, while a slightly, more loosely strung racket gives you more power. Several professional tennis players consistently serve over 130 miles per hour. Professional players often hit groundstrokes between 80 and 85 miles per hour. Professional racquetball players hits serves in excess of 190 miles per hour. Overhead smashes in badminton have been timed well over 230 miles per hour.

Cycling continues to emphasize streamlining and lightening the bike and the rider. Bicycle frames of chrome-molybdenum are exceptionally light and strong. The shape of the frame, the seat and the helmet has been contoured for aerodynamic benefits. Aerobars put the rider's arms in the center of the bike, reducing drag. Helmets weigh approximately six ounces and have visors to improve aerodynamics. Carbon-fiber disc wheels, titanium seat rails and aluminum handlebars lighten, yet also strengthen the bicycle further.

Courts and playing surfaces vary greatly from sport to sport. There is no official or standardized surface for badminton or tennis courts. A court may be indoors or outdoors; it may be concrete, asphalt, clay, grass, synthetic, or wood. During the 1993 World Track and Field Championships in Tokyo, Japan, the now famous Mike Powell-Carl Lewis long jump competition took place in which both men broke Bob Beaman's 23-year old world record. Powell now holds the record at 29 feet, 4.5 inches. Six men went under ten seconds during the 100 meter dash final with Lewis setting the then world record time of 10.86 seconds. The men's 4x100 relay world record was also broken. These record performances were attributed to a new, very firm track surface, nicknamed the "magic carpet". Shortly afterward, this track was declared illegal. According to the International Amateur Athletic Federation, an illegally hard track has a force reduction rate of 0.34 or less. The hardness of a track is described in terms of this force of reduction rating which places the relative hardness of a running surface on a scale ranging from 0.00 for concrete to 1.00 for sand. Harder tracks are faster tracks because they rebound the pounding foot faster. The foot of a male runner touches the ground for only about 0.083 seconds on an average track. A harder track, similar to the one in Atlanta used for the 1996 Summer Olympics had a force reduction rating of 0.36 and because the track was harder, the rebound was faster than average, about 0.079 seconds. Several athletes complained of having leg cramps after running on the Atlanta track. John Smith (1996) theorized that the high incidence of leg cramps was due to the hardness of the track. "When the feet are rebounding from the track faster than an athlete is accustomed to, Smith said, it sends shock waves back through the legs, which in turn can cause cramps."

Anxiety

You vary in your response to drills or learning situations. Every situation differs in the degree of stress and anxiety produced. Even instructions which may be very clear to someone else may be completely confusing to you. Fear, self-doubt, nervousness or apprehension can also unnerve some or embarrass others. You must have an environment in which even a timid, shy player will not be afraid to try. Warming-up or following a set routine often sets the tone for successful competition. Patterns of activity, such as, habits, traditions, rituals or even superstitions are often used to build confidence.

Fear of failure may serve as a motivator for success or predispose you to failure itself. Some players use the situation to "psych themselves up" and are really excited about the competition. Others seem to "psych themselves out" by making the situation more important than it really is and completely fail. If a player is tight or tense, both mental and physical mistakes are more likely to occur.

Strategy

In many sports, strategy and/or tactics are the most neglected aspect of play. Players should be adequately prepared to cope with all the fundamentals of competition, as well as, all the situations that might be confronted in actual games. Practice should include the basic mechanics necessary to perform, the methods needed to be successful and the development of individual skills.

Baseball players must do their mental homework between pitches in order to anticipate any potential situation or problem that arises. Basketball teams prepare to play and/or defend against both zone and person-to-person defenses, half-court traps, and full-court presses. Individual decision making, timing and one's strengths and weaknesses may affect the outcome of the game. Practice should consist of learning specific situations so well that you do not have to think; you react. If you are a runner on first base and a fly ball is hit to right field, you should automatically go half-way to second base. If the ball is caught, you can easily return to first; if the ball falls in or is dropped, you will make it safely to second. A defensive back in football must learn to interpret or react to the subtle movements that a wide receiver makes and not be fooled or faked out of position. Learning these situations so well that you do not have to think is called a **conditioned reflex**. It is the result of a well learned motor skill.

The ability to react or respond quickly to any situation in sports is very important. Athletes are often thought to have good reactions or reflexes. **Reflexes** are unconscious responses to stimuli that do not require information to be processed in the brain. **Reflex time** is usually described as an involuntary response to a stimulus which does not require one to think or consciously make a decision. Therefore, this unconscious reflex cannot be improved with practice. Fielding a "bad hop" in baseball or softball or quickly removing your hand from a hot oven are examples of reflex time. **Reaction time** is the period between a stimulus and a response, when the response requires thinking or is voluntary. Reaction time varies greatly and those individuals with faster reaction time are usually better athletes. Because it refers to conscious responses to expected or unexpected stimuli, reaction time can be improved with practice. Reducing the time that it takes you to get out of the blocks at the start of a race is an example.

Motivation

Motivation is the process of you being energized and stimulated to want to learn. You learn by doing, but only if you understand and are interested in what you are doing. This also entails controlling your behavior and structuring learning situations to encourage yourself to work harder and stay focused on the immediate task. The learning environment should assist in regulating, controlling and directing your energy towards being a more successful player.

Players, teachers and coaches can attempt to enhance motivation in several ways. One way is to control your **level of excitement** or arousal. Many players can be motivated by their coach just talking to them, while others must be hit upside the head with the proverbial two-by-four, just to get their attention.

Also, your drills or tasks to be accomplished must be appropriate for your skill level. If are really well prepared, you are more likely to have a better performance. If you feel prepared and well conditioned, you develop confidence and a winning attitude. You expect to succeed. Some anticipatory response is probably good; your adrenalin is flowing, your heart rate is increased and your senses are on edge, you're ready for the competition. Generally, your best performance results from a level of alertness or arousal somewhere between hyperventilation and boredom.

Motivation can also be increased by proper **reinforcement**. Reinforcement provides rewards or awards designed to motivate a change in your behavior. Reinforcement may range from favorable comments made by the teacher or coach to the possibility of competing for millions of dollars in prize money as a professional athlete. There are also social reinforcers, such as, becoming a member of a group or a team of their peers. Coaches and teachers should provide activities that makes recognition readily available. This may consist of success in challenge matches, contests or competitive drills.

Various material rewards can serve as reinforcers. Trophies, medals, ribbons, patches or t-shirts are often awarded for participation. Letters, letter jackets or blankets are common awards for successful varsity competition. Another important form of reinforcement is the activity itself. If the game is fun and interesting, if the practice sessions are challenging and beneficial and if you feel that progress is being made, you will have little trouble remaining interested and motivated.

Another technique for increasing your motivation is to obtain **feedback** or information. You can use various forms of feedback to change or correct your performance while practicing or competing. Feedback may be visual in nature. You get information following every shot or rally simply by observing your results, or by observing other players executing their shots. You can see if your shots are in or out. Some research indicates that visual feedback alone, even without physical practice, can improve your quality of play. Modern technology allows anyone to watch the very best athletes in any sport. Watching the proper form or technique of experts on a video tape allows you to observe the correct way to perform the strokes and serves or the correct way to perform other skills. You may also videotape yourself and see how closely your form resembles theirs. Some studies have gone so far as to edit out all of the improper techniques and only record the strokes that were executed well. Then the subject observes himself or herself performing the stroke correctly. You also receive a form of internal feedback called kinesthetic feel during and after each stroke. Proprioceptors in the joints and muscles sense where your body is in space, relative to the oncoming ball in tennis for example. You are aware of where your racket is even though you cannot see it. You sense if the stroke felt good and you can see if the results was good. Verbal feedback, usually in the form of constructive criticism, gives you information from either your coach, teacher or trained partner. This information, collected over time, allows you to develop better form, strokes and consistency.

Psychological interventions include considerations, such as, your ability to concentrate and mentally prepare for competition. **Concentration** is your ability to shut out any outside, extraneous interference or keep a more task-oriented focus. **Mental practice** or cognitive restructuring intervention involves reviewing game situations over in your mind, perceiving yourself executing good shots and/or winning games. A recent U.S. national champion in table tennis claimed to spend one to one and half hours a day on mental training, such as, visualization, relaxation, goal setting and listening to tapes. **Mental rehearsal or imagery** involves closing your eyes and visualizing yourself winning or playing well. Also pausing to take some deep breaths and relaxing seems to improve your ability to concentrate. **Relaxation intervention** seems to decrease the likelihood of being distracted and helps to control your anxiety. Before competition, holding your breath prior to your initial movement allows you to react more quickly during competition. Grunting or forcefully expelling air from your lungs during the execution of a lift in weight training or during a tennis stroke seems to give you more power.

A relatively new method of enhancing your ability to relax and concentrate is **sensory deprivation**. By isolating yourself with no outside interference or distraction in a sensory deprivation chamber, your thoughts and perceptions seem to become more focused. The Alpha Chair, an egg shaped audio-visual device used at the U.S. Olympic Training Center, surrounds you with speakers and as you watch a videotape of one of your best performances, you listen to your audio description of the performance.

The most elusive, and promising edge in psychological preparation for sports competition is what has been called "the sweet spot in time", when mind and body are synchronized in perfect harmony for athletic performance. In sports, it is sometimes referred to as the state of flow, in the groove or "in the zone". Another common way of expressing it is by saying the player is "treed", meaning they are playing above their normal standard of play or way over their head. It is the condition during an athletic performance when time seems to slow down, objects appear larger than life, pain is blocked out, and everything is instinctive or second nature. When an athlete hits this sweet spot, they experience a moment of perfection. Nothing can go wrong. If research can determine how to trigger this peak mental state, athletes may be capable of reaching even greater physical and mental accomplishments.

Numerous research studies indicate that sport psychological interventions can improve athletic performance. However, harmful interventions, such as, poor advice, incorrect coaching, a misdiagnosed injury or encouragement by a trainer or coach to play with an injury may result in harmful consequences. Trainers, coaches, physicians or other health professionals should have the proper training and credentials in order to be effective in medical or psychological intervention. Some psychological performance enhancing interventions may not be effective in producing a positive change in behavior, but a well-informed and alert athlete may increase his potential for success.

Readiness

Readiness to learn seems to depend upon both physi8ological and psychological needs. Children appear to learn more readily and faster if they are healthy and strong. Maslow's Hierarchy of Needs has often been cited as an example of the process required to attain self-actualization in learning. Physical needs, such as: (1) the satisfaction of hunger, thirst, sex; (2) the feeling of safety, order, stability; (3) a sense of belonging or being loved; (4) the fulfillment of esteem, including self-respect and one's experienci8ng of success; all lead to the last step (6) of self-actualization.

The normal goals of physical activity probably should include the following:

1. to have fun;

2. to enjoy the company of friends;

3. to develop strength, endurance and become more fit;

4. to become a member of an individual or team sport;

5. to develop a better physique or to be better looking; and

6. to get up and move around and experience some relief from the confinement of the classroom setting.

Educators have known for a long time that a child who gains confidence from sports often performs better in the classroom as well. Exercise and movement seem to increase one's ability to focus and/or concentrate on written work. However, recent research provides evid3ence that there is a psychological connection between exercise and learning. The U.S. Surgeon General's Report (1997) cited several studies which seem to indicate that exercise boosts learning.

The findings suggest that exercise helps produce neurotrophins, chemicals that build brain cells and gets the brain in better shape to learn. In addition to increasing neurotrophin production, research indicates that exercise improves the brain's blood flow. Complex movements may also multiply the brain's nerve connections, aiding in the processing of information. William Greenough, a neuroscientist at the University of Illinois, states that, "through exercise, the brain is getting itself in better condition for sustained use. Overall, you have very convincing data that intellectual performance is dependent on being in good physical condition." In Greenough's experimental research (1997) on the link between movement and the brain, rats that completed complex motor tasks had more nerve connections and a better flow of brain nutrients than did rats who performed more simple tasks or were sedentary. Neurophysiologist, Carla Hannaford (1997) recently published Smart Moves, a book about the movement-learning link which cites Greenough's research and a Canadian study in which 500 children who participated in an additional hour of exercise every day performed significantly better on written exams than did less active children.

Although fitness is considered a significant asset to an exercise program, there are some concerns about children engaging in strength training programs. It is not until adulthood that all the physiological mechanisms for strength development are achieved. It is widely accepted that strength training improves athletic performance in adults and adolescents, but very few studies have been performed regarding the effect of strength training on children's athletic performance, particularly prepubescent children. Research indicates that very intense, heavy resistant weight training and long distance, high impact running increase the risk for injury because the young athlete's bones are not completely ossified. Cartilage and muscle are more susceptible to damage during heavy lifting, especially during periods of rapid growth. There also seems to be conflicting reports on the effects of a a regular exercise program for preadolescent girls. Some research suggests that a regular exercise program prevents the onset of puberty and thus allows the female to grow taller by several inches. This would appear to be an advantage for any female athlete, especially in sports like basketball and volleyball. Other research indicates that if young adolescent female athletes exercise too intensely, they may experience ammenorhea which could lead to excessive bone loss.

Competitive gymnastics is a prime example, in which the smaller athlete has an advantage. In 1972, the average female gymnast on the U.S. Olympic team was 5'3" tall and weighed 103 pounds. In 1992, the average height was 4'9" and 86 pounds. The lower center of gravity along with the shorter he3ight allows the gymnast to perform faster rotations and more complex movements on the balance beam, the uneven parallel bars, during vaulting and on the floor exercise. Puberty signifies the beginning of the end for the female gymnaast's competitive career. In a sport in which statistics show the smallest and strongest win, the change in physical shape and size from that of a girl into that of a woman works against the female athlete and increases the difficulty level in almost every gymnastic event. Gymnastics revolves around balancing and tumbling activities. Gravity works against the mature, more developed, heavier and taller female athlete. As they change shape and their center of gravity shifts; it is more difficult to balance. As the female gymnast grows taller, their limbs grow longer and they slow down. Thus, the career of a competitive gymnast is seemingly very short, approximately five years at the most.

Also, special considerations need to be addressed relative to making the exercise program safe, productive and enjoyable for the young athlete. Prior to beginning any exercise program, children should be mature enough to understand and follow directions and safety rules. A pre-participation physical examination should be performed to screen for pre-existing problems, injuries, conditions or diseases. Proper supervision and instruction should be provided at all times. The teacher or coach should have some prior training in order to design and develop the exercise program appropriately and effectively. In all sports and exercise activities there is the potential for adverse effects caused by the psychological stress of the participation itself. Small and Smith (1996) state that, "if the demands imposed on the child by the coach, trainer or parents are greater than the resources of the child, stress will result." Stress can also occur if the demands are too low and there is little challenge. This can lead to boredom and potentially even disciplinary problems. Decreased self-esteem can also result if too much emphasis is placed on successful performance during athletic competition. In all sports, there is the potential for adverse effects caused by the stress of participating in any given activity.

In general, all exercise programs for children should be well supervised, with the proper techniques being taught and should be designed based on the individual physical and emotional needs as well as the maturity of the athlete. Weight lifting with maximal amounts of weights should be avoided. Also free weights pose a greater safety due to the need for greater neuromuscular control which the younger athlete will not possess.

Before signing up for a sports program, a child's emotional and physical development should be scrutinized. The sport that matches his or her physical and emotional levels should be selected. Age, maturity, temperament, personality, physical size and safety are factors which will affect each child's level of enjoyment of any activity or sport. The following questions should be asked: Is the coach a good teacher and well-prepared? What level of commitment is required by the coach and/or league? Is the primary objective to win at all costs or to have fun? Ultimately, what are the results attempted to gain by the child's participation in sports? Hopefully, the child will develop new skills, get the exercise he or she needs, and have fun.

Talent Identification

Talent identification is one of the latest attempts to discover the illusive qualities that make an athlete a champion. Historically, the United States has made very little attempt at searching out the champion athlete. We have gradually over time allowed the population sample to grow in number of participants and have let the cream of the crop rise to the top. Only recently have women athletes begun to participate on a much, broader scale. Title IX legislation (1972) was instrumental in providing greater access to athletic participation at every level. The first collegiate athletic scholarships for women were awarded in 1975. The first Olympic Marathon which allowed women participants was in 1984. Since 1984, the world record for the women's marathon has improved by over thirty-five minutes. During the same time period, the world record for the men's marathon has only improved approximately two minutes. Gender equity, the success of women's professional sports (most recently the WNBA) and the proliferation of other individual and team sports at the interscholastic and collegiate levels have provided greater opportunities for women in sports. Dr. Brian Whipp, UCLA Physiologist, in *Can Science Build a Champion Athlete?* (1993) makes the observation in an effort to explain the continued improvement of athletic performances, "If I would put the most weight on a single factor, I would say it's the broadening of the sample of the prople involved in the athletic events. Because the wider the sample of the entire human race, the more likely you are to match the intrinsic genetic make-up of the athlete. So naturally, as the sample broadens, what you'll see is improvement in performance." Hopefully, this broader sampling of the human population will allow all athletes to continually improve and achieve their true potential.

Charles Dillman, Deputy Executive Director of the United States Olympic Committee, concedes that most Olympic sports have no established scholastic or developmental program. He suggests that there probably needs to be some type of selection process established to identify potentially, talented athletes in the United States. Some structured process should be developed to discover physical characteristics early on; specific physical traits that would predispose children for success in certain, specific sports. Nick Bolliterri's Tennis Academy in Florida is probably the only example in the United States which can remotely be credited with some form of talent identification. Pete Sampras, Andre Agassi and Jim Courier are all former number one ranked players on the Association of Tennis Players (ATP) tour for professional tennis. They are all former students at the Bolliterri Tennis Academy.

The former Soviet Union and other European Eastern Block countries have been involved in talent identification for decades. Records indicate that the Soviet Union was a leader in talent identification for their elite athletes. An example of a test that was used to identify specific athletic ability was the support time test. This test had young athletic children jump from a height, approximately three feet, down onto a force platform and rebound up into the air. This test measured the length of time that the feet were in contact with the force platform during the transition from landing from the jump and the subsequent take-off. Approximately 10,000 eight to twelve year old children were tested and only twelve had a support time of less than one-tenth of a second. This indicated that they would be successful at sports that required explosive running or jumping ability, such as, basketball, volleyball or track and field jumping events.

Romania has been very successful in using talent identification for their Olympic gymnastics program. Every year approximately 5,000 five-year old girls apply for the gymnastics program. Only 200 are selected to be admitted. From five to seven, children are encouraged to play, jump, run and work on their athletic skills in a play environment. Only the best children advance to the Olympic Gym. This two-year long selection process identifies the children who are the most athletic, strongest and most coordinated. They must also have demonstrated that they have little fear in performing on the various apparatus. At age eight, the serious work begins. The atmosphere becomes much more competitive. Only one or two children of the original 200 selected will make it to the Olympic Team. Constant, year-round repetitive training to practice and refine the necessary skills for competitive gymnastics also prevents the onset of puberty. This serves to lengthen the relatively short career of the competitive gymnast.

East Germany used talent identification in a number of Olympic sports, especially, sports which required explosive movement and speed. Track and field running and throwing events, swimming and weight lifting were areas which received special attention and were especially successful. In recent years, Australia and China have used an East German model for their talent identification programs. China has been particularly successful in swimming. Australia copies a program for identifying competitive rowers which was very successful.

The United States has had many great and talented athletes over the years. But there have been very few who were deliberately selected through a structured, deliberate system. Most U.S. athletes begin athletic participation because of the influence of a role model, such as, a parent, a coach or a professional athlete. Their relative interest level seems to be a product of various factors, including, enjoyment of the activity, successful participation, or peer pressure. The development of a talent identification process that could select children at an early age would be the equivalent of building a better mousetrap. Parents would probably welcome the opportunity for their children to experience success at certain sports. Parents would also make fewer poor choices for their children in sports where the child had a very limited chance of success. There are so many opportunities for children in organized sports, such as ballet, baseball, basketball, football, gymnastics, martial arts, soccer, softball, swimming, and tennis to name a few. Parents often seem to use these as a form of baby-sitting service to get their children out of the house and to give the parents some release time as well. This is not altogether a negative situation, but the child

171

would certainly enjoy these attempts at structured activity more if they experienced some success. Grice and Hnizdor (1999) developed a working model for identifying talent in specific sports using a three-digit composite known as **KidTest**, a **T**alent **ID**entification **E**valuation **S**cores of **TIDES**. Norms were established for students, kindergarten through fifth grade. An example of the **KidTest TIDESGRAM** is shown in Figures 10.1 and 10.2.

The intervention of science and technology into sports may allow the athlete the opportunity to achieve his true potential. Dillman (1993) indicated that athletes 40 years ago were probably achieving approximately 80% of their potential. Today with more knowledge and newer technology, he suggests that we may be achieving 90% of that potential. Dillman concludes, "And I think most of us who have looked at this area are astonished at what the human can do and because of that, believe that we can even go much further." The impact of science and technology along with the utilization of concepts such as talent identification provide optimism for the development of the future champion athlete.

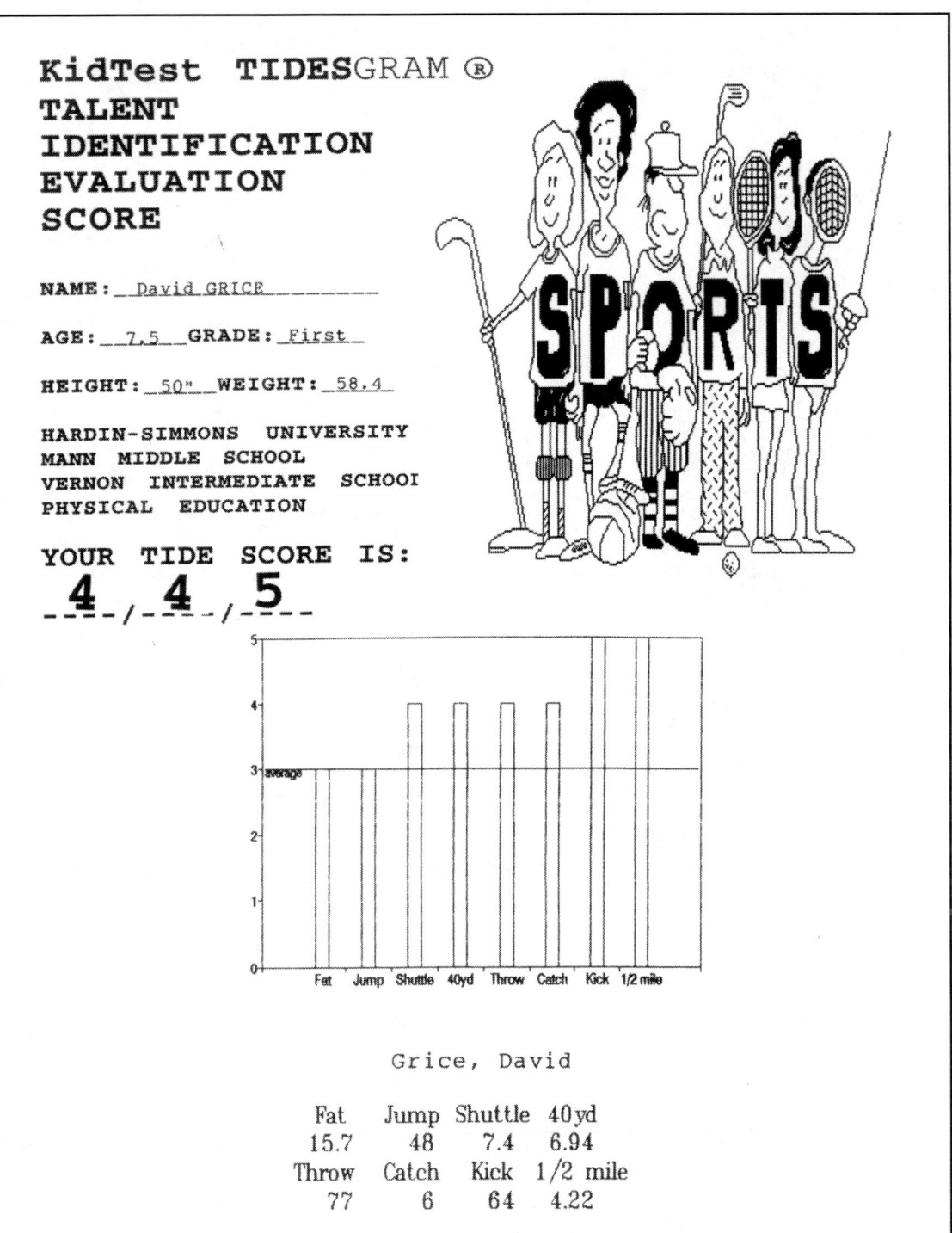

Figure 11-1. KidTest TIDESGRAM Front Page

KidTest TALENT IDENTIFICATION EVALUATION SCORE

SPORTS	TIDE Score	Aerobic	Motor	Coordination
1.	Archery	1	3	2
2.	Badminton	3	2	5
3.	Ballet	3	3	5
4.	Baseball	2	4	5
5.	Basketball	5	4	4
6.	Bowling	1	3	3
7.	Football	2	4	4
8.	Golf	1	3	4
9.	Gymnastics	2	4	4
10.	Handball	3	3	5
11.	Martial Arts	2	4	3
12.	Racquetball	3	3	5
13.	Recreational Sports			
	Bicycling	3	2	3
	Frisbee-Horseshoe/Darts	1	2	2
	Horseback Riding	1	2	3
	Rollerblade/Skateboarding	2	2	3
	Rollerskating	2	2	2
14.	Skiing			
	Downhill	3	5	5
	Cross-Country	5	3	4
	Water	4	4	4
15.	Soccer			
	Wings, Forwards, Strikers	4	5	5
	Goalie	3	5	4
	Halfback, Fullback	3	3	3
16.	Softball	2	4	5
17.	Swimming			
	Sprints/50-200 meters (all strokes)	3	4	5
	400-800 meters	4	4	4
	1500 meters (freestyle)	5	3	3
18.	Tennis	3	2	5
19.	Track and Field			
	Sprints/100-200 meters	2	5	3
	400-800 meters	3	4	3
	5000 meters (5K)	5	4	2
	1000 meters (10K)	5	5	2
	Marathon/Triathlon	5	5	3
20.	Volleyball	2	2	4

KidTest TIDESGRAM ®

The TIDES KidTest provides a means of evaluating the potential talent that your child may exhibit for success in specific sports. It is a subjective evaluation based on their performance on various tests in the areas of aerobic power, motor skills and coordination. The results are shown as their TIDES score, a three-digit composite, each of which are on a scale from 1-5.

The suggested sports which your child would seem to have the most potential for success are high-lighted and recommended by order of choice as follows:

FIRST CHOICE
Soccer, Swimming, Water Skiing

SECOND CHOICE
Baseball, Basketball, Racquetball

THIRD CHOICE:
Badminton, Tennis, Soccer Goalie
Track and Field (400-800 meters)

Figure 11-2. KidTest TIDESGRAM Back Page

Study Questions

1. What is meant by the term, motivation?

2. Give three examples of reinforcement as it applies to sports.

3. How does internal feedback differ from external or visual feedback?

4. Generally, where should your level of excitement or arousal be to result in your best performance?

5. What does it mean to be "in the zone"?

6. You are playing third base, and a ground ball hit directly at you takes a bad bounce. What is the time referred to between seeing the bad bounce and moving your hands and glove?

7. The gun sounds to start the beginning of a 5-Kilometer run. What is the time called between the sound of the gun and your first movement?

References

1. Eckrich J. & Widule, A. (1993). The effects of video observational training on video and live observational proficiency. *Research Quarterly for Exercise and Sport, 64,* A-86.

2. Jambor, E.A. & Weekes, E.M. (1955). Video feedback: Make it more effective. *Journal of Physical Education, Recreation and Dance.* February, 66, 48-50

3. Jerome, J. (1980). *The sweet spot in time.* New York: Avon Books.

4. Kirschenbaum, D., McCann, S., Meyers, A. & Williams, J. (1995). Roundtable: The use of sport psychology to improve sport performance. *Gatorade Sports Science Institute, 6,* 1-4.

5. Kohl, R.M., Fisicaro, S.A. & Erbaugh, S.J. (1993). Alternating actual and imagery practice; preliminary theoretical considerations. *Research Quarterly for Exercise and Sport, 63,* 162-170.

6. Mathias, K.E., Adams, T.M., II, Sterns, B., & Mayo, C. (1993). An investigation of the effects of an interactive videodisc application on freestyle and butterfly swimming skill acquisition. *Research Quarterly for Exercise and Sport, 64,* A-90.

7. Murphy, C. & Murphy, B. (1975). Psychological aspects of teaching tennis. *Tennis for the Player, Teacher and Coach* (pp. 42-56). Philadelphia: Saunders.

8. Wulf, G., Horstmann, G. & Choi, B. (1995). Does mental practice work like physical practice without information feedback? *Research Quarterly for Exercise and Sport, 66,* 262-267.

Key Terms from Chapter 11

Anxiety—Apprehension or uneasiness over an impending event which may cause fear or fearful concern.

Conditioned Reflex—Being able to respond to a stimulus or situation so well that you do not have to consciously make a decision to do so.

Feedback—Information processed to produce changes that improve performance .

Friction—The force that resists relative motion between two surfaces in contact with each other. This contact or rubbing between the two surfaces provides traction and often produces heat.

Level of Excitement—The optimum level of alertness or arousal at which most individuals perform best.

Reaction Time—The time interval from the presentation of a stimulus to the initiation of a response which requires conscious thought.

Reflexes—Responses to stimuli that do not require information to be processed in the brain. Reflexes occur virtually automatically at the spinal level. An example of a spinal reflex is the "knee jerk or myotatic reflex" or the patellar tendon reflex.

Reflex Time—The time interval between a stimulus and the initiation of a response that involves a nerve impulse passing inward from a receptor to a nerve center and thence outward to an effector (muscle or gland) without reaching the level of consciousness.

Reinforcement—A stimulus such as a reward which produces the desired response.

Sensory Deprivation—The removal of sensation or the interference of reception and interpretation of sensory stimuli, such as, heat, light, sound, pressure or any particular motion.

Strategy—A careful plan or method employed to accomplish a goal.

LABORATORY APPLICATIONS

12
SKILL TECHNIQUES

Before attempting to mechanically analyze sports, one must be familiar with the skill techniques and/or the teaching points necessary to perform sports skills. In order to become cognizant of sports techniques complete the following worksheet designating the skill techniques in operation in the fundamental skills you select.

Directions: Select two fundamental skills from each of the four sections listed. Analyze each fundamental for technique, i.e., list teaching points. Teaching points are to be stated in sentence statement form in the space provided on the worksheet.

Section A

Fundamental Activity—Walking

Fundamental Activity—Carrying

Fundamental Activity—Pulling

Angling—Spin - Casting - Grip and Stance

Archery—Bracing the Bow

Balance Beam—Front Scale

Bowling—Stance and Holding the Ball

Golf—Stance and Grip

Field Hockey—Holding and Carrying the Stick

Handball—Stance

Modern Dance—Leap

Modern Dance—Jump

Modern Dance—Slide

Skiing—Walking

Surfing—Stance

Lacrosse—Catching the Ball

Section B

Angling—Fly Casting
Badminton—Forehand
Badminton—Overhead
Golf—Wood Shot
Field Hockey—Dribble
Field Hockey—Push Pass
Table Tennis—Forehand Slice
Table Tennis—Forehand Top Spin
Water Skiing—Crossing the Wake
Volleyball—Overhand Service
Handball—Forehand Shot
Shuffleboard—Shot
Soccer—Passing
Speedball—Drop Kick

Section C

Diving—Jack knife
Diving—Forward One and a Half with a Full Twist
Snow Skiing—Walking
Snow Skiing—Stem Turn
Tumbling—Forward Roll
Tumbling—Standing Back Somersault
Side Horse—Straddle Dismount Forward from Front Rest
Side Horse—Single Leg Circle Left Full Left
Parallel Bars—Front Uprise from Upper Arm Hang
Parallel Bars—Cross Shoulder Balance
Parallel Bars—Kip Up
Parallel Bars—Front Dismount
Trampoline—Cradle
Trampoline—Back Somersault to Feet (Pike)
Trampoline—Back Cody
Trampoline—Back Somersault with 1/2 Twist
Trampoline—Seat Drop Full Twist Seat Drop

Section D

Archery—Nocking, Drawing, and Loosing the Arrow
Balance Beam—One Knee Mount
Basketball—Lay-up Shot
Basketball—One Hand Set Shot
Bowling—Four Step Delivery Straight Ball
Boxing—Right Hook
Fencing—The Retreat
Football—Screen Block
Water Polo—Dribbling
Water Polo—Pick up
Water Polo—Catching the Ball
Weight lifting—Snatch
Wrestling—Escape
Lacrosse—Picking up a Ground Ball
Softball—Pitching
Speedball—Pass

SECTION A

Skill _____   Name _____

Teaching Points

1. _____
   _____

2. _____
   _____

3. _____
   _____

4. _____
   _____

5. _____
   _____

6. _____
   _____

7. _____
   _____

8. _____
   _____

SECTION A

Skill _____   Name _____

Teaching Points

1. _____
   _____

2. _____
   _____

3. _____
   _____

4. _____
   _____

5. _____
   _____

6. _____
   _____

7. _____
   _____

8. _____
   _____

SECTION B

Skill _____   Name _____

Teaching Points

1. _____

   _____

2. _____

   _____

3. _____

   _____

4. _____

   _____

5. _____

   _____

6. _____

   _____

7. _____

   _____

8. _____

   _____

SECTION B

Skill _____   Name _____

Teaching Points

1. _____

   _____

2. _____

   _____

3. _____

   _____

4. _____

   _____

5. _____

   _____

6. _____

   _____

7. _____

   _____

8. _____

   _____

SECTION C

Skill _____   Name _____

Teaching Points

1. _____
   _____

2. _____
   _____

3. _____
   _____

4. _____
   _____

5. _____
   _____

6. _____
   _____

7. _____
   _____

8. _____
   _____

SECTION C

Skill _____   Name _____

Teaching Points

1. _____

   _____

2. _____

   _____

3. _____

   _____

4. _____

   _____

5. _____

   _____

6. _____

   _____

7. _____

   _____

8. _____

   _____

SECTION D

Skill _____   Name _____

Teaching Points

1. _____

   _____

2. _____

   _____

3. _____

   _____

4. _____

   _____

5. _____

   _____

6. _____

   _____

7. _____

   _____

8. _____

   _____

SECTION D

Skill _____   Name _____

Teaching Points

1. _____

   _____

2. _____

   _____

3. _____

   _____

4. _____

   _____

5. _____

   _____

6. _____

   _____

7. _____

   _____

8. _____

   _____

13

BODY MOVEMENT
AND STABILITY

1. Understanding of movement aids in the teacher learning process and promotes optimum performance.

2. The mechanical mechanisms of the human body (struts, arches, levers, hinges, ball and sockets, pulleys, wheel and axle, cables, etc.) powered by muscles produce that wonderful human experience—movement.

3. Before learning about principles of movement and stability one must know definitions of terms describing stability and movements.

    A. Balance _____

         _____

    B. Center of Gravity _____

         _____

    D. Equilibrium _____

         _____

    E. Foot-Pounds _____

         _____

    F. Gravity _____

         _____

    G. Lever _____

         _____

    H. Mass _____

         _____

    I. Mechanical Advantage _____

         _____

J. Pulley _____

_____

K. Stability _____

_____

4. Planes of the Body are Sagittal or Anteroposterior; Frontal or lateral; Horizontal or transverse.

5. The three axes of the body are:
    A. Vertical axis that is perpendicular to the ground.
    B. The frontal axis that passes horizontally from side to side.
    C. The sagittal axis that passes horizontally from front to back.

6. Mechanical Mechanisms of the body. Examples:
    A. A keystone arch: _____

    _____

    B. The pulley and lever of a crane: _____

    _____

    C. A ball and socket: _____

    _____

    D. The struts of a bridge: _____

    _____

    E. The rigging of a ship: _____

    _____

    F. A simple hinge: _____

    _____

7. Bones of the body act as levers (a mechanical device) which creates mechanical advantage of strength or speed by producing a turning motion about an axis.

    A. A lever is characterized by a fulcrum or center of rotation, a force arm and a weight arm.
    B. The force arm is the distance from the fulcrum to the point where force is applied.
    C. The weight arm is the distance from the fulcrum to the center of gravity of the weight.

194

8. Most of the movements of the body are produced by third class levers. In the third class lever the force is located between the fulcrum and the weight.

    Examples: _____

    _____

    _____

    _____

9. Second class levers in the human body are thought not to exist or at least are controversial. In a second class lever the weight is between the fulcrum and the force.

    Possible Example: _____

    _____

10. In the first class lever the fulcrum is between the force and the weight.

    Examples: _____

    _____

11. A third class lever creates speed of movement while the second-class lever gives strength. The first class lever can either be one of strength or speed.

12. The correct application of stability in physical education activities makes a significant contribution to performance.

    A. The larger the base of support upon which a body rests the greater the stability.

        Examples: _____

        _____

        _____

        _____

    B. The farther the center of gravity is from the edge of the base in the direction of movement the greater the stability.

        Examples: _____

        _____

        _____

        _____

C. The heavier a person is, the greater his stability in a given position.

Examples: _____

_____

_____

_____

_____

D. The lower the center of gravity of a body the greater the stability.

Examples: _____

_____

_____

_____

_____

E. For equilibrium to be maintained the center of gravity must fall within the base of support.

Examples: _____

_____

_____

_____

_____

F. The greater the friction between the supporting surface and the parts of the body in contact with it, the greater the body's stability will be.

Examples: _____

_____

_____

_____

_____

G. In giving or receiving force one should widen his base in the direction of the force.

Examples: _____

_____

_____

_____

_____

13. To start quickly in one direction, create friction between the supporting surface and base, keep the center of gravity as high as possible and as near to the edge of the base in the direction of movement as possible and be in a position to create force.

Examples: _____

_____

_____

_____

_____

14. To stop quickly when in rapid movement, widen the base in the direction of movement, plant the forward foot to create friction, lower the center of gravity and place the center of gravity over the rear foot.

Examples: _____

_____

_____

_____

_____

Notes

14
LINEAR AND ROTARY MOVEMENT

1. Linear movement is a primary objective in most physical education activities.

2. Before learning the principles of linear and rotary movement one must know definitions of terms describing linear and rotary movement.

Acceleration _____

_____

Angular Speed _____

_____

Center of Rotation _____

_____

Degree _____

_____

Linear Motion _____

_____

Motion _____

_____

Projectile _____

_____

Radius _____

_____

Revolution _____

_____

Rotary Motion _____

_____

Rotary Speed _____

_____

Rotation _____

_____

Trajectory _____

_____

Velocity _____

_____

3. Movement is basic to most sports, i.e., they either employ movement as in sprinting or swimming or resist movement of others as in wrestling or football.

4. Movement may result in motion of the total body (running) or movement of some limb of the body (modern dance) or movement of an object by the body. (baseball)

5. Motion may be either vertical or horizontal or at an angle with the vertical or horizontal.

   Examples: _____

   _____

   _____

6. Many physical education activities are affected by the pull of gravity.

   Examples: _____

   _____

   _____

7. In many activities the force of gravity may be used conversely but is nevertheless present.

   Examples: _____

   _____

   _____

8. As an object becomes air borne, the path of its center of gravity is determined by initial velocity and direction. The trajectory that the object travels is not a parabola, due to air resistance.

   Example: _____

   _____

   _____

9. Path of Trajectory in a vacuum.
   1) A 45 degree angle of trajectory will travel the farthest horizontally if measured the same height above the surface from where it was released.
   2) An object thrown at the same number of degrees above 45 as one thrown below 45 will get the same distance but take a longer time.

10. If a person jumps into the air, the height to which the center of gravity can be raised above the floor cannot be changed by body movements, but the position of the center of gravity within the body can be changed.

    Examples: _____

    _____

    _____

11. In all types of activities where greatest distance is the goal, maximum initial velocity is desirable, with an initial angle of projection of the center of gravity of the object at an angle with the horizontal of approximately 30 degrees.

    Examples: _____

    _____

    _____

12. In certain activities where an object or body is released higher than the level of landing, the best angle of release is something less than 45 degrees when air resistance is not a factor.

Examples: _____

_____

_____

13. If time is an important factor in an air borne object then as flat a trajectory as possible to achieve the desired distance is desirable.

Examples: _____

_____

_____

14. If an increase in time is desired, then optimum height may gain time when the projection is greater than 45 degrees.

Examples: _____

_____

_____

15. Principle of the ends and the middle—When a body is in the air free of support, if the head and feet move down the hips move up and vice versa.

Examples: _____

_____

_____

16. Principle of transferring momentum from the part to the whole—Momentum of any part of the body can be transferred to the body as a whole. The direction of a limb (part) movement while in contact with a playing surface will be in the direction of the projected body movement. (whole)

Examples: _____

_____

_____

17. Rotary movement may be changed into or integrated with linear movement for optimum performance.

    Examples: _____

    _____

    _____

18. Linear velocity varies directly with the length of the radius when rotary velocity remains constant.

    Examples: _____

    _____

    _____

19. When linear velocity of a point about the center of rotation is held constant, the angular velocity is inversely proportional to the radius. (If the radius is reduced by one-half the angular velocity will be doubled.)

    Examples: _____

    _____

    _____

20. Movements of the body are generally brought about by rotary movement.

    Examples: _____

    _____

    _____

21. Clockwise rotation of the arms and shoulders counteract the counter clockwise torque of the legs.

    Examples: _____

    _____

    _____

NOTES

15
FORCE AND FACTORS AFFECTING FORCE

1. Force is essential to physical activity, for it takes force to create motion or to stop motion.

2. Before learning about the principles of force one must know definitions of terms used to describe force.

Applied Force _____

_____

Available Force _____

_____

Centrifugal Force _____

_____

Centripetal Force _____

_____

Effective Force _____

_____

Elasticity _____

_____

Force _____

_____

Friction _____

_____

Resultant Force _____

_____

Vector _____

_____

Work _____

_____

3. In the human body the primary source of force is strength derived from a muscle or combination of muscles.

4. There may be force without movement but there cannot be movement without force.

5. Force is inversely proportional to the time it takes to develop it.

Example: _____

_____

_____

6. The need for developing explosive power is paramount in activities requiring distance performance.

Examples: _____

_____

_____

7. Application of force and the direction force is applied is sometimes more important than brute force.

Examples: _____

_____

_____

8. The total of forces applied at the same time are limited to the weakest force.

   Examples: _____

   _____

   _____

9. To get maximum effective force from an implement, the grip must be firm on contact.

   Examples: _____

   _____

   _____

10. If it is desired to absorb a shock of a blow the shock should be:

    A. Spread over as large an area as possible.

       Examples: _____

       _____

       _____

    B. Transferred through as long a distance as possible.

       Examples: _____

       _____

       _____

11. For every action there is an equal and opposite reaction. For greatest distance keep in contact with ground.

    Examples: _____

    _____

    _____

12. The greater the centrifugal force, the greater the lean or banking necessary to balance the force.

    Examples: _____

    _____

    _____

13. To counteract centrifugal force one must lean to the inside, slow down, or cut a larger arc.

    Examples: _____

    _____

    _____

14. Since force creates motion, it is important that physical educators comprehend factors that affect force.

15. The angle of incidence equals the angle of refraction.

    Examples: _____

    _____

    _____

16. The coefficient of friction is dependent upon the composition of the two surfaces, the compression weight of the surfaces, the action between the two surfaces and the irregularity of the surfaces but is independent of the area of contact of the two surfaces.

    Examples: _____

    _____

    _____

17. Spin aids in stability in flight.

    Examples: _____

    _____

    _____

18. A fast spinning object will curve.

    Examples: _____

    _____

    _____

19. The reaction of a spinning object after contact with a flat surface is dependent upon the direction of spin.

    Examples: _____

    _____

    _____

20. In swimming, speed is developed as much by overcoming resistance as by increasing force.

    Examples: _____

    _____

    _____

21. Forward rotation is faster when a twist is brought into the movement.

    Examples: _____

    _____

    _____

22. In the human body, available force varies inversely with the speed of movement.

    Examples: _____

    _____

    _____

23. An understanding of the mechanical principles underlying skill techniques aid in the teaching learning process giving confidence to teacher and learner alike in the soundness of the fundamental taught, to the end that optimum performance will result.

NOTES

16

REVIEW WORKSHEET

Completion Review

Directions: Complete the following initial phrases with word or words needed to make applicable and correct statements of kinesiology.

1. Change of position of a body is called _____

2. The effect which one body exerts on another is called _____

3. That point at which all of the weight of an object may be considered to be concentrated is called the _____

4. Force that deflects a body from its linear path and compels it to move along a curve is called _____

5. Destroying or upsetting the equilibrium of a body is called _____

6. Rate of change of position is called _____

7. Produces or prevents motion or has a tendency to do so is called _____

8. A body which is at a state of rest is in _____

9. To upset a stance or position one must _____

10. The long jumper strives to remain in the air is _____

    _____

11. The hurdler should skim the hurdle as closely as possible in order to _____

    _____

12. The baseball player in taking a lead from a base should _____

    _____

13. A ball thrown at an initial velocity of 60 feet per second will travel _____
    and remain in the air _____ when thrown at an angle of 45 degrees
    than if it was thrown at an angle of 60 degrees.

14. A track man running a 100 yard dash is _____ in equilibrium.

15. A ball thrown at 80 feet per second will travel _____ thrown
    at an angle of 70 degrees than if it was thrown at an angle of 25 degrees.

16. If a performer is in the air free of support, the height to which the center of
    gravity can be raised above the floor _____

    _____

17. In throwing, jumping, or kicking activities where horizontal distance is the
    goal, the body or the object should be projected at an angle of approximately
    _____ and the _____ speed possible should be attained at
    the moment of release or take-off.

18. In throwing, jumping, or kicking activities in a vacuum where horizontal dis-
    tance is the goal, the body or the object should be projected at an angle of ap-
    proximately, but not _____ than 45 degrees.

19. When the angular velocity is constant, the linear velocity of a point about the
    center of rotation is directly proportional to the _____ and conversely.

20. There must be a/an _____ of forward linear motion with
    rotary motion in order to obtain the best results in many activities.

21. In swinging activities, lengthening the radius of rotation on the upswing will
    _____ the movement.

22. When converting rotary motion to linear motion, the greatest speed is transferred when the linear direction is at _____ angle to the radius connecting the point of release and the center of rotation.

23. In doing exercises that necessitate pulling the body up and then pushing it further upward, there should _____ between the pull-up and the push.

24. There is little difference between the stability of the wrestler in a down position on the mat and a football player in the _____ position

25. The state of a body in which there is no change in its motion is celled

_____ .

26. The rate of displacement is called _____

27. The rate of rotary motion is called _____

28. A continuing change of place or position is called _____

29. Two runners **A** and **B** each weigh 150 pounds. The center of gravity of each is the same distance from the ground. The center of gravity of **A** is six inches back of the edge of the base toward the direction where he will run. The center of gravity of **B** is directly over the edge. A will require _____ effort to upset his equilibrium.

20. Two linemen are in position on the line. **A** weighs 200 pounds. **B** weighs 175 pounds. All other factors are equal. It will take _____ to move **A**.

31. A runner takes a position at the starting line. Position **A** the center of gravity is 2.5 feet above the ground. In position **B** the center of gravity is 3 feet above the ground. It requires the least effort for him to upset his equilibrium and start running, in _____ if in both positions he assumes the same base with his center of gravity 3 inches back of the leading edge.

32. A football lineman takes a position with his center of gravity over the center of his base and 2 feet above the base. Position **A** has a base 12 by 12 inches. Position **B** has a base 18 by 24 inches. Position _____ is the most stable.

33. Two wrestlers each weighing 175 pounds take the referee's position on the mat. **A** takes a position with a base 18 by 18 inches with his center of gravity di-

rectly over the center of his base and 12 inches above the base. **B** takes a position with a base of 36 by 36 inches with his center of gravity directly over the center of his base and 24 inches above the base. _____ is the most stable wrestler's position.

34. A basketball player jumps into the air with both arms extended vertically overhead. Just before the maximum height is reached, one arm is forcibly lowered so that the center of gravity is lowered 2 inches in the body. The fingertips of the other hand _____ .

35. In diving and executing the jack-knife, when the legs and arms move down, the buttocks _____ .

36. A diver in executing a somersault from a tuck position went into a layout position so that the radius of rotation was increased by 1.5 feet. His angular velocity would _____ .

37. Two balls are thrown with a velocity of 70 ft./sec. One is thrown at an angle of 30 degrees while the other is thrown at an angle of 60 degrees. The 30-degree angle will get _____ .

38. In executing the giant swing _____ .

39. The radius of rotation of a skater who is spinning is 3 feet. She reduces her radius of rotation to 1.2 feet. Her angular velocity would _____ .

40. Two discus throwers spin with the same angular velocity. John has a reach of 4 feet from the center of the discus to the center of rotation. Jim's reach is 3 feet from the center of rotation to the center of the discus. John's discus on release would _____ initial velocity.

41. In all arm support activities the center of gravity must _____

42. If a performer is in the air free of support, the height to which the center of gravity can be raised above the floor _____ .

43. In throwing, jumping, or kicking activities where horizontal distance is the goal one should _____ .

44. When angular velocity is constant, the linear velocity of a point about a center of rotation is directly proportional to _____ .

45. In swinging exercises, to accelerate the movement on the upswing one must

_____ .

46. In doing exercises that necessitate pulling the body up and then pushing it further upward one should _____ .

47. When a limb is used to turn the body of another, the individual turned should

_____ .

48. If it is desired to absorb the shock of a blow, a fall, a throw, or a kick the shock should _____

49. In throwing or pushing activities, one or both feet are in contact with the ground because _____ .

50. In general, force should be applied _____

_____

51. The direction of flight of a ball which has been struck depends upon _____

_____

52. The speed of the flight of a struck ball depends upon _____ and _____ .

53. The reaction produced by air on a thrown object depends upon _____ and _____ .

54. In the human body, the available force varies inversely with _____

_____

55. In jumping activities, the depth of the crouch is determined by _____

_____

56. A muscle contracts with more force when first _____

_____

57. A muscle will quickly lose its elasticity if _____

_____

58. Body movements are adapted more to speed than to strength because _____

_____

59. Twister movements which are started before the body is air-borne will be _____

_____

60. Twister movements which are started after the body is air-borne will be _____

_____

61. When a twister is brought into the movement, forward rotation will be _____

_____

62. Every body continues in its state of rest or of uniform motion in a straight line
    except _____

63. The acceleration of a body is directly proportional to _____

_____

64. In a head stand, the hands should be kept well back of the head because _____

_____

65. Activities on the horse necessitate that the center of gravity be kept over the
    hands of support. This is accomplished by _____

_____

66. As a pole vaulter goes over the bar his feet are up. The feet are then dropped to

_____

67. The initial problem of the gymnast on the flying rings is that of being given
    potential energy. This is accomplished by _____

_____

68. In the Sargent jump, to get the greatest height _____

_____

69. The most significant factor in putting the shot is _____

_____

70. The firmness of the area where the shot hits the ground affects the distance of the put because _____

71. The function of the "the windup" in pitching suggests the principle of _____

72. Increase in muscular strength is brought about by _____

_____

73. Skillful, efficient performance in a particular technique can be developed by

_____

74. The easiest and safest pyramids are those _____

_____

75. The kneeling position in rowing represents a compromise position which combines the advantages of _____ and _____

76. In carrying a heavy load one compensates for this weight by leaning unless

_____

77. When landing from a jump in order to land without undue shock one should

_____

78. In order to land without undue shock from a fall one should _____

_____

79. When catching a ball the hands should _____

_____

80. A football player is standing braced and rigid. At what point will it take the least force to push him off his feet? _____

_____

81. The length of Joe's arm is 50% greater than Bill's arm. If all other factors are the same, who could stand and throw the discus the farthest? _____

_____

82. A person who has both legs amputated above the knees is fitted to artificial legs which are _____

because _____

83. In throwing, in catching, and in batting objects one can control his balance more readily if he _____

84. The wearing of cleats and rubber soled shoes aids in _____

_____

85. Beginners learning to perform balance stunts can minimize disturbing visual stimuli by _____

86. Of the three, the rowboat, the human body, the canoe, which meet the least resistance from the water? _____

Why? _____

87. A coasting sled on level ground comes to a stand still because of _____

_____

88. Extending the arms horizontally while pirouetting on ice skates will _____

_____

89. In pendulum exercises on the bar the time to execute your exercise is when _____ because _____

90. In tipping a basketball, the legs should be held straight at the time of the tip because _____

_____

91. If constant angular velocity is maintained by a shot putter when the shot is held against the neck, and when the shot is held at a point on the shoulder, which will give the greater linear velocity? _____

_____

92. A high spinning tennis ball near the net should be hit hard because _____

_____

93. The use of weights held in the hands until after the take-off in the long jump adds distance to the jump because _____

_____

94. The advantage in getting low and in close to an opponent so that the charge is more vertical than horizontal is _____

_____

95. A lighter football player can compensate for the difference in weight of his opponent in order to stop the opponent by

_____

96. The stance which a football player assumes is determined by _____

_____

97. The value in pacing oneself in distance running is to _____

_____

98. A head wind may increase the distance of the discus throw b _____

_____

99. Imparting spin to a football gives it _____

_____

100. Explosive power is of great importance in developing force because _____

_____

Overview

Directions: List the principles that satisfy the following initial statements.

1. A persons stability is determined by:

2. To start quickly in one direction an athlete must follow the following fundamentals:

3. A basketball player to stop quickly when in rapid motion must:

4. The three factors which should be emphasized in the long jump are:

5. A few general characteristics of skillful performance which are easily recognized are:

6. Common opposing forces of movement in sports are:

7. Some points to remember in reducing water resistance when swimming are:

8. Four methods which may be used to overcome centrifugal force are:

9. Three activities in which performers strive for height are:

10. Three activities in which performers try to return to earth and continue their performance are:

17
COACHING POINTS WORKSHEET

As a teacher of Physical Education or a coach of one of the various sports, it is important that one understands and can interpret to the learner the reason a certain sport technique is used. Learning is enhanced if this explanation is based upon sound mechanical principles. Below are listed certain basic sport techniques. Justify each of these techniques relating them to sound mechanical principles of movement.

1. Swing arms forward and upward in the take-off in the standing broad jump.

2. Flick your wrist at the moment of release in pitching a baseball.

3. The developing of explosive power is important in getting distance from a punt.

4. A heavier football player meets the ball carrier head on, the lighter player might do better at an angle.

5. On the start of a race one should reduce the angle of projection.

6. Use starting blocks for a quick start.

7. The human body is built for speed rather than strength.

8. In executing hanging activities in gymnastics the moment arm should be as short as possible.

9. Elevate your hips in the track start.

10. Emphasize throwing arm forward in starting quickly.

11. Swing arms while running.

12. Chop stride while starting.

13. In running, keep center of gravity on a straight line.

14. On long races, run at a uniform speed.

15. Bend the knee after the foot leaves the ground in the push-off while running.

16. Reduce acceleration before hitting take-off board in the long jump.

17. In hurdling, raise the trunk as little as necessary as the hurdle is cleared.

18. In hurdling, return the first foot over the hurdle to the ground as quickly as possible.

19. Take equal strides between hurdles.

20. In the pole vault, the center of gravity of the body should be directly below the hands as the pull-up is made.

21. On clearing the bar, a pole vaulter should use the jack-knife movement.

22. A football player running directly into the line, is hit at a 90 degree angle by the linebacker, will gain yardage and pick up speed at the moment of contact.

23. Bend arms at take-off when using rigid pole and keep arms straight when using fiberglass pole.

24. Warm-up vaults and total vaults should be limited.

25. Strive for height in the long jump.

26. The ideal angle of take off in the long jump is approximately 25 degrees.

27. Spring step before the take-off in the high jump.

28. The velocity of the shot should continually increase from the start across the circle until release.

29. Create power for the shot put.

30. Rotate through 180 degrees in putting the shot.

31. Continually increase the velocity of shot from the start to the release.

32. The putting foot should be in contact with the ground during the thrust of the shot.

33. The angle of put for the shot is less than 45 degrees.

34. Holding the shot away from the neck gives greater velocity to the shot before the reverse.

35. Attain as many degrees of rotation as possible in the discus throw.

36. Other things being equal the person with the longest arm should become a better discus thrower.

37. Keep arm extended when throwing the discus.

38. Release the discus when the throwing arm is in line with the shoulder.

39. Impart spin to the discus.

40. Throw into a slight wind with the discus when possible.

41. Release the discus at about a 30 degree angle.

42. Take advantage of running in throwing the javelin.

43. Throw the javelin at approximately a 30 degree angle.

44. Baseball pitchers should start pitch with striding foot back of the pitcher's rubber.

45. Do not palm the ball while throwing.

46. Throw ball from finger tips.

47. Recoil in catching the ball.

48. A right-handed batter can develop the greater velocity in running to first base.

49. Do not hop when taking a lead off of a base.

50. Flatten body out on ground when sliding into a base.

51. On hitting a ball extend bat with arms straight.

52. A bunted ball will more likely deviate from its angle of incidence more than a hard hit ball.

Name: _____

53. Hit a slow ball harder than a fast ball to get the same distance.

54. Keep feet in contact with the ground when taking a lead off base.

55. Run through first base.

56. Lean toward the infield when rounding first base.

57. Swing the leg across the median line of the body in punting a football.

58. A football charge should be more vertical than horizontal.

59. A ball carrier should use the straight arm if being tackled.

60. The angle of lean of a driving fullback partially determines the magnitude of forces on contact.

61. Put spin on a football when throwing.

62. Hop on last step before punting a football.

63. Drop a football from as short a distance as possible when punting.

64. The body leaves the ground after the football is punted.

65. Kick low into the wind and high with the wind.

66. In starting and stopping quickly plant both feet.

67. In place kicking, contact the ball below the center of gravity of the ball.

68. In falling on a loose football spread out over the ground and ball.

69. The stance a football player takes depends to a larger extent on the objective of the offensive formation.

70. Get low and close to the man to be blocked so that the charge is more vertical than horizontal.

71. Be relaxed catching a football.

72. Football pads are built to spread the force of impact over a larger area.

73. Keep the head between the arms when entering the water.

74. Drop the heels as the push-off starts in the racing start.

75. Extend toes and thrust arms upward on the swimming start.

76. Keep the hands and arms at 90 degrees with the direction of movement in the water as long as possible.

77. A diver leans when diving off a board.

78. The height of the hurdle in diving determines the height of the dive.

79. Throw hand close to major axis of the body to begin twist in diving.

80. A good basketball shooter puts reverse spin on the basketball.

81. A high jumper and basketball player will get greater height by stepping or hopping before the take-off.

82. Arch of a basketball can compensate for inaccuracies in shooting.

83. In basketball jumping extend the legs downward and swing the arm downward sharply just before the maximum height of the jump is attained.

84. A basketball player should have his feet flat on the floor, knees bent and thrust arms upward at the beginning of a jump.

85. Catch a basketball as far away from the body as possible.

86. The golf club used determines the distance.

87. Hitting a golf ball off center will cause it to slice off hook.

88. In driving in golf, grip the club firmly on impact.

89. Take a good stance in addressing the golf ball.

90. In serving in tennis the head of the racquet is forward of the hand.

91. Make sure you take a good grip with the tennis racquet.

92. In returning a tennis ball the racquet should be held at arms length.

93. In rope climbing the center of gravity should be directly below the hands.

94. The front arm should be kept straight in driving a golf ball.

95. Snap the wrists before impact in baseball, golf ball, etc.

96. Serve volleyball by striking ball in upper right quadrant, in overhead serve.

97. Wear good shoes while playing basketball.

98. Take advantage of effective force in running.

99. The stance an athlete takes is partially determined by his strength.

100. Slow a bowling ball down in order to get a greater curve.

18
SPORT ACTIVITY ANALYSIS

Instructions

On the following pages are a number of pictures of common sport activities. The list is obviously not exhaustive by any means. Evaluate each of these by suggesting coaching points, teaching cues and identifying biomechanical principles that could apply to each skill.

18.1 Racquetball Serve

Coaching Points:

1. _____

_____

2. _____

_____

3. _____

_____

Teaching Cues:

1. _____

_____

2. _____

_____

3. _____

_____

Mechanical Principles:

1. _____

_____

2. _____

_____

3. _____

_____

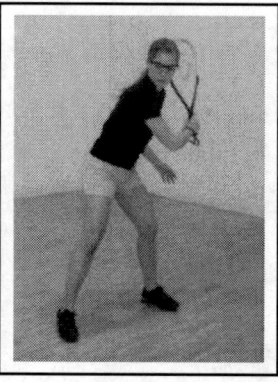

18.2 Racquetball Backhand

Coaching Points:

1. _____

_____

2. _____

_____

3. _____

_____

Teaching Cues:

1. _____

_____

2. _____

_____

3. _____

_____

Mechanical Principles:

1. _____

_____

2. _____

_____

3. _____

_____

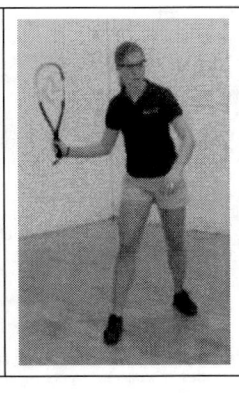

18.3 Racquetball Forehand

Coaching Points:

1. _____

_____

2. _____

_____

3. _____

_____

Teaching Cues:

1. _____

_____

2. _____

_____

3. _____

_____

Mechanical Principles:

1. _____

_____

2. _____

_____

3. _____

_____

18.4 Badminton Clear

Coaching Points:

1. _____

_____

2. _____

_____

3. _____

_____

Teaching Cues:

1. _____

_____

2. _____

_____

3. _____

_____

Mechanical Principles:

1. _____

_____

2. _____

_____

3. _____

_____

18.5 Basketball Layup

Coaching Points:

1. _____

_____

2. _____

_____

3. _____

_____

Teaching Cues:

1. _____

_____

2. _____

_____

3. _____

_____

Mechanical Principles:

1. _____

_____

2. _____

_____

3. _____

_____

18.6 Basketball Jump Shot

Coaching Points:

1. _____

   _____

2. _____

   _____

3. _____

   _____

Teaching Cues:

1. _____

   _____

2. _____

   _____

3. _____

   _____

Mechanical Principles:

1. _____

   _____

2. _____

   _____

3. _____

   _____

18.7 Martial Arts Absorbing Shock

Coaching Points:

1. _____

_____

2. _____

_____

3. _____

_____

Teaching Cues:

1. _____

_____

2. _____

_____

3. _____

_____

Mechanical Principles:

1. _____

_____

2. _____

_____

3. _____

_____

18.8 Olympic Weight Lifting Clean

Coaching Points:

1. _____

_____

2. _____

_____

3. _____

_____

Teaching Cues:

1. _____

_____

2. _____

_____

3. _____

_____

Mechanical Principles:

1. _____

_____

2. _____

_____

3. _____

_____

18.9 Olympic Weight Lifting Jerk

Coaching Points:

1. _____

   _____

2. _____

   _____

3. _____

   _____

Teaching Cues:

1. _____

   _____

2. _____

   _____

3. _____

   _____

Mechanical Principles:

1. _____

   _____

2. _____

   _____

3. _____

   _____

18.10 Olympic Weight Lifting Snatch

Coaching Points:

1. _____

_____

2. _____

_____

3. _____

_____

Teaching Cues:

1. _____

_____

2. _____

_____

3. _____

_____

Mechanical Principles:

1. _____

_____

2. _____

_____

3. _____

_____

18.11 Softball Fielding

Coaching Points:

1. _____

_____

2. _____

_____

3. _____

_____

Teaching Cues:

1. _____

_____

2. _____

_____

3. _____

_____

Mechanical Principles:

1. _____

_____

2. _____

_____

3. _____

_____

18.12 Gymnastics Front Scale

Coaching Points:

1. _____

_____

2. _____

_____

3. _____

_____

Teaching Cues:

1. _____

_____

2. _____

_____

3. _____

_____

Mechanical Principles:

1. _____

_____

2. _____

_____

3. _____

_____

18.13 Gymnastics Head Stand and Hand Stand

Coaching Points:

1. _____

   _____

2. _____

   _____

3. _____

   _____

Teaching Cues:

1. _____

   _____

2. _____

   _____

3. _____

   _____

Mechanical Principles:

1. _____

   _____

2. _____

   _____

3. _____

   _____

18.14 Power Lifting Bench Press

Coaching Points:

1. _____

_____

2. _____

_____

3. _____

_____

Teaching Cues:

1. _____

_____

2. _____

_____

3. _____

_____

Mechanical Principles:

1. _____

_____

2. _____

_____

3. _____

_____

18.15 Power Lifting Dead Lift

Coaching Points:

1. _____

_____

2. _____

_____

3. _____

_____

Teaching Cues:

1. _____

_____

2. _____

_____

3. _____

_____

Mechanical Principles:

1. _____

_____

2. _____

_____

3. _____

_____

18.16 Power Lifting Squat

Coaching Points:

1. _____

_____

2. _____

_____

3. _____

_____

Teaching Cues:

1. _____

_____

2. _____

_____

3. _____

_____

Mechanical Principles:

1. _____

_____

2. _____

_____

3. _____

_____

18.17 Tennis Forehand

Coaching Points:

1. _____

   _____

2. _____

   _____

3. _____

   _____

Teaching Cues:

1. _____

   _____

2. _____

   _____

3. _____

   _____

Mechanical Principles:

1. _____

   _____

2. _____

   _____

3. _____

   _____

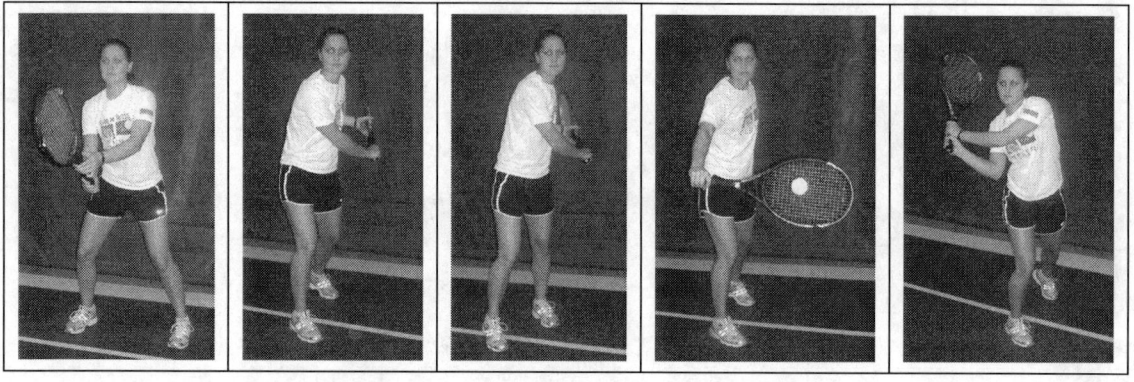

18.18 Tennis Backhand

Coaching Points:

1. _____

   _____

2. _____

   _____

3. _____

   _____

Teaching Cues:

1. _____

   _____

2. _____

   _____

3. _____

   _____

Mechanical Principles:

1. _____

   _____

2. _____

   _____

3. _____

   _____

18.19 Tennis Volley

Coaching Points:

1. _____

_____

2. _____

_____

3. _____

_____

Teaching Cues:

1. _____

_____

2. _____

_____

3. _____

_____

Mechanical Principles:

1. _____

_____

2. _____

_____

3. _____

_____

18.20 Tennis Two Hand

Coaching Points:

1. _____

_____

2. _____

_____

3. _____

_____

Teaching Cues:

1. _____

_____

2. _____

_____

3. _____

_____

Mechanical Principles:

1. _____

_____

2. _____

_____

3. _____

_____

19
MECHANICAL ANALYSIS

Directions: On the following pages, coaching points for selected Physical Education skills are listed. In the space to the right of each coaching point write in the mechanical principle illustrated.

Basketball—Two-Handed Chest Pass

Coaching Points	Mechanical Principles
1. The ball is held in both hands, the fingers spread on the sides of the ball slightly to the rear, with the thumbs pointed toward the inside.	1. _____ _____ _____ _____
2. The ball is retained in a position about chest height directly in front of the body and about one foot from the body.	2. _____ _____ _____ _____
3. Knees should be slightly flexed and the body slightly bent forward. The feet should be shoulder width apart.	3. _____ _____ _____
4. The ball is brought back toward the chest, the elbows are held in close, and wrists are extended.	4. _____ _____ _____
5. The arms are bent and the wrists cocked as the center of gravity is shifted forward.	5. _____ _____ _____
6. The back foot pushes against the floor to create force in the direction of movement.	6. _____ _____
7. The elbows are kept close to the body and the ball is released by extending the arms fully, snapping the wrists, and stepping in the direction of the pass.	7. _____ _____ _____ _____
8. The final impetus is put on the ball by the wrist snap ending with palms facing outward.	8. _____ _____ _____

Basketball—Catching the Ball

Coaching Points	Mechanical Principles
1. Receiver should have eyes directly on approaching ball.	1. _____ _____
2. Receiver should move in the direction of the approaching ball in order to meet it.	2. _____ _____ _____
3. Body should be slightly crouched and in a relatively good maneuvering position.	3. _____ _____ _____
4. The posture of the person catching the basketball should be such that his hands and arms are free to absorb the shock of the impact of the catch.	4. _____ _____ _____ _____ _____
5. In catching the ball, the fingers should be comfortably spread and relaxed.	5. _____ _____ _____
6. As the ball comes into the hands, the fingers should be closed around it.	6. _____ _____ _____
7. The hands should be allowed to "give" with the ball.	7. _____ _____
8. Shift the weight from the forward foot to the back foot.	8. _____ _____

Jump Ball

Coaching Points	Mechanical Principles
1. Feet should be separated and staggered.	1. _____ _____
2. Flexion of ankle, knee, and hip joint with trunk inclined slightly forward.	2. _____ _____ _____
3. Extend both legs forcefully.	3. _____ _____
4. Arms should swing upward and one arm should be forced down just before height of jump is reached.	4. _____ _____ _____ _____
5. All movement should be as nearly vertical as possible.	5. _____ _____
6. As feet touch floor, ankle, knee and hip joints flex.	6. _____ _____

Basketball — One Hand Jump Shot

Coaching Points	**Mechanical Principles**
1. The ball is held in both hands, at about chest level, with fingers and thumb of right hand comfortably spread.	1. _____ _____ _____ _____
2. The ball is brought up with both hands as the jump is started. With the shooting hand in back of the ball and the balancing hand on the side.	2. _____ _____ _____ _____ _____ _____
3. Both knees flex slightly, and the jump is made as the ball is raised directly above the head to a height of about six to twelve inches. The right elbow is flexed at approximately a 90 degree angle.	3. _____ _____ _____ _____ _____ _____
4. At the height of the jump, the legs are extended, the ball is released toward the basket by releasing the left hand from the ball and using a combination of right arm and wrist, giving power and aim to the ball. The ball is shot with backspin.	4. _____ _____ _____ _____ _____ _____ _____ _____
5. Follow through with the shooting arm.	5. _____ _____
6. Attempt to land on the take-off place.	6. _____ _____
7. The head is kept up and the eyes are on the front of the rim of the basket.	7. _____ _____ _____

Badminton — Service

Coaching Points	Mechanical Principles
1. Stand in comfortable position with weight evenly distributed, and on balls of feet.	1. _____ _____ _____
2. In singles, the left foot will usually be forward for the right-handed server.	2. _____ _____ _____
3. Drop the shuttle from a low height.	3. _____ _____
4. The backswing is specific to the server, depth of serve, racket, type of shuttle, etc.	4. _____ _____ _____
5. Swing the racket forward with a straight arm.	5. _____ _____
6. Have the wrist cocked as the arm is swinging forward.	6. _____ _____
7. Extend the wrist at the point of contact.	7. _____ _____
8. Follow through with the swing.	8. _____
9. Allow the momentum of the followthrough to bring you around into a "set" position.	9. _____ _____ _____

Three Point Balanced Football Stance

Coaching Points	Mechanical Principles
1. The feet are shoulder width with either the right or left foot back, use a heel and toe combination.	1. _____ _____ _____
2. The hand that is down corresponds to the foot that is staggered while the other arm rests comfortable across the thigh of the leg.	2. _____ _____ _____ _____ _____
3. Shoulders and hips should be on a straight line.	3. _____ _____
4. Head up and eyes looking directly ahead.	4. _____ _____

Football — Defensive Line Stance (4 Point)

Coaching Points	Mechanical Principles
1. The feet and hands should be at least shoulder width.	1. _____ _____
2. The stance should be one that will allow the defensive lineman to react to a drive block, cross block, trap, etc.	2. _____ _____ _____ _____
3. The center of gravity should be lower than the track start.	3. _____ _____
4. The body weight should be mostly on the balls of the feet.	4. _____ _____
5. The back should be parallel to the ground.	5. _____ _____
6. The head should be in a position conducive to seeing any movement by the offensive line.	6. _____ _____ _____
7. When the defensive man fires out, he should take short quick steps.	7. _____ _____

Dodging

Coaching Points	Mechanical Principles
1. Dodging consists of quickly changing the direction of the motion of the body.	1. _____ _____ _____
2. Throw one foot ahead of the center of gravity and lean away from the direction of the original motion.	2. _____ _____ _____
3. The knees are bent to drop the center of gravity near the base.	3. _____ _____
4. The amount of lean and dip depends on the speed with which the player is moving.	4. _____ _____ _____
5. The player springs quickly and forcefully in another direction.	5. _____ _____

Forward Pass

Coaching Points	Mechanical Principles
1. Stand with left foot forward.	1. _____ _____
2. Weight shifts to the right allowing hips to rotate to the right.	2. _____ _____
3. Grip of the football depends on the size of the hand of the passer (hold with two hands).	3. _____ _____ _____
4. Bring ball behind ear with elbow and wrist cocked.	4. _____ _____
5. Rotate hips as arm is brought forward.	5. _____ _____
6. The trunk, shoulders and spine rotate to the left.	6. _____ _____
7. Rotate the shoulders, arm and wrist forward.	7. _____ _____
8. Wrist is uncocked.	8. _____ _____
9. Ball rolls off fingers as it is released.	9. _____ _____
10. Arm continues down across body as body rotates in direction of throw.	10. _____ _____ _____

Football — Catching (Over the Receiver's Shoulder)

Coaching Points	**Mechanical Principles**

1. To catch the ball over the shoulder, the receiver should extend his hands so that the palms are facing the ball with the little fingers almost touching each other.

1. _____
   _____
   _____
   _____
   _____

2. The elbows should be close together: The hands and elbows actually form a basket.

2. _____
   _____
   _____

3. The hands should give with the force of the ball and lessen the impact of the ball and make it easier to hold.

3. _____
   _____
   _____
   _____

4. If necessary to leap into the air for the ball, the receiver takes off from one foot and lands on the opposite foot.

4. _____
   _____
   _____
   _____

5. Watch the ball until it is securely held in the hands.

5. _____
   _____

267

Football — Punt

Coaching Points	Mechanical Principles
1. The right foot should be slightly in front of the left foot.	1. _____ _____
2. The knees should be flexed slightly and the position should be one that will allow the punter to move quickly to the right or left or to jump to catch a bad snap.	2. _____ _____ _____ _____ _____
3. The first step is a short jab step with the right foot. The second step is a hop.	3. _____ _____ _____
4. The right leg is flexed so that it is almost touching the gluteal group.	4. _____ _____
5. As the left foot contacts the ground, the right leg starts forward and the ball is dropped with the nose slightly down.	5. _____ _____ _____ _____
6. The lower leg and right front are extended as the entire leg is thrown in an arc toward the midline of the body.	6. _____ _____
7. The boney portion and the right side of the foot should contact the ball near the minor axis of the ball.	7. _____ _____ _____ _____
8. As contact is made with the ball the knee should be locked.	8. _____ _____
9. The kicking foot should end up in front of the left shoulder.	9. _____ _____

268

Golf — Iron Shot

Coaching Points	Mechanical Principles
1. Ball is opposite the center of the body.	1. _____ _____
2. Feet are a short stride apart (closer than shoulder width) and the club is a few degrees short of perpendicular to the line of flight.	2. _____ _____ _____ _____
3. Club leads on the backswing, left arm is straight, pivoting around a vertical line of balance.	3. _____ _____ _____
4. Head remains still and the eyes focus on the ball.	4. _____ _____
5. The clubhead position at the top of the backswing is slightly more than vertical. (Shorter than wood shot)	5. _____ _____ _____ _____
6. Left side (right handed golfer) leads on the forward swing, left arm is straight.	6. _____ _____ _____
7. Wrists uncock just before contacting the ball.	7. _____ _____
8. Ball is contacted on the downswing.	8. _____ _____
9. Hips rotate to the left as the club head follows through to a vertical position.	9. _____ _____ _____

Tumbling — Hand-Head Stand

Coaching Points	**Mechanical Principles**

1. The hands are placed on the floor and slightly wider than shoulder width with the fingers pointed forward and spread apart.

   1. _____
      _____
      _____
      _____

2. The closer the hands are placed between the feet, the easier the press will be.

   2. _____
      _____
      _____

3. The front part of the head is placed on the floor about a foot in front of the hands.

   3. _____
      _____

4. From this position the hips are raised slowly by pushing hard with the arms until the center of gravity is over the points of support.

   4. _____
      _____
      _____
      _____
      _____

5. From this position the legs are raised overhead and at the same time close together.

   5. _____
      _____
      _____

6. The balance should be held in a slight arch with the weight primarily on the front of the head, but not completely removed from the hands.

   6. _____
      _____
      _____
      _____
      _____

Tumbling — Kip Up

Coaching Points	Mechanical Principles
1. Lie down on back. Raise straight legs upward and roll backward into a kip position. Place hands on mat with thumbs in.	1. _____ _____ _____ _____
2. Slowly roll downward and kick straight legs upward and outward.	2. _____ _____ _____
3. At the same time push off forcefully with hands and arch the back.	3. _____ _____ _____
4. Land on the balls of feet with toes pointed outward, with feet under body and knees straight.	4. _____ _____ _____
5. Flex the hips upon landing.	5. _____ _____
6. Keep arms stretched overhead with the head back.	6. _____ _____

Tumbling — Running Forward Somersault

Coaching Points	Mechanical Principles
1. Take a short running approach, skipping on the left foot and as you bring the right foot forward, raise arms overhead and land on both feet.	1. _____ _____ _____ _____
2. Swing arms upward as the take-off is executed.	2. _____ _____
3. Tuck the chin to the chest and circle arms forward and downward until both shins are grasped forming a tuck position.	3. _____ _____ _____ _____
4. During the somersault, the chest should be close to the knees and the heels close to the buttocks.	4. _____ _____ _____
5. Slightly before completing the somersault, shoot out of the tuck position and land on mat in upright position with the knees slightly flexed.	5. _____ _____ _____ _____ _____

Tumbling — Round Off

Coaching Points	**Mechanical Principles**
1. Take a good run, skip on the right foot and bring the left foot forward.	1. _____ _____ _____
2. Place the left foot on the ground, bend forward at the waist and place the left hand on the mat about two feet in front of the left foot.	2. _____ _____ _____ _____ _____
3. Kick the right foot overhead followed by the left and place the right hand on the mat in front and slightly to the left of the left hand.	3. _____ _____ _____ _____
4. The hands and arms pivot to the left and the body turns to the left.	4. _____ _____
5. The fingers of both hands are pointing toward the left edge of the mat.	5. _____ _____ _____
6. When the feet pass overhead execute a half turn. Snap the feet down from the waist and simultaneously push off the mat by extending the shoulders and flexing the wrists.	6. _____ _____ _____ _____ _____ _____
7. Land on both feet facing in the direction opposite from that of starting. When the feet strike the ground, bounce off the balls of the feet.	7. _____ _____ _____ _____ _____
8. Keep the eyes trained on a spot about six inches in front of the hands during the entire trick.	8. _____ _____ _____

Flank Vault

Coaching Points	Mechanical Principles
1. The running approach should be fast and smooth. Begin with a slow start, quickly increasing speed. The last couple of strides should be floating steps, maintaining the existing speed, in preparation for the takeoff, or hurdle; there should be no hesitation.	1. _____ _____ _____ _____ _____ _____ _____ _____
2. The last contact with the floor should be made two to three feet from the take-off board.	2. _____ _____ _____
3. As the vaulter comes down, both feet should contact the board at the greatest spring. At the time of contact the body should be leaning backwards, slightly.	3. _____ _____ _____ _____ _____
4. As the vaulter comes down on the board, ankles, knees, and hips should flex, but the upper body should remain erect.	4. _____ _____ _____ _____
5. With the push-off the body should uncoil and the arms should be thrust forward and upward in preparation for the vault.	5. _____ _____ _____ _____
6. In the pre-flight, the hips should be driven high and the body should be held in a stretched position until contact is made with the horse.	6. _____ _____ _____ _____ _____

Flank Vault (continued)

Coaching Points	Mechanical Principles

7. Hand contact on top of the horse should only be momentary. Elbows remain straight throughout the vault, but hands and wrists execute a forceful push-off.

7. _____
_____
_____
_____
_____

8. For the flank vault, the vaulter should begin from a two-foot take-off, place both hands on top of the horse. Lift the hips and legs high and sideways so that the side of the body is horizontal to the horse. As the legs pass over the horse, extend the hips to a horizontal position and raise the top arm.

8. _____
_____
_____
_____
_____
_____
_____
_____
_____
_____

9. The landing should be made with the knees and hips flexed.

9. _____
_____

Parallel Bars — Hand Stand

Coaching Points	Mechanical Principles
1. When executing the handstand from a straight arm support position, swing from the shoulders with the arms held straight.	1. _____ _____ _____ _____
2. When ready to swing to the hand stand, arch at the front end of the swing and keep the body arched throughout the back swing.	2. _____ _____ _____ _____
3. Allow the feet to swing over the head, keeping the shoulders over the hands.	3. _____ _____ _____
4. Flex the arms slightly if needed, if going off balance, grip hard with the hands to maintain the balance. Lean the head forward until the balance point is approached.	4. _____ _____ _____ _____ _____
5. In returning from the hand balance position, do not allow the body to swing freely back to the straight arm support position. Slow down the swing with the shoulders and upper back muscles by leaning forward slightly.	5. _____ _____ _____ _____ _____ _____

Back Hip Circle Mount Uneven Parallel Bars

Coaching Points	Mechanical Principles
1. After two foot take-off on reuther board, grasp low bar and allow shoulders to go forward keeping arms straight.	1. _____ _____ _____ _____
2. Extend body completely to reach a horizontal position. Shoulders are forward of low bar.	2. _____ _____ _____
3. Bring body to bar.	3. _____ _____
4. When hips contact bar, flex and continue with back hip circle.	4. _____ _____
5. Body opens as hips come over top of bar.	5. _____ _____

Glide Kip
Uneven Parallel Bars
Horizontal and Parallel Bars

Coaching Points	**Mechanical Principles**

Starting position:
    Standing facing low bar, arms
    extended, shoulders relaxed

1. Jump up and forward, lifting hips backward. Hips stay flexed as body glides under bar to an extended position.

1. _____
   _____
   _____
   _____

2. After reaching full extension; body pikes sharply; ankles are lifted to bar.

2. _____
   _____
   _____

3. Legs are lifted upward until bar is at hip level, then swing outward and downward, pushing down with arms and rotating grip to finish in front support.

3. _____
   _____
   _____
   _____
   _____

Overhand Throw

Coaching Points	Mechanical Principles
1. Stand with the left foot forward.	1. _____ _____
2. Rotation and weight shift to the right. Rotate hips and torso to the right.	2. _____ _____ _____ _____
3. Bring arm back behind head with the wrist cocked.	3. _____ _____
4. Ball is held with first two fingers on top, thumb underneath, and the third and fourth fingers on the side.	4. _____ _____ _____ _____ _____
5. Rotate hips forward as arm is brought forward.	5. _____ _____
6. The trunk, shoulders, and spine bend laterally, rotating to the left.	6. _____ _____
7. Medial rotation of shoulders, arm and wrist rotate forward.	7. _____ _____
8. Wrist is uncocked.	8. _____ _____
9. Ball rolls off fingers as it is released.	9. _____ _____
10. Release ball at desired angle.	10. _____ _____
11. Arm continues down across body, as body rotates in direction of throw.	11. _____ _____ _____

Softball — Fielding Ground Ball

Coaching Points	Mechanical Principles
1. Body position should be in the line as that of the ball.	1. _____ _____
2. Waiting position, one is ready for action in any direction.	2. _____ _____
3. Flex the knees and bend over at the waist.	3. _____ _____
4. Relax hands and fingers.	4. _____ _____
5. Field the ball slightly to the inside of the forward foot.	5. _____ _____
6. Field the ball on the short hop whenever possible or at the apex of the long hop.	6. _____ _____ _____
7. Shift the weight from the slightly extended forward foot to the back foot.	7. _____ _____ _____

Softball — Bunting

Coaching Points	Mechanical Principles
1. Batter stands in a position for a normal swing. As pitcher releases the ball he rotates his body at the hips, a 90 degree angle with the starting position. He twists up on his right toe and left heel and bends his knees and waist to a 45 degree angle.	1. _____ _____ _____ _____ _____ _____ _____
2. The hands slide up the bat to just below the brand on the bat. The arms are extended toward the pitcher. The bat is parallel with the ground. The grip is firm on the bat.	2. _____ _____ _____ _____ _____ _____
3. The bat is moved up and down in a parallel line with flight of the ball. The ball strikes the bat. As ball makes contact, the hands recoil the bat.	3. _____ _____ _____ _____ _____
4. The angle of projection depends on the angle of the bat when contact is made with the ball.	4. _____ _____ _____

Hitting

Coaching Points	Mechanical Principles
1. The feet are about shoulder width apart, with the knees flexed, and the trunk slightly bent, weight is slightly to the back leg.	1. _____ _____
2. The position of the hands on the bat must be adjusted to the strength of the grip, wrists, arms, and the weight of the bat.	2. _____ _____ _____ _____
3. The front foot should be moved in the direction of the pitch.	3. _____ _____
4. As the foot is placed, the body starts to rotate at the shoulder and hips.	4. _____ _____ _____
5. The forearms extend, and as the ball is met, the wrists are extended.	5. _____ _____ _____
6. The bat should be swung in line with the ball, and the ball should be met out in front of the plate so that the bat is at right angles to the line of the shoulders and with the arms fully extended.	6. _____ _____ _____ _____ _____ _____
7. At impact, both the grip and rigidity of the back leg must be firm.	7. _____ _____
8. The swing must be timed to meet the ball at the proper angle if the ball is to be placed.	8. _____ _____ _____

Forward Swimming Start

Coaching Points	Mechanical Principles
1. Swimmer assumes standing position on the block and wraps his toes over the front edge.	1. _____ _____ _____
2. Upon the command, the swimmer bends forward at the trunk and bends his knees slightly. Arms are placed in front and hang straight down with palms facing back. Center of gravity is above the balls of his feet.	2. _____ _____ _____ _____ _____ _____ _____ _____
3. When the gun fires, the swimmer moves arms upward, outward, and forward. Knees are flexed. Body movement is forward.	3. _____ _____ _____ _____ _____
4. Arms begin to move backward in swing. With center of gravity in front of body, the swimmer falls toward the water. Hips and knees flexed.	4. _____ _____ _____ _____ _____ _____
5. Arms continue to make the circular swinging motion and begin to move forward. Hips and knees start to extend.	5. _____ _____ _____ _____
6. Arm swing stops with arms below and in front of swimmer. Ankles extend, followed by push from the big toes.	6. _____ _____ _____ _____
7 Swimmer is completely extended in the air. Hands are together and toes are pointed.	7. _____ _____ _____
8. Hands enter water first, followed by rest of body.	8. _____ _____

Back Crawl Stroke

Coaching Points	Mechanical Principles
1. Body should be as streamlined or horizontal as possible and still permit the arms and legs to perform their function.	1. _____ _____ _____ _____
2. Arm enters water directly over shoulder with little finger entering first.	2. _____ _____ _____
3. The arm sinks into the water and as the pull is initiated, the elbow begins to bend. The swimmer rotates on his longitudinal axis to put that shoulder more into the water.	3. _____ _____ _____ _____ _____ _____
4. Elbow continues to bend as the arm pulls to midline of the swimmer.	4. _____ _____ _____
5. At the end of the pull, the hand is pressed downward to help raise the shoulder.	5. _____ _____ _____
6. The arm starts its recovery as the body rolls to the other side. Arm continues recovery as it reaches above the shoulder.	6. _____ _____ _____ _____
7. Repeat stroke without pause. Use continuous stroking.	7. _____ _____

Back Crawl Stroke

Coaching Points	Mechanical Principles
1. Body should be as streamlined or horizontal as possible and still permit the arms and legs to perform their function of creating propulsion.	1. _____ _____ _____ _____ _____
2. Hand enters water with palm facing downward and elbow high.	2. _____ _____
3. Hand continues to sink downward for the catch. As the hand presses downward, the elbow starts to bend.	3. _____ _____ _____ _____
4. Hand begins to move toward center line of body. As pulling hand accomplishes ½ of pull the head starts to rotate on its longitudinal axis.	4. _____ _____ _____ _____ _____
5. Head turns to side but does *not* lift out of the water. Hand continues to press backward.	5. _____ _____ _____
6. As swimmer inhales, the hand completes the pull and begins the recovery. Head rotates so that face goes back into water as swimmer recovers with high elbow recovery.	6. _____ _____ _____ _____ _____

Swimming — Breast Stroke

Coaching Points	Mechanical Principles
1. During the whip kick, the knees should be flexed approximately 90 degrees on the recovery. Rotate the feet outward.	1. _____ _____ _____ _____
2. The circular, whipping action should press out, back, and in.	2. _____ _____
3. The knees should separate no more than body width apart. Full leg extension as the kick finishes.	3. _____ _____ _____
4. The arm pull uses a deep catch (6-8 in.). The pull takes the hands diagonally outward and downward until they are about twelve inches apart, then the elbows bend slightly and the arms rotate medially.	4. _____ _____ _____ _____ _____ _____ _____
5. The arm power should start slowly and build-up to maximum.	5. _____ _____
6. The elbows should never go beyond shoulder level to the pull.	6. _____ _____
7. The recovery takes the hands under the chin and shoots them forward.	7. _____ _____ _____
8. Glide in a full extension. Lift the head just high enough to breathe.	8. _____ _____

Forward Approach

Coaching Points	Mechanical Principles
1. Diver assumes a natural standing position.	1. _____ _____
2. Diver leans forward and takes his first step. The arms move backwards.	2. _____ _____
3. Forward movement of the diver is continued. Arms begin to swing forward in the sagital planes.	3. _____ _____ _____
4. Left knee is lifted and flexed. Right leg pushes by extending the knee and ankle.	4. _____ _____ _____
5. Arms reach above the head with all elbow joints extended. The body is lifted off the board.	5. _____ _____ _____
6. As body begins to return to the board both knees are extended, arms press downward through the transverse plane of the body.	6. _____ _____ _____ _____
7. As the body depresses the board, the knees and hips flex. Weight of body continues to depress the board.	7. _____ _____ _____ _____
8. As the board returns from the press, the knees are extended and then the hips.	8. _____ _____ _____
9. The arms reach out in the sagital plane.	9. _____ _____
10. The body is completely extended as the body leaves the board.	10. _____ _____

Forward Dive — Pike Position

Coaching Points	Mechanical Principles

Coaching Points

1. Diver leaves the board with all joints extended. He is leaning slightly forward as the board lifts him into the air.

2. Once in the air, the direction and height of the dive cannot be changed.

3. Diver begins to push his hips upward and flexes at the hips. Arms reach for toes.

4. Diver touches his ankles at the apex of the dive. The diver holds this position while the body spins until the hips and shoulders are in an almost vertical position.

5. The legs begin to move away from the body and the arms are moved away from the legs. The rotation motion begins to slow.

6. The body straightens out until the hips and body are completely extended. The rotation of the body is stopped.

7. The diver enters the water in a vertical position with all joints extended.

Mechanical Principles

1. _____

2. _____

3. _____

4. _____

5. _____

6. _____

7. _____

Reverse Dive — Somersault — Pike Position

Coaching Points	Mechanical Principles
1. Diver leaves the board with all joints extended. He is leaning slightly forward as the board lifts him into the air.	1. _____ _____ _____ _____
2. Once in the air, the direction and height of the dive cannot be changed.	2. _____ _____ _____
3. The legs with the knees extended are brought up as the hands move to meet the legs in front of the chest. Hips rotate downward.	3. _____ _____ _____ _____
4. As the diver assumes the pike position the velocity of rotation increases.	4. _____ _____ _____
5. The pike position is kept tight by flexing the elbows and pulling in the legs.	5. _____ _____ _____
6. When the diver "spots" the water, he releases his knees and begins to straighten out of the pike.	6. _____ _____ _____

Diving Gainer (Tuck Position)

Coaching Points	Mechanical Principles
1. The approach of a running dive includes three steps and a jump.	1. _____
2. As the jump begins the arms are lifted to a point just above shoulder height and the leg opposite the take-off foot should be lifted so that the thigh is at right angles to the body.	2. _____
3. The diver will land near the end of the board on both feet as the arms are brought down.	3. _____
4. As the board is depressed the knees are flexed and the arms are brought to a position of extension.	4. _____
5. When the peak of the dive is reached, the diver should bring his knees to his chest and grap his knees with his hands.	5. _____
6. His head should be thrown back and this position should be held until the flip is completed.	6. _____
7. The legs should be straightened out and the arms put along the side.	7. _____
8. The toes should be pointed with the body straight as the diver enters the water.	8. _____

Diving — Forward One and a Half with Half Twist

Coaching Points	Mechanical Principles
1. The angle of lean must be small so that greater height can be reached.	1. _____ _____ _____
2. As the reach is made in the take off, the hips are lifted up and over the body as the shoulders and head are lowered with the chin in toward the chest as the body rotates forward.	2. _____ _____ _____ _____ _____ _____
3. The hands grasp the back of the knees and the elbows are held close to the hips.	3. _____ _____ _____
4. The legs are extended and the feet plantar flexed (toes pointed).	4. _____ _____
5. As the body falls from the peak of the dive and is in the V position, the trunk is held firm and the opening from the pike position is begun.	5. _____ _____ _____ _____ _____
6. The legs are pressed down and the head is pressed backward with the chin in.	6. _____ _____ _____
7. To start the half twist, movement of the arms in one direction will cause the body to move in the opposite direction.	7. _____ _____ _____ _____
8. Bring one arm in next to the body and the radius of rotation is shorter.	8. _____ _____ _____
9. The legs are driven backward and upward as the trunk remains firm as the body becomes straight for the entry into the water.	9. _____ _____ _____ _____

Tennis — Drive Service

Coaching Points	Mechanical Principles

Coaching Points

1. The body should be turned slightly sideways in relation to the net, with the left foot forming about a 45-degree angle with the baseline and the right foot parallel to the baseline.

2. The ball is thrown high enough so the arm will be fully extended when the racket hits the ball.

3. As the ball is thrown into the air, the weight of the body is shifted to the rear foot.

4. The racket is brought to the ball with a slight wrist action, and the ball met with a straight-arm stretch.

5. The rear foot should be in contact with the ground, with the leg rigid and extended, until after the ball has been contacted.

6. The racket face should contact the ball at a downward angle.

Mechanical Principles

1. _____
_____
_____
_____
_____
_____

2. _____
_____
_____

3. _____
_____
_____

4. _____
_____
_____
_____

5. _____
_____
_____
_____

6. _____
_____

Tennis — Forehand Drive

Coaching Points	Mechanical Principles
1. The body should be sideways to the net so the shoulders are parallel to the sideline.	1. _____ _____ _____
2. The backward swing of the racket should be executed with an extended arm and firm wrist, carrying the racket head on the hip level to a point opposite the right hip.	2. _____ _____ _____ _____ _____ _____
3. During the backswing, the weight of the body shifts to the right foot, and the upper body is pivoted to the right from the hips.	3. _____ _____ _____ _____
4. The knees are bent slightly.	4. _____ _____
5. The point of impact is opposite the left hip, and the arm should be fully extended.	5. _____ _____ _____
6. Continue to follow-through in the direction you wish the ball to go.	6. _____ _____

Name: _____

Tennis — Backhand Drive

Coaching Points	Mechanical Principles

Coaching Points

1. Eyes should be focused on the ball.

2. The body is turned with the right side toward net, weight on left foot.

3. Keep the fingers closed and the hand slightly tense so racket will be firm.

4. Bring the racket head back to the hip, and keep the elbow in close to the body.

5. Meet the ball squarely in front of the right knee.

6. Hit slightly beneath the center of the ball.

7. The weight is shifted forward when the ball is contacted with the knees slightly relaxed and with a little trunk rotation.

8. Let the racket head pull the elbow out so that the right arm is fully extended on the follow-through. The action describes that of a flowing movement and in a plane parallel to the ground.

9. Finish with the palm of the right hand turned up.

Mechanical Principles

1. _____

2. _____

3. _____

4. _____

5. _____

6. _____

7. _____

8. _____

9. _____

Track — Sprinters Bunch Start

Coaching Points	Mechanical Principles
1. The runner sets his blocks so the front foot is 12 to 20 inches from the starting line and the toes of the rear foot back about 11 inches or almost even with heel of the front.	1. _____ _____ _____ _____ _____ _____
2. Hands should be separated about the width of the shoulders and placed immediately behind and parallel to the starting line.	2. _____ _____ _____ _____ _____
3. Weight should be shifted forward until shoulders are directly over or slightly in front of hands.	3. _____ _____ _____ _____
4. Supporting hands, with thumb and index finger parallel and just behind starting line.	4. _____ _____ _____
5. Head should be down and the eyes focused down the track a few feet.	5. _____ _____
6. Knees should be kept directly in front of feet and pointing straight forward.	6. _____ _____ _____ _____
7. On the command of "Set" the sprinter raises his hips to a position slightly above the level of his head, while keeping both feet firmly against the blocks.	7. _____ _____ _____ _____ _____ _____
8. The body is inclined forward with shoulders approximately four inches in front of hands.	8. _____ _____ _____
9. First step out of blocks must come straight forward, not too long or too short, with the sprinter's power staying behind his hips.	9. _____ _____ _____ _____
10. Thrust opposite arm forward at gun.	10. _____ _____

Track Running (Distance)

Coaching Points	Mechanical Principles
1. The foot plant is flat. The roll to the inside comes through in the ball of the foot followed by a strong push.	1. _____ _____ _____ _____
2. The posture is held erect, with the flat back position of the lumbar spine flexed.	2. _____ _____ _____
3. When the feet leave the ground, float through the air.	3. _____ _____
4. The lower half of the rear leg is tucked and held high. The runner rolls in squarely over the lead foot. The lead foot is now under the body.	4. _____ _____ _____ _____ _____
5. The arms are bent to approximately ninety degrees and carried high. The forearms are parallel with the track.	5. _____ _____ _____ _____
6. There is a full driving extension of the rear leg followed by a firm push of the rear foot. The chest is thrust well forward. The hip and knee of the lead leg are now in a flexed position.	6. _____ _____ _____ _____ _____
7. Maintain a constant pace and stride.	7. _____ _____

Track — Discus

Coaching Points	Mechanical Principles

1. Hold the discus with the first joint of the fingers.

   1. _____
      _____

2. Place both feet near the back of the circle and rotate body on the backswing so that he is facing opposite from direction of movement.

   2. _____
      _____
      _____
      _____
      _____

3. Rotation should be as fast as the thrower can move and still maintain his balance.

   3. _____
      _____
      _____

4. Release arm needs to be straight when releasing the discus.

   4. _____
      _____

5. Need to release discus at right angle to radius connecting the center of rotation with release point.

   5. _____
      _____
      _____
      _____

6. Discus should be released at 35 degrees when head wind is less than 14 mph.

   6. _____
      _____
      _____

7. The discus should be released so as to let it spin in the air.

   7. _____
      _____

Shot Put

Coaching Points	Mechanical Principles
1. The shot is held upon the base of the first three fingers with the thumb in front.	1. _____ _____ _____
2. The shot putter's back is toward the front of circle. The left arm with elbow bent is pointed outward at shoulder height. The right foot is supporting most of the weight, with the left foot back.	2. _____ _____ _____ _____ _____ _____ _____
3. Putter starts the shift by lowering head and shoulders to where they are horizontal to the ground.	3. _____ _____ _____
4. Putter bends right knee to his greatest point of lifting power with his body weight on the ball of his foot.	4. _____ _____ _____ _____
5. Weight starts falling toward toe board with a powerful drive from the right leg and foot. Simultaneously, the left leg is kicking forward or toward toe board.	5. _____ _____ _____ _____ _____
6. The push starts as soon as the right foot is in the center of the circle.	6. _____ _____ _____
7. The weight of the body transfers to the left leg during delivery with both feet on the ground.	7. _____ _____ _____

Track — Javelin Throw

Coaching Points	Mechanical Principles

Coaching Points

1. To attain the speed essential, the thrower should approach the scratch line from a distance of 80 to 100 feet.

2. The run-up is relaxed; the javelin is carried overhead with the point slightly lower than the tail.

3. In executing the front cross step, cross step is slightly shorter than preceding steps, while the throwing step is extended.

4. Upon execution of the throw the forward foot or breaking foot is planted.

5. The flexed back leg then drives up into the hip.

6. The hips snap forward and the trunk flexes.

7. The free arm is thrust outward and downward away from the body.

8. The throwing arm follows ballistically, elbow leading to propel the javelin into flight from a point above the head.

9. A good and complete follow-through and a final wrist flip complete the throw.

Mechanical Principles

1. _____
_____
_____
_____

2. _____
_____
_____

3. _____
_____
_____
_____

4. _____
_____
_____

5. _____
_____

6. _____
_____

7. _____
_____
_____

8. _____
_____
_____
_____

9. _____
_____
_____

Track High Jump —
Fosbury Flop — Right Foot Take Off

Coaching Points	**Mechanical Principles**

1. The jumper runs to the bars at an angle of approximately 45 degrees and as he nears the bar changes direction to make a curve close to the bar in a direction nearly parallel to the bar as he plants his foot to make the take off.

   1. _____
   _____
   _____
   _____
   _____
   _____
   _____

2. The foot away from the bar is the take off foot. The final stride prior to jumping should be long, the take off foot stamped down as hard as possible with the leg in a fairly rigid position. The leg near the bar is swung upward as forcefully as possible.

   2. _____
   _____
   _____
   _____
   _____
   _____
   _____

3. The jump take off is vertical, near the bar so that the maximum force is used in gaining height and lean is reduced to a minimum.

   3. _____
   _____
   _____
   _____

4. Kick the free leg.

   4. _____
   _____

5. The back is toward the bar on take off. This means a body rotation of 90 degrees. The rotation can be accomplished by:

   5. _____
   _____
   _____
   _____

Track High Jump —
Fosbury Flop — Right Foot Take Off (continued)

Coaching Points	Mechanical Principles

a) A backward thrust of the right arm

b) A small rotation of the shoulders in a clockwise direction

c) A swing by the bent left leg

_____
_____
_____
_____
_____

6. When the shoulders rise above the bar, arch the back, which makes the head and shoulders and legs drop as the back is arched to clear the bar.

6. _____
_____
_____
_____
_____

7. When the back clears the bar, start to straighten the legs so they can clear the bar.

7. _____
_____
_____

8. Straighten the back and move the head forward. This will prevent the legs from knocking the bar off the standard.

8. _____
_____
_____
_____

9. After clearing the bar tuck the chin in, straighten the legs and hold at an angle of approximately 90 degrees with the body.

9. _____
_____
_____
_____

Pole Vault

Coaching Points	Mechanical Principles
1. Low pole carry on sprint like approach, square shoulders.	1. _____ _____
2. As much speed as possible should be developed in direction of vault.	2. _____ _____
3. Take off foot in line with and directly behind the pole, body extended, until lift off ground.	3. _____ _____ _____
4. On upswing keep knees in close to the body and the pole, extend after catapulting action of pole is nearly completed.	4. _____ _____ _____ _____
5. As much speed as possible at the point and motion should be continued without pause as the body rotates.	5. _____ _____ _____ _____
6. Final push with arms is completed only after pole is straight.	6. _____ _____
7. After release of pole and the center of gravity is above the cross bar, vigorously raise the arms above the head.	7. _____ _____ _____ _____

Underhand Volleyball Serve (Right Handed)

Coaching Points	Mechanical Principles
1. Stand facing net with left foot forward and feet shoulder distance apart.	1. _____ _____ _____
2. The left arm extended across the front of the body.	2. _____ _____
3. The ball rests on palm of left hand.	3. _____ _____
4. The right arm is swung straight back.	4. _____ _____
5. Then move right hand forward to strike ball with the heel of the hand. (palm forward)	5. _____ _____ _____
6. The head should be bent slightly forward.	6. _____ _____
7. As ball is struck step forward with left foot.	7. _____ _____
8. Follow-through with the swing of your right arm.	8. _____ _____

Volleyball Set Up

Teaching Points	Mechanical Principles
1. Get feet into a position pointing toward the ball and the player to whom it will be passed.	1. _____ _____ _____
2. Assume a crouch position.	2. _____ _____
3. Let the ball come to you. Do not jump to meet it.	3. _____ _____
4. As contact with ball is made, body should be extended.	4. _____ _____
5. As body is being extended, the arms then start extending.	5. _____ _____ _____
6. Keep a rigid position with hands and body as contact with ball is made. (not stiff)	6. _____ _____ _____
7. Ball contacted so that pads of all fingers and the thumbs touch it.	7. _____ _____

Volleyball — Spike

Teaching Points	Mechanical Principles
1. Two to five steps approach perpendicular to net.	1. _____ _____
2. Heels are planted in front of the body, hips, legs, and ankles flex.	2. _____ _____
3. Two foot take off, extension follows, arms swing forcefully upward.	3. _____ _____ _____
4. During jump from the floor, striking arm is flexed and cocked with the upper body rotated to the right.	4. _____ _____ _____ _____
5. Left arm is extended and raised above and in front of head.	5. _____ _____
6. Right elbow brought forward and upward in front of shoulder.	6. _____ _____
7. Arm fully extended, shoulder lifted, hand snapped for contact.	7. _____ _____
8. Ball directed downward, with movement of striking hand.	8. _____ _____
9. Landing, legs flexed and feet shoulder width apart.	9. _____ _____

20
SKILL ANALYSIS

Directions: Select two fundamental skills from each of the four sections listed.

1. Analyze each fundamental for technique, i.e., list teaching points. Teaching points are to be in sentence statement form.

2. Give a mechanical analysis of each teaching point listed.

Section A

Fundamental Activity — Lifting

Fundamental Activity — Pushing

Angling — *Fly-Casting* — Grip and Stance

Archery — Addressing the Target

Badminton — Stance and Grip

Balance Beam — Balance Seat

Boxing — On Guard Position

Fencing — The Guard

Wresting — Referees Position

Modern Dance — Run

Modern Dance — Gallop

Modern Dance — Skip

Speedball — Foot Trap

Weightlifting — Military Press

Soccer — Knee Trap

Section B

Angling — *Spin* — Casting

Badminton — Backhand

Basketball — Dribble

Field Hockey — Drive

Field Hockey — Flick

Table Tennis — Grip and Service

Water Skiing — Getting Up

Tennis — American Twist — Service

Tennis — Overhead Shot

Handball — Service

Lacrosse — Cradling and Throwing

Soccer — Dribbling

Soccer — Heading

Speedball — Punt

Section C

Diving — Forward one and a Half

Snow Skiing — Kick Turn

Snow Skiing — Snow Plow

Tumbling — High Arm-to-Arm

Side Horse — Front Scissors

Parallel Bars — Back Circle Mount to "Front Thigh Leaning Rest

Parallel Bars — Shoulder Circle Forward

Parallel Bars — Rear Dismount

Trampoline — Front Somersault to Feet (Tuck)

Trampoline — Barani

Trampoline — Swivel Hips

Trampoline — Barrel Roll

Section D

Baseball — Pitching

Balance Beam — Pirouette

Basketball — Two Hand Set Shot

Basketball — One Hand Bounce Pass

Bowling — Four Step Delivery — Hook Ball

Boxing — Straight Right

Fencing — The Advance

Fencing — The Lunge

Football — Screen Block

Water Polo — One Hand Shoulder Pass

Water Polo — Press and Catch

Weightlifting — Clean and jerk

Wrestling — Standing Take-Down

Wrestling — Break Down and Hold

Skiing — Down Hill Running and Breaking

Speedball — One Arm Baseball Pass

Swimming — Elementary Backstroke

Skill _____   Name _____

SECTION A

Teaching Points   **Mechanical Analysis**

1. _____   1. _____

   _____   _____

   _____   _____

2. _____   2. _____

   _____   _____

   _____   _____

3. _____   3. _____

   _____   _____

   _____   _____

4. _____   4. _____

   _____   _____

   _____   _____

5. _____   5. _____

   _____   _____

   _____   _____

Skill _____   Name _____

SECTION A

Teaching Points   **Mechanical Analysis**

1. _____   1. _____

   _____   _____

   _____   _____

2. _____   2. _____

   _____   _____

   _____   _____

3. _____   3. _____

   _____   _____

   _____   _____

4. _____   4. _____

   _____   _____

   _____   _____

5. _____   5. _____

   _____   _____

   _____   _____

Skill _____   Name _____

SECTION A

Teaching Points   **Mechanical Analysis**

1. _____   1. _____

   _____   _____

   _____   _____

2. _____   2. _____

   _____   _____

   _____   _____

3. _____   3. _____

   _____   _____

   _____   _____

4. _____   4. _____

   _____   _____

   _____   _____

5. _____   5. _____

   _____   _____

   _____   _____

Skill _____   Name _____

SECTION A

Teaching Points	Mechanical Analysis

1. _____

_____

_____

2. _____

_____

_____

3. _____

_____

_____

4. _____

_____

_____

5. _____

_____

_____

1. _____

_____

_____

2. _____

_____

_____

3. _____

_____

_____

4. _____

_____

_____

5. _____

_____

_____

Skill _____   Name _____

SECTION B

Teaching Points	Mechanical Analysis

1. _____

   _____

   _____

2. _____

   _____

   _____

3. _____

   _____

   _____

4. _____

   _____

   _____

5. _____

   _____

   _____

1. _____

   _____

   _____

2. _____

   _____

   _____

3. _____

   _____

   _____

4. _____

   _____

   _____

5. _____

   _____

   _____

Skill _____   Name _____

SECTION B

Teaching Points   **Mechanical Analysis**

1. _____   1. _____

   _____   _____

   _____   _____

2. _____   2. _____

   _____   _____

   _____   _____

3. _____   3. _____

   _____   _____

   _____   _____

4. _____   4. _____

   _____   _____

   _____   _____

5. _____   5. _____

   _____   _____

   _____   _____

Skill _____   Name _____

SECTION B

| Teaching Points | Mechanical Analysis |

1. _____

   _____

   _____

2. _____

   _____

   _____

3. _____

   _____

   _____

4. _____

   _____

   _____

5. _____

   _____

   _____

1. _____

   _____

   _____

2. _____

   _____

   _____

3. _____

   _____

   _____

4. _____

   _____

   _____

5. _____

   _____

   _____

Skill _____   Name _____

SECTION B

Teaching Points   **Mechanical Analysis**

1. _____   1. _____

   _____   _____

   _____   _____

2. _____   2. _____

   _____   _____

   _____   _____

3. _____   3. _____

   _____   _____

   _____   _____

4. _____   4. _____

   _____   _____

   _____   _____

5. _____   5. _____

   _____   _____

   _____   _____

Skill _____   Name _____

SECTION C

Teaching Points   **Mechanical Analysis**

1. _____   1. _____

   _____   _____

   _____   _____

2. _____   2. _____

   _____   _____

   _____   _____

3. _____   3. _____

   _____   _____

   _____   _____

4. _____   4. _____

   _____   _____

   _____   _____

5. _____   5. _____

   _____   _____

   _____   _____

Skill _____   Name _____

SECTION C

Teaching Points   Mechanical Analysis

1. _____   1. _____

   _____   _____

   _____   _____

2. _____   2. _____

   _____   _____

   _____   _____

3. _____   3. _____

   _____   _____

   _____   _____

4. _____   4. _____

   _____   _____

   _____   _____

5. _____   5. _____

   _____   _____

   _____   _____

Skill _____ Name _____

SECTION C

Teaching Points **Mechanical Analysis**

1. _____ 1. _____

   _____   _____

   _____   _____

2. _____ 2. _____

   _____   _____

   _____   _____

3. _____ 3. _____

   _____   _____

   _____   _____

4. _____ 4. _____

   _____   _____

   _____   _____

5. _____ 5. _____

   _____   _____

   _____   _____

Skill _____   Name _____

SECTION C

Teaching Points	Mechanical Analysis

1. _____

   _____

   _____

2. _____

   _____

   _____

3. _____

   _____

   _____

4. _____

   _____

   _____

5. _____

   _____

   _____

1. _____

   _____

   _____

2. _____

   _____

   _____

3. _____

   _____

   _____

4. _____

   _____

   _____

5. _____

   _____

   _____

322

Skill _____   Name _____

SECTION D

Teaching Points   **Mechanical Analysis**

1. _____   1. _____

   _____   _____

   _____   _____

2. _____   2. _____

   _____   _____

   _____   _____

3. _____   3. _____

   _____   _____

   _____   _____

4. _____   4. _____

   _____   _____

   _____   _____

5. _____   5. _____

   _____   _____

   _____   _____

Skill _____   Name _____

SECTION D

Teaching Points   **Mechanical Analysis**

1. _____   1. _____

   _____   _____

   _____   _____

2. _____   2. _____

   _____   _____

   _____   _____

3. _____   3. _____

   _____   _____

   _____   _____

4. _____   4. _____

   _____   _____

   _____   _____

5. _____   5. _____

   _____   _____

   _____   _____

Skill _____   Name _____

SECTION D

Teaching Points	Mechanical Analysis

1. _____

    _____

    _____

2. _____

    _____

    _____

3. _____

    _____

    _____

4. _____

    _____

    _____

5. _____

    _____

    _____

1. _____

    _____

    _____

2. _____

    _____

    _____

3. _____

    _____

    _____

4. _____

    _____

    _____

5. _____

    _____

    _____

Skill _____   Name _____

SECTION D

Teaching Points	Mechanical Analysis

1. _____

   _____

   _____

2. _____

   _____

   _____

3. _____

   _____

   _____

4. _____

   _____

   _____

5. _____

   _____

   _____

1. _____

   _____

   _____

2. _____

   _____

   _____

3. _____

   _____

   _____

4. _____

   _____

   _____

5. _____

   _____

   _____

21
GLOSSARY

Acceleration is the rate of change of velocity.

Air resistance is the effect that the air current produces on an object moving through the air.

Angular Velocity is the rate of rotary motion.

Available force is the amount of force available in the human body for external work.

Center of gravity is that point at which all of the weight of an object may be considered to be concentrated.

Centrifugal force is the force which is equal in magnitude to the centripetal force but pulls away from the center of rotation.

Centripetal force is the force that deflects a body from its linear path and compels it to move along a curve.

Circular motion is the motion of a body along a curved path of constant radius.

Efficiency is the ratio of the actual mechanical advantage to the ideal mechanical advantage; the ratio of the output to the input.

Elasticity is the characteristic of an object that allows it to rebound after contact.

Energy is the ability to do work.

Equilibrium is the state of a body in which there is no change in its motion.

Force is that which produces or prevents a motion, or has a tendency to do so.

Mechanical advantage is the ratio of the distance the effort force moves to the distance the resistance force moves.

Impact is a striking of objects together made with forcible contact.

Inertia is the property of matter which requires that a force be exerted on it in order to change its position or motion.

Input is the product of the effort force and the distance through which it acts.

Kinetic energy is the energy due to the motion of a mass.

A law is a statement of scientific fact concerning natural phenomena.

Linear motion is motion along a line.

Mass is the measure of the quantity of matter or measure of the weight of a body divided by the pull of gravity.

Momentum is the product of the mass of an object and its velocity.

Motion is a continuing change of place or position.

Parallel forces are forces acting in the same or opposite direction.

Potential energy is stored energy, or energy due to the position of a mass.

Power is the time-rate of doing work.

Resultant force is the single force which has the same effect as two or more forces acting in the same direction.

Restitution of a body is that characteristic that causes it to resume its original shape after forcible contact.

Rotary motion is motion about a point which acts as a pivot.

Speed is the rate of motion.

Spin is rotation of an object in flight.

Stability is the degree of equilibrium that a body possesses.

Stability in flight is the ability of an object to remain on course.

Torque is the product of a force and the length of the moment arm on which it acts.

Velocity is the rate of displacement.

Water resistance is the effect that movement through water causes on produced force.

Weight is the measure of the attractive force of the earth for a body.

Work is the amount of energy expended in moving an object a specified distance.

Name _____

Definition of Additional Terms

Term	Definition

_____   _____

_____   _____

_____   _____

_____   _____

_____   _____

_____   _____

_____   _____

_____   _____

Name _____

Definition of Additional Terms

Term | Definition

_____ _____

_____

_____ _____

_____

_____ _____

_____

_____ _____

_____

_____ _____

_____

_____ _____

_____

_____ _____

_____

_____ _____

_____

Definition of Additional Terms

Term	Definition
_____	_____
	_____
_____	_____
	_____
_____	_____
	_____
_____	_____
	_____
_____	_____
	_____
_____	_____
	_____
_____	_____
	_____
_____	_____
	_____

Definition of Additional Terms

Term	Definition
_____	_____
	_____
_____	_____
	_____
_____	_____
	_____
_____	_____
	_____
_____	_____
	_____
_____	_____
	_____
_____	_____
	_____
_____	_____
	_____
_____	_____
	_____
_____	_____
	_____

22
MECHANICAL PRINCIPLES

1. Everybody continues in a state of rest or uniform motion in a straight line unless acted upon by an outside force.

2. The greater the acceleration of a body the greater the force causing it and conversely.

3. For every action there is always an opposite reaction.

4. The larger the area of the base on which a body rests the greater the stability and conversely.

5. The farther the center of gravity is from the forward edge of the base in the direction of movement the greater the stability and conversely.

6. The heavier the body the greater the stability and conversely.

7. The lower the center of gravity of a body the greater the stability and conversely.

8. For equilibrium to exist, the center of gravity must fall within the base.

9. When a body is in the air free of support, the principle of the ends and the middle functions, i.e., when the head and feet move up the hips move down and conversely.

10. In arm support activities the center of gravity should be as nearly as possible over the point of support.

11. A body in the air free of support may change position of the center of gravity in his body by movement of the limbs.

12. A body in the air free of support cannot change the path his center of gravity will take or the height of the center of gravity above the floor.

13. In projecting a body through the air to gain the greatest distance the body should be projected at maximum velocity and at an angle of approximately 30 degrees.

14. When angular velocity of an object about a center of rotation is constant, the linear velocity of an object about the center of rotation increases as the length of the radius increases and conversely.

15. When linear velocity remains constant, angular velocity increases as the length of the radius of rotation is shortened and conversely.

16. In swinging exercises on the bar, a shortening of the radius of rotation on the upswing and lengthening of the radius of rotation on the downswing accelerates the motion and conversely.

17. In order to obtain best results there should be an integration of rotary and linear motion.

18. When converting rotary motion to linear motion of a body, the greatest velocity is obtained when the linear direction is at a tangent to the arc of rotation.

19. Movement should be continuous when performing activities that requires a transfer from a pull action to a push action or vice-versa.

20. When generating force in a series, each successive force should be started at the point of greatest velocity but least acceleration.

21. The total effective force may be no greater than the sum of forces in a series.

22. When forces are applied simultaneously they are limited by the weakest of the group of forces.

23. Force may be exerted without creating motion but there cannot be motion without force.

24. The principle of transfer of momentum from the part to the whole—by movement of the limbs of the body this movement is transferred to the body as a whole.

25. The direction that a body free of support will take is determined by the resultant of force which set it in motion.

26. Objects travel toward earth at a rate of 32 feet per second/per second until they encounter air resistance.

27. Third-class levers are useful in producing movements of great range and speed at the expense of force.

28. Second class levers produce movements of great force at the expense of speed and distance.

29. First class levers may produce either speed or force or be in balance for both.

30. The mechanical advantage of a lever is represented by the ratio of the length of the force arm divided by the length of the weight arm.

31. The longer the force arm the greater the momentum force and conversely.

32. Force must be applied at right angles to the lever in order to gain maximum effective force.

33. In order to lessen the shock of a blow, fall, throw, or kick, the shock should be spread over as large an area as possible and/or through as long a distance as possible.

34. The longer the radius of rotation the greater the centrifugal force with angular velocity and weight constant.

35. In order to gain maximum effective force, applied force should be as directly as possible in the direction of the intended motion.

36. In running a curve the greater the centrifugal force, the greater the lean or banking necessary in order to balance this force.

37. When a ball meets a surface, the angle of rebound is greater than the angle of incidence.

38. Friction is independent of the area of contact of the two surfaces.

39. The reaction of air on an object in flight is dependent upon the active surface area of the body over which the air stream passes and the velocity of the air stream with respect to the body.

40. The spin of an object in flight has a stabilizing effect upon it.

41. Topspin on a ball causes a lower angle of rebound, a longer bounce and more roll.

42. Back spin on a ball causes a higher angle of rebound, a shorter bounce and less roll.

43. A ball with clockwise spin curves to the right and bounces to the right after contact with the surface.

44. A ball with counter clockwise spin curves to the left and bounces to the left after contact with the surface.

45. When an object is propelled at a height above the ground, to get maximum distance the angle of trajectory is less than 45 degrees if the distance is measured to the spot at which it hits the ground, even when not affected by air resistance.

46. In swimming, overcoming water resistance is as important as increasing force.

47. The larger the area contacted by a moving object the less force of impact per unit area and vice versa.

48. Muscular strength is developed by overloading the muscles.

49. The quicker a muscle can accelerate an object the greater the force it can produce.

50. The greater the spin of rotation in relation to the forward velocity of a ball, the greater will be the deviation from a vertical plane.

Additional Principles

1. _____
_____

2. _____
_____

3. _____
_____

4. _____
_____

5. _____
_____

6. _____
_____

7. _____
_____

8. _____
_____

9. _____
_____

10. _____
_____

Additional Principles

1. _____
   _____

2. _____
   _____

3. _____
   _____

4. _____
   _____

5. _____
   _____

6. _____
   _____

7. _____
   _____

8. _____
   _____

9. _____
   _____

10. _____
    _____

23
APPLIED PRINCIPLES

1. In most sports activities, the optimum position requires a compromise between stability and position to perform.

2. In order to start quickly in a given direction keep the center of gravity near the forward edge of the base in the direction of movement, as high as possible, in a position to exert effective force, and good friction with the running surface.

3. For greatest stability, increase the area of the base, lower the center of gravity and get good friction with the playing surface.

4. In order to stop quickly, increase the area of the base in the direction of movement, keep the center of gravity low, move the center of gravity over the trailing edge of the base and have good friction with the running surface.

5. When striking a ball, additional velocity may be gained by bending a joint.

6. In order to turn a person by imparting force through a limb, the person being turned must counteract that force.

7. To get maximum effect from blows that are struck with an implement held in the hand, the grip must be as firm as possible at the moment of impact.

8. Angular movement in the body is counterbalanced by rotation in the opposite direction.

9. In creating greater force, one or both feet should be in firm contact with the surface.

10. The velocity of a struck ball depends upon the weight and striking force of the ball and bat and the restitution of the ball and bat.

11. In the human body, the available force varies inversely with the speed of movement.

12. The stronger the muscles the greater the depth of the crouch in gaining maximum height and conversely.

13. A muscle contracts with more force when first put under stretch.

14. A muscle will quickly lose its elasticity if it is put under stretch too often and for too long period of time.

15. The human body is adapted more to speed than to strength because the body operates largely under a system of third class levers.

16. Body movements that are away from the longitudinal axis of the body after the body is air-borne will be in the opposite direction from the direction of rotation.

17. Body movements that are executed close to the longitudinal axis of a body that is airborne will be in the same direction as the rotation.

18. Body movements that are away from the longitudinal axis of a body and that are started before the body is air-borne will be in the direction of rotation.

19. Forward rotation is speeded up when a twist is brought into the movement.

20. When horizontal distance is the goal, kick a ball at an angle greater than 45 degrees with the wind and much less than an angle of 45 degrees against the wind.

21. A spinning bowling ball may hook instead of curve when the initial force is great and the linear velocity of the ball slows down so it will curve into the pins.

22. In catching a basketball, catch the ball at the farthest point from the body to decrease the time and distance for interception.

23. A base runner rounding first base may counteract centrifugal force by any of these ways, namely by leaning, by slowing down or by taking a wide arc.

24. In running and walking, a clockwise rotation of the legs is counter-bounced by a counter-clockwise rotation of the arms.

25. If a rifle shot was released horizontally to a floor and another bullet was dropped to the floor at the same instance and from the same height, both bullets would contact the surface at the same time but some distance apart.

26. In walking, when the left foot is forward, the right arm is forward.

27. A basketball player's center of gravity must travel a specified parabola but he can change his body position in relation to his center of gravity and appear to hang in the air.

28. An old basketball player may compensate for his lack of accuracy by arching the ball higher in order to enlarge the area of the basket to the ball on the downward flight.

29. A long jumper will slow his acceleration the last three strides before hitting the takeoff board in order to have more available force for jumping.

30. The depth of crouch a basketball player takes in jumping depends on the strength in his muscles.

Name _____

Additional Principles

1. _____
   _____

2. _____
   _____

3. _____
   _____

4. _____
   _____

5. _____
   _____

6. _____
   _____

7. _____
   _____

8. _____
   _____

9. _____
   _____

10. _____
    _____

Name _____

Additional Principles

1. _____
   _____

2. _____
   _____

3. _____
   _____

4. _____
   _____

5. _____
   _____

6. _____
   _____

7. _____
   _____

8. _____
   _____

9. _____
   _____

10. _____
    _____

Appendix A
ANSWERS TO CHAPTER PROBLEMS

Chapter 3

1a. .500, .9659, .8660
1b. .9063, .6428, .1737
1c. .3640, .8391, 1.000
2a. 500 lbs.
2b. 1/5 or .20
3. 8 feet from daughter
4. 42.43 lbs.
5a. 160 lbs.
5b. 467.81 lbs.
6a. 430.26 lbs.
6b. 1979.22 lbs.
7a. 60 lbs.
7b. 620 lbs.
7c 1240 lbs.
8a. 147.08 lbs.
8b. 769.33 lbs.
9a. weight = 25 lbs., forearm= 12.5 lbs.
9b. 216.51 lbs.
10. 1439.56 lbs.

Chapter 4

1a. 12 miles/hour, 5.87 yd/sec.
1b. 58.67 feet
1c. 96.6 ft/sec., 80.5 ft., 257.6 ft.
2. 147.99 ft/sec., 0.372 sec.
3. 31.18 ft/sec.
4. 6.73 ft/sec., 10.37 ft.
5. 45 degrees, 9.25 ft!
6. 5.13 ft.
7. 1.53 sec, 44,44 ft., 1.18 secs., 38.84 ft.

8. Erin , 223.6 ft.
9. 222.93 ft., 36.99 ft.

Chapter 5

1. 1175 in-lbs.
2a. 1050 in-lbs.
2b. 369.46 in-lbs.
3a. Jill
3b. 72.21 in-lbs.
4a. 1781.45 in-lbs.
4b. 518.25 in-lbs.
5a. position b
5b. **A** takes 2× as much force
6a. 525 in-lbs.
6b. **B** is twice as stable as **A**
7a. the second position
7b. by 251.22 in-lbs.
8. 1500 in-lbs.
9. The fingertips will go higher.

Chapter 6

1. 6 radians/sec.
2. 314 ft.
3. 4.19 radians/sec.
4. 10.47 radians/sec.
5. John   45 ft./sec. for John, 42 ft./sec. for Jack
6. 35 ft./sec.
7. 471.2 ft.
8. 6 radians/sec.
9. 4.5 ft./sec.
10. 91.13 ft., 106.95 ft., 15.82 ft.

Chapter 7

1a. 75 lbs.
1b 150 ft/sec/sec
2. 625 lbs.

3. 33.56 degrees
4. 200 lbs.
5a 655.74 lbs.
5b. 40.32 degrees
6a 519.62 lbs.
6b. 424.26 lbs.
7. 321.39 lbs.
8. 22.5 lbs.
9. 7.13 degrees
10a. 50 lbs.
10b. 133.33 ft/sec/sec
11. 18.75 lbs.
12a. 162.5 lbs.
12b. 281.46 lbs.
13a. 69.46 lbs.
13b. 282.84 lbs.
14. 59.04 degrees
15a. 433.01 lbs.
15b. 34.72 degrees
15c. 434.05 lbs.
16. 38 degrees
17a. 112.5 lbs.
17b. 29.36 degrees
18a. 19.78 lbs.
18b. 79.1 lbs.
19. 62.5 lbs.
20. 18.75 mm/sec.
21. 0.825
22. 38.66 degrees
23. 200 lbs.
24. 16.67 mm/sec.
25. 300 lbs.